CAN'T HURT ME

MASTER YOUR MIND AND
DEFY THE ODDS

CAN'T
HURT
ME

DAVID GOGGINS

LIONCREST
PUBLISHING

CAN'T HURT ME
Master Your Mind and Defy the Odds

ISBN 978-1-5445-1228-0 *Hardcover*
     978-1-5445-1227-3 *Paperback*
     978-1-5445-1226-6 *Ebook*
     978-1-5445-1229-7 *Audiobook*

TO THE UNRELENTING VOICE IN MY HEAD
THAT WILL NEVER ALLOW ME TO STOP.

CONTENTS

CONTENTS

WARNING ORDER

TIME ZONE: **24/7**

TASK ORGANIZATION: **SOLO MISSION**

1. **SITUATION:** You are in danger of living a life
   so comfortable and soft that you will die
   without ever realizing your true potential.

2. **MISSION:** To unshackle your mind. Ditch the
   victim's mentality forever. Own all aspects
   of your life completely. Build an unbreakable
   foundation.

3. **EXECUTION:**

   a. Read this cover to cover. Study the
      techniques within, accept all ten challenges.
      Repeat. Repetition will callous your mind.

   b. If you do your job to the best of your
      ability, this will hurt. This mission is
      not about making yourself feel better. This
      mission is about being better and having a
      greater impact on the world.

   c. Don't stop when you are tired. Stop when
      you are done.

4. **CLASSIFIED:** This is the origin story of a hero.
   The hero is you.

BY COMMAND OF: **DAVID GOGGINS**

SIGNED: _____

RANK AND SERVICE: **CHIEF , U.S . NAVY SEALS, RETIRED**

INTRODUCTION

DO YOU KNOW WHO YOU REALLY ARE AND WHAT YOU'RE capable of?

I'm sure you think so, but just because you believe something doesn't make it true. Denial is the ultimate comfort zone.

Don't worry, you aren't alone. In every town, in every country, all over the world, millions roam the streets, dead-eyed as zombies, addicted to comfort, embracing a victim's mentality and unaware of their true potential. I know this because I meet and hear from them all the time, and because just like you, I used to be one of them.

I had a damn good excuse too.

Life dealt me a bad hand. I was hom broken, grew up with beat downs, was tormented in school, and called *nigger* more times than I could count.

We were once poor, surviving on welfare, living in government-subsidized housIng, and my depression was smothering. I lived life at the bottom of the barrel, and my future forecast was bleak as fuck.

Very few people know how the bottom feels, but I do. It's like quicksand. It grabs you, sucks you under, and won't let go. When life is like that it's easy to drift and continue to make the same comfortable choices that are killing you, over and over again.

But the truth is we all make habitual, self-limiting choices. It's as natural as a sunset and as fundamental as gravity. It's how our brains are wired, which is why motivation is crap.

Even the best pep talk or self-help hack is nothing but a temporary fix. It won't rewire your brain. It won't amplify your voice or uplift your life. Motivation changes exactly nobody. The bad hand that was my life was mine, and mine alone to fix.

So I sought out pain, fell in love with suffering, and eventually transformed myself from the weakest piece of shit on the planet into the hardest man God ever created, or so I tell myself.

Odds are you have had a much better childhood than I did, and even now might have a damn decent life, but no matter who you are, who your parents are or were, where you live, what you do for a living, or how much money you have, you're probably living at about 40 percent of your true capability.

Damn shame.

We all have the potential to be so much more.

Years ago, I was invited to be on a panel at the Massachusetts Institute of Technology. I'd never set foot in a university lecture hall as a student. I'd barely graduated high school, yet I was at one of the most prestigious institutions in the country to discuss mental toughness with a handful of others. At some point in the discussion an esteemed MIT professor said that we each have genetic limitations. Hard ceilings. That there are some things we just can't do no matter how mentally tough we are. When we hit our genetic ceiling, he said, mental toughness doesn't enter into the equation.

Everyone in that room seemed to accept his version of reality because this senior, tenured professor was known for researching mental toughness. It was his life's work. It was also a bunch of bull shit, and to me he was using science to let us all off the hook.

I'd been quiet until then because I was surrounded by all these smart people, feeling stupid, but someone in the audience noticed the look on my face and asked if I agreed. And if you ask me a direct question, I won't be shy.

"There's something to be said for living it instead of studying it," I said, then turned toward the professor. "What you said is true for most people, but not 100 percent. There will always be the 1 percent of us who are willing to put in the work to defy the odds."

I went on to explain what I knew from experience. That anybody can become a totally different person and achieve what so-called experts like him claim is impossible, but it takes a lot of heart, will, and an armored mind.

Heraclitus, a philosopher born in the Persian Empire back in the fifth century BC, had it right when he wrote about men on the battlefield. "Out of every one hundred men," he wrote, "ten shouldn't even be there, eighty are just targets, nine are the real fighters, and we are lucky to have them, for they make the battle. Ah, but the one, one is a warrior ... "

From the time you take your first breath, you become eligible to die. You also become eligible to find your greatness and become the One Warrior. But it is up to you to equip yourself for the battle ahead. Only you can master your mind, which is what it takes to live a bold life filled with accomplishments most people consider beyond their capability.

I am not a genius like those professors at MIT, but I am that One Warrior. And the story you are about to read, the story of my fucked-up life, will illuminate a proven path to self-mastery and empower you to face reality, hold yourself accountable, push past pain, learn to love what you fear, relish failure, live to your fullest potential, and find out who you really are.

Human beings change through study, habit, and stories. Through my story you will learn what the body and mind are capable of when they're driven to maximum capacity, and how to get there. Because when you're driven, whatever is in front of you, whether it's racism, sexism, injuries, divorce, depression, obesity, tragedy, or poverty, becomes fuel for your metamorphosis.

The steps laid out here amount to the evolutionary algorithm, one that obliterates barriers, glimmers with glory, and delivers lasting peace.

I hope you're ready. It's time to go to war with yourself.

CHAPTER ONE

I SHOULD HAVE BEEN A STATISTIC

WE FOUND HELL IN A BEAUTIFUL NEIGHBORHOOD. IN 1981, Williamsville offered the tastiest real estate in Buffalo, New York. Leafy and friendly, its safe streets were dotted with dainty homes filled with model citizens. Doctors, attorneys, steel plant executives, dentists, and professional football players lived there with their adoring wives and their 2.2 kids. Cars were new, roads swept, possibilities endless. We're talking about a living, breathing American Dream. Hell was a corner lot on Paradise Road.

That's where we lived in a two-story, four-bedroom, white wooden home with four square pillars framing a front porch that led to the widest, greenest lawn in Williamsville. We had a vegetable garden out back and a two-car garage stocked with a 1962 Rolls Royce Silver Cloud, a 1980 Mercedes 450 SLC, and, in the driveway, a sparkling new 1981 black Corvette. Everyone on Paradise Road lived near the top of the food chain, and based on appearances, most of our neighbors thought that we, the so-called happy, well-adjusted Goggins family, were the tip of that spear. But glossy surfaces reflect much more than they reveal.

They'd see us most weekday mornings, gathered in the driveway at 7 a.m. My dad, Trunnis Goggins, wasn't tall but he was handsome and built like a boxer. He wore tailored suits, his smile warm and open. He looked every bit the successful businessman on his way to work. My mother, Jackie, was seventeen years younger, slender and beautiful, and my brother and I were clean cut, well dressed in jeans and pastel Izod shirts, and strapped with backpacks just like the other kids. The white kids. In our version of affluent America, each driveway was a staging ground for nods and waves before parents and children rode off to work and school. Neighbors saw what they wanted. Nobody probed too deep.

Good thing. The truth was, the Goggins family had just returned home from another all-nighter in the hood, and if Paradise Road was Hell, that meant I lived with the Devil himself. As soon as our neighbors shut the door or turned the corner, my father's smile morphed into a scowl. He barked orders and went inside to sleep another one off, but our work wasn't done. My brother, Trunnis Jr., and I had somewhere to be, and it was up to our sleepless mother to get us there.

I was in first grade in 1981, and I was in a school daze, for real. Not because the academics were hard—at least not yet—but because I couldn't stay awake. The teacher's sing—song voice was my lullaby, my crossed arms on my desk, a comfy pillow, and her sharp words—once she caught me dreaming—an unwelcome alarm clock that wouldn't stop blaring. Children that young are infinite sponges. They soak up language and ideas at warp speed to establish a fundamental foundation upon which most people build life-long skills like reading and spelling and basic math, but because I worked nights, I couldn't concentrate on anything most mornings, except trying to stay awake.

Recess and PE were a whole different minefield. Out on the playground staying lucid was the easy part. The hard part was the hiding. Couldn't let my shirt slip. Couldn't wear shorts. Bruises were red flags I couldn't show because if I did, I knew I'd catch even more. Still, on that playground and in the classroom I knew I was safe, for a little while at least. It was the one place he couldn't reach me, at least not physically. My brother went through a similar dance in sixth grade, his first year in middle school. He had his own wounds to hide and sleep to harvest, because once that bell rang, real life began.

The ride from Williamsville to the Masten District in East Buffalo took about a half an hour, but it may as well have been a world away. Like much of East Buffalo, Masten was a mostly black working-class neighborhood in the inner city that was rough around the edges; though, in the early 1980s, it was not yet completely ghetto as fuck. Back then the Bethlehem Steel plant was still humming and Buffalo was the last great American steel town. Most men in the city, black and white, worked solid union jobs and earned a living wage, which meant business in Masten was good. For my dad, it always had been.

By the time he was twenty years old he owned a Coca-Cola distribution concession and four delivery routes in the Buffalo area. That's good money for a kid, but he had bigger dreams and an eye on the future. His future had four wheels and a disco funk soundtrack. When a local bakery shut down, he leased the building and built one of Buffalo's first roller skating rinks.

Fast-forWard ten years and Skateland had been relocated to a building on Ferry Street that stretched nearly a full block in the heart of the Masten District. He opened a bar above the rink, which he named the Vermillion Room. In the 1970s, that was the place to be in East Buffalo, and it's where he met my mother when she was just nineteen and he was thirty-six. It was her first time away from home. Jackie grew up in the Catholic Church. Trunnis was the son of a minister, and knew her language well enough to masquerade as a believer, which appealed to her. But let's keep it real. She was just as drunk on his charm.

Trunnis Jr. was born in 1971. I was born in 1975, and by the time I was six years old, the roller disco craze was at its absolute peak. Skateland rocked every night. We'd usually get there around 5 p.m., and while my brother worked the concession stand—popping corn, grilling hot dogs, loading the cooler, and making pizzas—I organized the skates by size and style. Each afternoon, I stood on a step stool to spray my stock with aerosol deodorizer and replace the rubber stoppers. That aerosol stink would cloud all around my head and live in my nostrils. My eyes looked permanently bloodshot. It was the only thing I could smell for hours. But those were the distractions I had to ignore to stay organized and on hustle. Because my dad, who worked the Dl booth, was always watching, and if any of those skates went missing, it meant my ass. Before the doors opened I'd polish the skate rink floor with a dust mop that was twice my size.

Skateland, age six

At around 6, p.m., my mother called us to dinner in the back office. That woman lived in a permanent state of denial, but her maternal instinct was real, and it made a big fucking show of itself, grasping for any shred of normalcy. Every night in that office, she'd set out two electric burners on the floor, sit with her legs curled behind her, and prepare a full dinner—roast meat, potatoes, green beans, and dinner rolls, while my dad did the books and made calls.

The food was good, but even at six and seven years old I knew our "family dinner" was a bullshit facsimile compared to what most families had. Plus, we ate fast. There was no time to enjoy it because at 7 p.m. when the doors opened, it was show time, and we all had to be in our places with our stations prepped. My dad was the sheriff, and once he stepped into the DJ booth he had us triangulated. He scanned that room like an all-seeing eye, and if you fucked up you'd hear about it. Unless you felt it first.

The room didn't look like much under the harsh, overhead house lights, but once he dimmed them, the show lights bathed the rink in red and glanced off the spinning mirror ball, conjuring a skate disco fantasy. Weekend or weeknight, hundreds of skaters piled through that door. Most of the time they came in as a family, paying their $3 entrance fee and half-dollar skate fee before hitting the floor.

I rented out the skates and managed that entire station by myself. I carried that step stool around like a crutch. Without it, the customers couldn't even see me. The bigger-sized skates were down below the counter, but the smaller sizes were stored so high I'd have to scale the shelves, which always made the customers laugh. Mom was the one and only cashier. She collected everyone's cover charge, and to Trunnis, money was everything. He counted the people as they came in, calculating his take in real time so he had are high idea of what to expect when he counted out the register after we closed up. And it had better all be there.

All the money was his. The rest of us never earned a cent for our sweat. In fact, my mother was never given any money of her own. She had no bank account or credit cards in her name. He controlled everything, and we all knew what would happen if her cash drawer ever came up short.

None of the customers who came through our doors knew any of this, of course. To them, Skateland was a family-owned-and-operated dream cloud. My dad spun the fading vinyl echoes of disco and funk and the early rumbles of hip hop. Bass bounced off the red walls, courtesy of Buffalo's favorite son Rick James, George Clinton's Funkadelic, and the first tracks ever released by hip hop innovators Run DMC. Some of the kids were speed skating. I liked to go fast too, but we had our share of skate dancers, and that floor got funky.

For the first hour or two the parents stayed downstairs and skated, or watched their kids spin the oval, but they would eventually leak upstairs to make their own scene, and when enough of them made their move, Trunnis slipped out of the DJ booth so he could join them. My dad was considered the unofficial mayor of Masten, and he was a phony politician to the core. His customers were his marks, and what they didn't know was that no matter how many drinks he poured on the house and bro hugs he shared, he didn't give a fuck about any of them. They were all dollar signs to him. If he poured you a drink for free, it was because he knew you would buy two or three more.

While we had our share of all-night skates and twenty-four-hour skate marathons, the Skateland doors typically closed at 10 p.m. That's when my mother, brother, and I went to work, fishing bloody tampons out of shit-filled toilets, airing the lingering cannabis haze out of both bathrooms, scraping bacteria-loaded gum off the rink floor, cleaning the concession kitchen, and taking inventory. Just before midnight, we'd slog into the office, half-dead Our mother would tuck my brother and me beneath a blanket on the office sofa, our heads opposite one another, as the ceiling shook with the sound of bass-heavy funk.

Mom was still on the clock.

As soon as she stepped inside the bar, Trunnis had her working the door or hustling downstairs like a booze mule to fetch cases of liquor from the basement. There was always some menial task to perform and she didn't stop moving, while my father kept watch from his corner of the bar where he could take in the whole scene. In those days, Rick James, a Buffalo native and one of my father's closest friends, stopped by whenever he was in town, parking his Excalibur on the sidewalk out front. His car was a billboard that let the hood know a Superfreak was in the house. He wasn't the only celebrity that came through. OJ Simpson was one of the NFL's biggest stars, and he and his Buffalo Bills teammates were regulars, as was Teddy Pendergrass and Sister Sledge. If you don't know the names, look them up.

Maybe if I had been older, or my father had been a good man, I might have had some pride in being part of a cultural moment like that, but young kids aren't about that life. It's almost like, no matter who our parents are and what they do, we're all born with a moral compass that's properly tuned. When you're six, seven, or eight years old, you know what feels right and what feels way the fuck off. And when you are born into a cyclone of terror and pain, you know it doesn't have to be that way, and that truth nags at you like a splinter in your jacked up mind. You can choose to ignore it, but the dull throbbing is always there as the days and nights bleed together into one blurred memory.

Some moments do stick out though, and one I'm thinking of right now still haunts me. That was the night my mom stepped into the bar before she was expected and found my dad sweet talking a woman about ten years her junior. Trunnis saw her watching and shrugged while my mother eyeballed him and slugged two shots of Johnnie Walker Red to calm her nerves. He noticed her reaction and didn't like it one damn bit.

She knew how things were. That Trunnis ran prostitutes across the border to Fort Erie in Canada. A summer cottage belonging to the president of one of Buffalo's biggest banks doubled as his pop-up brothel. He introduced Buffalo bankers to his girls whenever he needed a longer line of credit, and those loans always came through. My mom knew the young woman she was watching was one of the girls in his stable. She'd seen her before. Once, she walked in on them fucking on the Skateland office sofa, where she tucked her children in damn near every night. When she found them together, the woman smiled at her. Trunnis shrugged. No, my mom wasn't clueless, but seeing it with her own eyes always burned.

Around midnight, my mother drove with one of our security guards to make a bank deposit. He begged her to leave my father. He told her to leave that very night. Maybe he knew what was coming. She did too, but she couldn't run because she had no independent means whatsoever, and she wasn't going to leave us in his hands. Plus, she had no rights to community property because Trunnis had always refused to marry her, which was a riddle she was only then starting to solve. My mother came from a solid, middle class family, and had always been the virtuous type. He resented that, treated his hookers better than the mother of his sons, and as a result he had her trapped. She was 100 percent dependent, and if she wanted to leave, she'd have to walk with nothing at all.

My brother and I never slept well at Skateland. The ceiling shook too much because the office was directly below the dance floor. When my mother walked in that night I was already awake.

She smiled, but I noticed the tears in her eyes and remember smelling the scotch on her breath when she scooped me up in her arms as tenderly as she could. My father trailed in after her, sloppy and annoyed. He pulled a pistol from beneath the cushion where I slept (yes, you read that right, there was a loaded gun under the cushion on which I slept at six years old!), flashed it at me, and smiled before concealing it beneath his pant leg in an ankle holster. In his other hand were two brown paper shopping bags filled with nearly $10,000 in cash. So far it was a typical night.

My parents didn't speak on the drive home, though the tension between them simmered. My mom pulled into the driveway on Paradise Road just before 6 a.m., a little early by our standards. Trunnis stumbled from the car, disabled the alarm, dropped the cash on the kitchen table, and went upstairs. We followed him, and she tucked us both into our beds, kissed me on the forehead, and turned out the light before slipping into the master suite where she found him waiting, stroking his leather belt. Trunnis didn't appreciate being glared at by my mom, especially in public.

"This belt came all the way from Texas just to whip you," he said, calmly. Then he started swinging it, buckle first. Sometimes my mother fought back, and she did that night. She threw a marble candlestick at his head. He ducked and it thudded the wall. She ran into the bathroom, locked the door, and cowered on the toilet. He kicked the door down and backhanded her hard. Her head slammed into the wall. She was barely conscious when he grabbed a fistful of her hair and dragged her down the hall.

By then my brother and I had heard the violence, and we watched him drag her all the way down the stairs to the first floor, then crouch over her with the belt in his hand. She was bleeding from the temple and the lip, and the sight of her blood lit a fuse in me. In that moment my hatred overcame my fear. I ran downstairs and jumped on his back, slammed my tiny fists into his back, and scratched at his eyes. I'd caught him off guard and he fell to one knee. I wailed on him.

" Don't hit my mom!" I yelled. He tossed me to the ground, stalked toward me, belt in hand, then turned toward my mother.

"You're raising a gangster," he said, half-smiling.

I curled into a ball when he started swinging his belt at me. I could feel bruises rise on my back as my mom crawled toward the control pad near the front door. She pressed the panic button and the house exploded in alarm. He froze, looked toward the ceiling, mopped his brow with his sleeve, took a deep breath, looped and buckled his belt, and went upstairs to wash off all that evil and hate. Police were on their way, and he knew it.

My mother's relief was short-lived. When the cops arrived, Trunnis met them at the door. They looked over his shoulder toward my mom, who stood several paces behind him, her face swollen and caked with dried blood. But those were different days. There was no #metoo back then. That shit didn't exist, and they ignored her. Trunnis told them it was all a whole lot of nothing. Just some necessary domestic discipline.

"Look at this house. Does it look like I mistreat my wife?" He asked. "I give her mink coats, diamond rings, I bust my ass to give her everything she wants, and she throws a marble candlestick at my head. She's spoiled."

The police chuckled along with my father as he walked them to their car. They left without interviewing her. He didn't hit her again that morning. He didn't have to. The psychological damage was done. From that point on it was clear to us that as far as Trunnis and the law were concerned it was open season, and we were the hunted.

Over the next year, our schedule didn't change much and

the beatings continued, while my mother tried to paper over the darkness with swatches of light. She knew I wanted to be a Scout, so she signed me up for a local troop. I still remember putting on that navy blue Cub Scout button down one Saturday. I felt proud wearing a uniform and knowing at least for a few hours I could pretend that I was a normal kid. My mom smiled as we headed for the door. My pride, her smile, wasn't just because of the damn Cub Scouts. They rose up from a deeper place. We were taking action to find something positive for ourselves in a bleak situation. It was proof that we mattered, and that we weren't completely powerless.

That's when my father came home from the Vermillion Room.

"Where you two going?" He glared at me. I stared at the floor. My mother cleared her throat.

"I'm taking David to his first Cub Scout meeting," she said, softly.

"The hell you are!" I looked up, and he laughed as my eyes welled up with tears. "We're going to the track."

Within the hour we'd arrived at Batavia Downs, an old-school harness horse race track, the type where jockeys ride behind the horses in lightweight buggies. My dad grabbed a racing form as soon we stepped through the gate. For hours, the three of us watched him place bet after bet, chain smoke, drink scotch, and raise holy hell as every pony he bet on finished out of the money. With my dad raging at the gambling gods and acting a fool, I tried to make myself as small as possible whenever people walked by, but I still stuck out. I was the only kid in the stands dressed like a Cub Scout. I was probably the only black Cub Scout they'd ever seen, and my uniform was a lie. I was a pretender.

Trunnis lost thousands of dollars that day, and he wouldn't shut up about it on the drive home, his raspy throat raw from nicotine. My brother and I were in the cramped back seat and whenever he spat out the window, his phlegm boomeranged into my face. Each drop of his nasty saliva on my skin burned like venom and intensified my hate. I'd long since learned that the best way to avoid a beat down was to make myself as invisible as possible, avert my eyes, float outside my body, and hope to go unnoticed. It was a practice we'd all honed over the years, but I was done with that shit. I would no longer hide from the Devil. That afternoon as he veered onto the highway and headed home, he continued to rave on, at:}d I mad-dogged him from the back seat. Have you ever heard the phrase, "Faith Over Fear"? For me it was Hate Over Fear.

He caught my eyes in the rearview mirror.

"You got something to say?!"

"We shouldn't have gone to the track anyway," I said.

My brother turned and stared at me like I'd lost my damn mind. My mother squirmed in her seat.

"Say that one more time." His words came slow, dripping with dread. I didn't say a word, so he started reaching behind the seat trying to smack me. But I was so small, it was easy to hide. The car veered left and right as he was half-turned in my direction, punching air. He'd barely touched me, which only stoked his fire. We drove in silence until he caught his breath. "When we get home, you're gonna take your clothes off," he said.

That's what he'd say when he was ready to bestow ·a serious beat down, and there was no avoiding it. I did what I was told. I went into my bedroom and took off my clothes, walked down the hall to his room, closed the door behind me, turned the lights off, then laid across the comer of the bed with my legs dangling, my torso stretched out in front of me, and my ass exposed. That was the protocol, and he'd designed it for maximum psychological and physical pain.

The beatings were often brutal, but the anticipation was the worst part. I couldn't see the door behind me, and he'd take his time, letting my dread build. When I heard him open the door, my panic spiked. Even then the room was so dark I couldn't see much with my peripheral vision, and couldn't prepare for the first smack until his belt hit my skin. It was never just two or three lickings either. There was no particular count, so we never knew when or if he was gonna stop.

This beating lasted minutes upon minutes. He started on my butt, but the sting was so bad I blocked it with my hands, so he moved down and started whipping my thighs. When I dropped my hands to my thighs he swung at my lower back. He belted me dozens of times, and was breathless, coughing and slick with sweat by the time it was over. I was breathing heavy too, but I wasn't crying. His evil was too real and my hate gave me courage. I refused to give that motherfucker the satisfaction. I just stood up, looked the Devil in his eye, limped to my room, and stood in front of a mirror. I was covered in welts from my neck to the crease at the knees. I didn't go to school for several days.

When you're getting beat consistently, hope evaporates. You stifle your emotions, but your trauma off-gasses in unconscious ways. After countless beatings she endured and witnessed, this particular beat down left my mother in a constant fog, a shell of the woman I remembered from a few years before. She was distracted and vacant most of the time, except when he called her name. Then she'd hop-to like she was his slave. I didn't know until years later that she was considering suicide.

My brother and I took our pain out on each other. We'd sit or stand across from one another and he would throw punches as hard as he could at me. It usually started out as a game, but he was four years older, much stronger, and he connected with all his power. Whenever I'd fall, I'd get up and he'd hit me again, as hard as he could, yelling like a martial arts warrior at the top of his lungs, his face twisted with rage.

"You're not hurting me! Is that all you fucking have?" I'd shout back. I wanted him to know that I could take more pain than he could ever deliver, but when it was time to fall asleep and there were no more battles to fight, no place to hide, I wet the bed. Nearly every night.

My mother's every day was a lesson in survival. She was told she was worthless so often she started to believe it. Everything she did was an effort to appease him so he wouldn't beat her sons or whip her ass, but there were invisible trip wires in her world and sometimes she never knew when or how she set them off until after he slapped the shit out of her. Other times she knew she teed herself up for a vicious beat down.

One day I came home early from school with a nasty earache and laid down on my mother's side of their bed, my left ear throbbing in excruciating pain. With each throb my hate spiked. I knew I wouldn't be going to the doctor because my father didn't approve of spending his money on doctors or dentists. We didn't have health insurance, a pediatrician, or a dentist. If we got injured or sick, we were told to shake it off because he wasn't down to pay for anything that didn't directly benefit Trunnis Goggins. Our health didn't meet that standard, and that pissed me the fuck off .

After about ⬚half hour, my mother came upstairs to check on me and when I rolled onto my back she could see blood dribbling down the side of my neck and smeared all over the pillow.

"That's it," she said, "come with me."

She got me out of bed, dressed me, and helped me to her car, but before she could start the engine, my dad chased us down.

"Where you think you're going?!"

"The emergency room," she said as she turned the ignition. He reached for the handle but she peeled out first, leaving him in her dust. Furious, he stomped inside, slammed the door, and called out to my brother.

"Son, get me a Johnnie Walker!, Trunnis Jr. brought over a bottle of Red Label and a glass from the wet bar. He poured and poured and watched my dad down shot after shot. Each one fueled an inferno. "You and David need to be strong," he raved. "I'm not raising a bunch of faggots! And that's what you'll be if you go to the doctor every time you get a little boo boo, understand?" My brother nodded, petrified. "Your last name is Goggins, and we shake it off!"

According to the doctor we saw that night, my mother got me to the ER just in time. My ear infection was so bad that if we'd waited any longer, I would have lost my hearing in my left ear for life. She risked her ass to save mine and we both knew she'd pay for it. We drove home in eerie silence.

My dad was still stewing at the kitchen table by the time we turned onto Paradise Road, and my brother was still pouring him shots. Trunnis Jr. feared our father, but he also worshipped the man and was under his spell. As the first born son he was treated better. Trunnis would still lash out at him, but in his warped mind, Trunnis Jr. was his prince. "When you grow up I'm gonna want to see you be the man of your house," Trunnis told him. "And you're gonna see me be a man tonight."

Moments after we walked through the front door, Trunnis beat our mother senseless, but my brother couldn't watch. Whenever the beatings exploded like a thunderstorm overhead, he'd wait them out in his room. He ignored the darkness because the truth was way too heavy for him to carry. I always paid close fucking attention.

During the summers, there was no midweek respite from Trunnis, but my brother and I learned to hop on our bikes and stay far away for as long as we could. One day, I came home for lunc.h and entered the house through the garage like normal. My father usually slept deep into the afternoon, so I figured the coast was clear. I was wrong. My father was paranoid. He did enough shady deals to attract some enemies, and he'd set the alarm after we left the house.

When I opened the door, sirens screamed and my stomach dropped. I froze, backed up against the wall, and listened for footsteps. I heard the stairs creak and knew I was fucked. He came downstairs in his brown terrycloth robe, pistol in hand, and crossed from the dining room into the living room, his gun out front. I could see the barrel come around the corner slowly.

As soon as he cleared the corner he could see me standing just twenty feet away, but he didn't drop his weapon. He aimed it right between my eyes. I stared straight at him, blank as possible, my feet anchored to the floor boards. There was no one else in the house, and part of me expected him to pull the trigger, but by this time in my life I no longer cared if I lived or died. I was an exhausted eight-year-old kid, plain old fucking tired of being terrified of my father, and I was sick of Skateland too. After a minute or two he lowered his weapon and went back upstairs.

By now it was becoming clear that someone was going to die on Paradise Road. My mother knew where Trunnis kept his .38. Some days she timed and followed him—envisioned how it would play out. They'd take separate cars to Skateland, she'd grab his gun from beneath the office sofa cushions before he could get there, bring us home early, put us to bed, and wait for him by the front door with his gun in hand. When he pulled up, she'd step out the front door and murder him in his driveway—leave his body for the milkman to find. My uncles, her brothers, talked her out of it, but they agreed she needed to do something drastic or she'd be the one lying dead.

It was an old neighbor who showed her a way. Betty used to live across the street from us and after she moved they stayed in touch. Betty was twenty years older than my mom and had the wisdom to match. She encouraged my mother to plan her escape weeks in advance. The first step was getting a credit card in her name. That meant she had to re-earn Trunnis' trust because she needed him to cosign. Betty also reminded my mother to keep their friendship a secret.

For a few weeks Jackie played Trunnis, treated him like she did when she was a nineteen-year-old beauty with stars in her eyes. She made him believe she worshipped him again, and when she slipped a credit card application in front of him, he said he'd be happy to score her a little buying power. When the card arrived in the mail, my mother felt its hard plastic edges through the envelope as relief saturated her mind. She held it at arms length and admired it. It glowed like a golden ticket.

A few days later she heard my father talking shit about her on the phone to one of his friends, while he was having breakfast with my brother and me at the kitchen table. That did it. She walked over to the table and said, "I'm leaving your father. You two can stay or you can come with me."

My dad was stunned silent and so was my brother, but I shot out of that chair like it was on fire, grabbed a few black garbage bags, and went upstairs to start packing. My brother eventually started gathering his things too. Before we left, the four of us had one last pow wow at that kitchen table. Trunnis glared at my mother, filled with shock and contempt.

"You have nothing and you are nothing without me," he said. "You're uneducated, you don't have any money or prospects. You'll be a prostitute inside a year." He paused then shifted his focus to my brother and me. "You two are gonna grow up to be a couple of faggots. And don't think about coming back, Jackie. I'll have another woman here to take your place five minutes after you leave."

She nodded and stood. She'd given him her youth, her very soul, and she was finally finished. She packed as little of her past as possible. She left the mink coats and the diamond rings. He could give them to his whore girlfriend as far as she was concerned.

Trunnis watched us load up into my mom's Volvo (the one vehicle he owned that he wouldn't ride in), our bikes already strapped to the back. We drove off slowly and at first he didn't budge, but before she turned the corner I could see him move toward the garage. My mother floored it.

Give her credit, she'd planned for contingencies. She figured he'd tail her, so she didn't head west to the interstate that would take us to her parent's place in Indiana. Instead, she drove to Betty's house, down a dirt construction road that my dad didn't even know about. Betty had the garage door open when we arrived. We pulled in. Betty yanked the door down, and while my father shot out on the highway in his Corvette to chase after us, we waited right under his nose until just before nightfall. By then we knew he'd be at Skateland, opening up. He wasn't going to miss a chance to make some money. No matter what.

Shit went wrong about ninety miles outside of Buffalo when the old Volvo started burning oil. Huge plumes of inky exhaust choked from the tail pipe and my mother spun into panic mode. It was as if she'd been holding it all in, stuffing her fear down deep, hiding it beneath a mask of forced composure, until an obstacle emerged and she fell apart. Tears streaked her face.

"What do I do?" My mom asked, her eyes wide as saucers. My brother never wanted to leave, and he told her to turn around. I was riding shotgun. She looked over expectantly. "What do I do?"

"We gotta go, mom," I said. "Mom, we gotta go."

She pulled into a gas station in the middle of nowhere. Hysterical, she rushed to a pay phone and called Betty.

"I can't do this, Betty," she said. "The car broke down. I have to go back!"

"Where are you?" Betty asked, calmly.

"I don't know," my mom replied. "I have no idea where I am!"

Betty told her to find a gas station attendant—every station had those back then—and put him on the phone. He explained we were just outside of Erie, Pennsylvania, and after Betty gave him some instructions, he put my mother back on the line.

"Jackie, there's a Volvo dealer in Erie. Find a hotel tonight and take the car there tomorrow morning. The attendant is going to put enough oil in the car to get you there." My mother was listening but she didn't respond. "Jackie? Are you hearing me? Do what I say and it will be okay."

"Yeah. Okay," she whispered, emotionally spent. "Hotel. Volvo dealer. Got it."

I don't know what Erie is like now, but back then there was only one decent hotel in town: a Holiday Inn, not far from the Volvo dealership. My brother and I followed my mom to the reception desk where we were hit with more bad news. They were fully booked. My mother's shoulders slumped. My brother and I stood on either side of her, holding our clothes in black trash bags. We were the picture of desperation, and the night manager saw it.

"Look, I'll set you up with some rollaway beds in the conference room," he said. "There's a bathroom down there, but you have to be out early because we have a conference starting at 9 a.m."

Grateful, we bedded down in that conference room with its industrial carpet and fluorescent lights, our own personal purgatory. We were on the run and on the ropes, but my mother hadn't folded. She laid back and stared at the ceiling tiles until we nodded off. Then she slipped into an adjacent coffee shop to keep an anxious eye on our bikes, and on the road, all night long.

We were waiting outside that Volvo dealership when the garage opened up, which gave the mechanics just enough time to source the part we needed and get us back on the road before their day was done. We left Erie at sunset and drove all night, arriving at my grandparents' house in Brazil, Indiana, eight hours later. My mom wept as she parked next to their old wooden house before dawn, and I understood why.

Our arrival felt significant, then and now. I was still only eight years old, but already in a second phase of life. I didn't know what awaited me—what awaited us—in that small, rural, Southern Indiana town, and I didn't much care. All I knew was that we'd escaped from Hell, and for the first time in my life, we were free from the Devil himself.

★ ★ ★

We stayed with my grandparents for the next six months, and I enrolled in second grade—for the second time—at a local Catholic school called Annunciation. I was the only eight-year-old in second grade,_ but none of the other kids knew I was repeating a year, and there was no doubt that I needed it. I could barely read, but I was lucky enough to have Sister Katherine as my teacher. Short and petite, Sister Katherine was sixty years old and had one gold front tooth. She was a nun but didn't wear the habit. She was also grumpy as hell and took no shit, and I loved her thug ass.

Second grade in Brazil

Annunciation was a small school. Sister Katherine taught all of first and second grade in a single classroom, and with only eighteen kids to teach, she wasn't willing to shirk her responsibility and blame my academic struggles, or anybody's bad behavior, on learning disabilities or emotional problems. She didn't know my backstory and didn't have to. All that mattered to her was that I turned up at her door with a kindergarten education, and it was her job to shape my mind. She had every excuse in the world to farm me out to some specialist or label me a problem, but that wasn't her style. She started teaching before labeling kids was a normal thing to do, and she embodied the no-excuses mentality that I needed if I was going to catch up.

Sister Katherine is the reason why I'll never trust a smile or judge a scowl. My dad smiled a hell of a lot, and he didn't give two shits about me, but grouchy Sister Katherine cared about us, cared about me. She wanted us to be our very best. I know this because she proved it by spending extra time with me, as much time as it took, until I retained my lessons. Before the year was out, I could read at a second grade level. Trunnis Jr. hadn't adjusted nearly as well. Within a few months he was back in Buffalo, shadowing my father and working that Skate land detail like he'd never left.

By then, we'd moved into a place of our own: a 600-square-foot, two-bedroom apartment at Lamplight Manor, a public housing block, that cost us $7 a month. My father, who earned thousands every night, sporadically sent $25 every three or four weeks (if that) for child support, while my mother earned a few hundred dollars a month with her department store job. In her off-hours she was taking courses at Indiana State University, which cost money too. The point is, we had gaps to fill, so my mother enrolle4 in welfare and received $123 a month and food stamps. They wrote her a check for the first month, but when they found out she owned a car they disqualified her, explaining that if she sold her car they'd be happy to help.

The problem is we lived in a rural town with a population of about 8,000 that didn't have a mass transit system. We needed that car so I could get to school, and so she could get to work and take night classes. She was hell-bent on changing her life circumstances and found a workaround through the Aide to Dependent Children program. She arranged for our check to go to my grandmother who signed it over to her, but that didn't make life easy. How far can $123 really go?

I vividly recall one night we were so broke we drove home on a gas tank that was near empty, to a bare refrigerator and a past due electric bill, with no money in the bank. Then I remembered that we had two 1nason jars filled with pennies and other loose change. I grabbed them off the shelf.

"Mom, let's count our change!"

She smiled. Growing up, her father had taught her to pick up the change she found on the street. He was molded by the Great Depression and knew what it was like to be down and out. "You never know when you might need it," he'd say. When we lived in Hell, carrying home thousands of dollars every night, the notion that we would ever run out of money sounded ludicrous, but my mother retained her childhood habit. Trunnis used to belittle her for it, but now it was time to see how far found money could take us.

We dumped that change out on the living room floor and counted out enough to cover the electric bill, fill the gas tank, and buy groceries. We even had enough to buy burgers at Hardee's on the way home. These were dark times, but we were managing. Barely. My mother missed Trunnis Jr. terribly, but she was pleased that I was adjusting and making friends. I'd had a good year at school, and from our first night in Indiana I hadn't wet the bed once. It seemed that I was healing, but my demons weren't gone. They were dormant. And when they came back, they hit hard.

★ ★ ★

Third grade was a shock to my system. Not just because we had to learn cursive when I was still getting the hang of reading block letters, but because our teacher, Ms. D, was nothing like Sister Katherine. Our class was still small, we had about twenty kids total, split between third and fourth grade, but she didn't handle it nearly as well and wasn't interested in taking the extra time I required.

My trouble started with the standardized test we took during our first couple of weeks of class. Mine came back a mess. I was still way behind the other kids and I had trouble building on lessons from the previous days, let alone the previous academic year. Sister Katherine considered similar signs as cues to dedicate more time with her weakest student, and she challenged me daily. Ms. D looked for a way out. Within the first month of class, she told my mother that I belonged in a different school. One for "special students."

Every kid knows what "special" means. It means you are about to be stigmatized for the rest of your damn life. It means that you are not normal. The threat alone was a trigger, and I developed a stutter almost overnight. My thought-to-speech flow was jammed up with stress and anxiety, and it was at its worst in school.

Imagine being the only black kid in class, in the entire school, and enduring the daily humiliation of also being the dumbest. I felt like everything I tried to do or say was wrong, and it got so bad that instead of responding and skipping like scratched vinyl whenever the teacher called my name, I often chose to keep quiet. It was all about limiting exposure to save face.

Ms. D didn't even attempt to empathize. She went straight to frustration and vented it by yelling at me, sometimes when she was leaning down, her hand on the back of my chair, her face just inches from my own. She had no idea the Pandora's box she was tearing open. Once, school was a safe harbor, the one place I knew I couldn't be hurt, but in Indiana it morphed into my torture chamber.

Ms. D wanted me out of her classroom, and the administration supported her until my mother fought for me. The principal agreed to keep me enrolled if my mother signed off on time with a speech therapist and put me into group therapy with a local shrink they recommended.

The psychologist's office was adjacent to a hospital, which was exactly where you'd want to put it if you were trying to make a little kid doubt himself. It was like a bad movie. The shrink set up seven chairs in a semicircle around him, but some of the kids wouldn't or couldn't sit still. One child wore a helmet and banged his head against the wall repeatedly. Another kid stood up while the doctor was mid-sentence, walked toward a far corner of the room, and pissed in the trash can. The kid sitting next to me was the most normal person in the group, and he had set his own house on fire! I can remember staring up at the shrink on my first day, thinking, *There's no way I belong here*

That experience kicked my social anxiety up several notches. My stutter was out of control. My hair started falling out, and white splotches bloomed on my dark skin. The doctor diagnosed me as an ADHD case and prescribed Ritalin, but my problems were more complex.

I was suffering from toxic stress.

The type of physical and emotional abuse I was exposed to has been proven to have a range of side effects on young children because in our early years the brain grows and develops so rapidly. If, during those years, your father is an evil motherfucker hell-bent on destroying everyone in his house, stress spikes, and when those spikes occur frequently enough, you can draw a line across the peaks. That's your new baseline. It puts kids in a permanent "fight or flight" mode. Fight or flight can be a great tool when you're in danger because it amps you up to battle through or sprint from trouble, but it's no way to live.

I'm not the type of guy to try to explain everything with science, but facts are facts. I've read that some pediatricians believe toxic stress does more damage to kids than polio or meningitis. I know firsthand that it leads to learning disabilities and social anxiety because according to doctors it limits language development and memory, which makes it difficult for even the most gifted student to recall what they have already learned. Looking at the long game, when kids like me grow up, they face an increased risk for clinical depression, heart disease, obesity, and cancer, not to mention smoking, alcoholism, and drug abuse. Those raised in abusive households have an increased probability of being arrested as a juvenile by 53 percent. Their odds of committing a violent crime as an adult are increased by 38 percent. I was the poster child of that generic term we've all heard before: "at-risk youth." My mother wasn't the one raising a thug. Look at the numbers and it's clear: if anyone put me on a destructive path it was Trunnis Goggins.

I didn't stay in group therapy for long, and I didn't take Ritalin either. My mom picked me up after my second session and I sat in the front seat of her car wearing a thousand-yard stare. "Mom, I'm not going back," I said. "These boys are crazy.". She agreed.

But I was still a damaged kid, and while there are proven interventions on the first way to teach and manage kids who suffer from toxic stress, it's fair to say that Ms. D didn't get those memos. I can't blame her for her own ignorance. The science wasn't nearly as clear in the 1980s as it is now. All I know is, Sister Katherine toiled in the trenches with the same malformed kid that Ms. D dealt with, but she maintained high expectations and didn't let her frustration overwhelm her. She had the mindset of, *Look, everybody learns in a different way and we're gonna figure out howy you learn.* She deduced that I needed repetition. That I needed to solve the same problems over and over again in a different way to learn, and she knew that took time. Ms. D was all about productivity. She was saying, *Keep up or get out.* Meanwhile, I felt backed into a corner. I knew that if I didn't show some improvement I would eventually be shipped out to that *special* black hole for good, so I found a solution.

I started cheating my ass off.

Studying was hard, especially with my fucked-up brain, but I was a damn good cheat. I copied friends' homework and scanned my neighbors' work during tests. I even copied the answers on the standardized tests that didn't have any impact on my grades. It worked! My rising test scores placated Ms. D, and my mother stopped getting calls from school. I thought I'd solved a problem when really I was creating new ones by taking the path of least resistance. My coping mechanism confirmed that I would never learn squat at school, and that I would never catch up, which pushed me closer toward a flunked out fate.

The saving grace of those early years in Brazil was that I was way too young to understand the kind of prejudice I would soon face in my new hick hometown. Whenever you're the *only* one of your kind, you're in danger of being pushed toward the margins, suspected and disregarded, bullied and mistreated by ignorant people. That's just the way life is, especially back then, and by the time that reality kicked me in the throat, my life had already become a full-fledged, fuck-you fortune cookie. Whenever I cracked it open, I got the same message.

You were born to fail !

CHALLENGE #1

My bad cards arrived early and stuck around a while, but every-one gets challenged in life at some point. What was your bad hand? What kind of bullshit did you contend with growing up? Were you beaten? Abused? Bullied? Did you ever feel insecure? Maybe your limiting factor is that you grew up so supported and comfortable, you never pushed yourself?

What are the current factors limiting your growth and suc-cess? Is someone standing in your way at work or school? Are you underappreciated and overlooked for opportunities? What are the long odds you're up against right now? Are you standing in your own way?

Break out your journal—if you don't have one, buy one, or start one on your laptop, tablet, or in the notes app on your smart phone—and write them all out in minute detail. Don't be bland with this assignment. I showed you every piece of my dirty laundry. If you were hurt or are still in harm's way, tell the story in full. Give your pain shape. Absorb its power, because you are about to flip that shit.

You will use your story, this list of excuses, these very good reasons why you shouldn't amount to a damn thing, to fuel your ultimate success. Sounds fun right? Yeah, it won't be. But don't worry about that yet. We'll get there. For now, just take inventory.

Once you have your list, share it with whoever you want. For some, it may mean logging onto social media, posting a picture, and writing out a few lines about how your own past or present cir-cumstances challenge you to the depth of your soul. If that's you, use the hashtags #badhand #canthurtme. Otherwise, acknowl-edge and accept it privately. Whatever works for you. I know it's hard, but this act alone will begin to empower you to overcome.

CHAPTER TWO

TRUTH HURTS

WILMOTHIRVING WAS A NEW BEGINNING. UP UNTIL HE met my mother and asked for her phone number, all I'd known was misery and struggle. When the money was good, our lives were defined by trauma. Once we were free of my father, we were swept under by our own PTSD-level dysfunction and poverty. Then, when I was in fourth grade, she met Wilmoth, a successful carpenter and general contractor from Indianapolis. She was attracted to his easy smile and laid-back style. There was no violence in him. He gave us permission to exhale. With him around it felt like we had some support, like something good was finally happening to us.

She laughed when they were together. Her smile was bright and real. She stood up a little straighter. He gave her pride and made her feel beautiful again. As for me, Wilmoth bec.ame as close to a healthy father figure as I've ever had. He didn't coddle me. He didn't te!l me he loved me or any of that fake-ass sappy shit, but he was there. Basketball had been an obsession of mine since grade school. It was the core of my relationship with my best friend, Johnny Nichols, and Wilmoth had game. He and I hit the courts together all the time. He showed me moves, tuned up my defensive discipline, and helped me develop a jump shot. The three of us celebrated birthdays and holidays together, and the summer before eighth grade, he got down on one knee and asked my mother to make it official.

With Wilmoth

Wilmoth lived in Indianapolis, and our plan was to move in with him the following summer. Though he wasn't nearly as rich as Trunnis, he made a nice living and we looked forward to city life again. Then in 1989, the day after Christmas, everything stopped.

We hadn't made the full time move to Indy yet, and he'd spent Christmas Day with us at my grandparents' place in Brazil. The next day, he had a basketball game in his men's league and he'd invited me to sub for one of his teammates. I was so excited I'd packed my bags two days early, but that morning he told me I couldn't come after all.

"I'm gonna keep you back here this time, Little David," he said. I dropped my head and sighed. He could tell I was upset and tried to reassure me. "Your mom is gonna drive up in a few days and we can play ball then."

I nodded, reluctantly, but I wasn't raised to pry into the affairs of adults and knew I wasn't owed an explanation or make-up game. My mother and I watched from the front porch as he backed out of the carport, smiled, and gave us that crisp single wave of his. Then he drove off.

It was the last time we'd ever see him alive.

He played in his men's league game that night, as planned, and drove home alone to the "house with the white lions." Whenever he gave directions to friends, family, or delivery guys, that's how he always described his ranch-style house, its driveway framed by two white lion sculptures elevated on pillars. He pulled between them and into the garage where he could enter the house directly, oblivious to the danger moving in from behind. He never did close that garage door.

They'd been staking him out for hours, waiting for a window, and as he climbed out from the driver's side door, they stepped from the shadows and fired from close range. He was shot five times in the chest. When he dropped to the floor of his garage, the gunman stepped over him and delivered a kill shot right between his eyes.

Wilmoth's father lived a few blocks away, and when he drove by the white lions the next morning, he noticed his son's garage door open and knew something was wrong. He walked up the driveway and into the garage where he sobbed over his dead son.

Wilmoth was just forty-three years old.

I was still at my grandmother's house when Wilmoth's mother called moments later. She hung up and motioned me to her side to break the news. I thought about my mom. Wilmoth had been her savior. She'd been coming out of her shell, opening up, ready to believe in good things. What would this do to her? Would God ever give her a damn break? It started as a simmer but within seconds my rage overwhelmed me. I broke free of my grandmother, punched the refrigerator, and left a dent.

We drove to our place to find my mother, who was already frantic because she hadn't heard from Wilmoth. She called his house just before we arrived, and when a detective picked up the phone it puzzled her, but she didn't expect this. How could she? We saw her confusion as my grandmother walked over, peeled the phone from her fingers, and sat her down.

She didn't believe us at first. Wilmoth was a prankster and this was just the kind of fucked-up stunt he might try to pull off. Then she remembered he'd been shot two months before. He'd told her the guys who'd done that weren't after him. That those bullets were meant for someone else, and because they merely grazed him, she decided to forget about the whole thing. Until that moment, she never suspected that Wilmoth had some secret street life she knew nothing about, and the police never did find out exactly why he was shot and killed. The speculation was that he was involved in a shady business deal or a drug deal gone bad. My mother was still in denial when she packed a bag, but she included a dress for his funeral.

When we arrived, his house was wrapped in a ribbon of yellow police tape like a fucked-up Christmas gift. This was no prank. My mom parked, ducked under the tape, and I followed right behind her to the front door. On the way, I remember glancing to my left trying to get a glimpse of the scene where Wilmoth had been killed. His cold blood was still pooled on the garage floor. I was a fourteen-year-old wandering through an active crime scene, but nobody, not my mother, not Wilmoth's family, and not even the police seemed disturbed by me being there, absorbing the heavy vibe of my would-be stepfather's murder.

As fucked up as it sounds, the police allowed my mom to stay in Wilmoth's house that night. Rather than stay alone, she had her brother-in-law there, armed with his two guns in case the killers came back. I wound up in a back bedroom at Wilmoth's sister's place, a dark and spooky house a few miles away, and left alone all night. The house was furnished with one of those analog, cabinet television sets with thirteen channels on a dial. Only three channels came in static-free, and I kept it on the local news. They ran the same tape on a loop every thirty minutes: footage of my mom and me ducking under police tape then watching Wilmoth get wheeled on a gurney toward a waiting ambulance, a sheet over his body.

It was like a horror scene. I sat there all alone, watching the same footage over and over. My mind was a broken record that kept skipping into darkness. The past had been bleak and now our sky-blue future had been blown the fuck up too. There would be no reprieve, only my familiar fucked-up reality choking out all light. Each time I watched, my fear grew until it filled the room, and still I could not stop.

A few days after we buried Wilmoth, and just after the new year, I boarded a school bus in Brazil, Indiana. I was still grieving, and my head was spinning because my mother and I hadn't decided whether or not we were staying in Brazil or moving to Indianapolis as planned. We were in limbo and she remained in a state of shock. She still hadn't cried over Wilmoth's death. Instead she became emotionally vacant again. It was as if all the pain she'd experienced in her life resurfaced as one gaping wound she disappeared into, and there was no reaching her in that void. In the meantime, school was starting up, so I played along, looking for any shred of normal I could hang onto.

But it was hard. I rode a bus to school most days, and my first day back, I couldn't shake a memory I'd buried from the year before. That morning, I slid into a seat above the back left tire overlooking the street as usual. When we arrived at school the bus pulled up to the curb, we needed to wait for the ones ahead of us to move before we could get off. In the meantime, a car pulled alongside us, and a cute, overeager little boy ran toward our bus carrying a platter of cookies. The driver didn't see him. The bus jerked forward

I noticed the alarmed look on his mother's face before the sudden crush of blood splattered my window. His mother howled in horror. She wasn't among us anymore. She looked and sounded like a fierce, wounded animal as she literally pulled the hair from her head by the roots. Soon sirens wailed in the distance and screamed closer by the second. The little boy was about six years old. The cookies were a present for the driver.

We were all ordered off the bus, and as I walked by the tragedy, for some reason—call it human curiosity, call it the magnetic pull of dark to dark—I peeked under the bus and saw him. His head was nearly as flat as paper, his brains and blood mingled under the carriage like spent oil.

For a full year I hadn't thought of that image even once, but Wilmoth's death reawakened it, and now it was all I could think about. I was beyond the pale. Nothing mattered to me. I'd seen enough to know that the world was filled with human tragedy and that it would just keep piling up in drifts until it swallowed me.

I couldn't sleep in bed anymore. Neither could my mother. She slept in her arm chair with the television on blast or with a book in her hands. For a little while, I tried to curl up in bed at night but would always wake in the fetal position on the floor. Eventually I gave in and bedded down low to the ground. Maybe because I knew if I could find comfort at the bottom place there would be no more falling.

We were two people in dire need of the fresh start we thought we had coming, so even without Wilmoth, we made the move to Indianapolis. My mother set me up for entry exams at Cathedral High School, a private college preparatory academy in the heart of the city. As usual, I cheated, and off a smart motherfucker too. When my acceptance letter and class schedule came in the mail the summer before freshman year, I was looking at a full slate of AP classes!

I hacked my way through, cheating and copying, and managed to make the freshman basketball team, which was one of the best freshman teams in the entire state. We had several future college players, and I started at point guard. That was a confidence boost, but not the kind I could build on because I knew I was an academic fraud. Plus, the school cost my mom way too much money, so after only one year at Cathedral, she pulled the plug.

I started my sophomore year at North Central High School, a

public school with 4,000 kids in a majority black neighborhood, and on my first day I turned up like some preppy-ass white boy. My jeans were definitely too tight, and my collared shirt was tucked into a waistline cinched with a braided belt. The only reason I didn't get completely laughed out of the building was because I could ball.

My sophomore year was all about being cool. I switched up my wardrobe, which was increasingly influenced by hip hop culture, and hung out with gang hangers and other borderline delinquents, which meant I didn't always go to school. One day, my mom came home in the middle of the day and found me sitting around our dining room table with what she described as "ten thugs." She wasn't wrong. Within a few weeks she packed us up and moved us back to Brazil, Indiana.

I enrolled at Northview High School the week of basketball tryouts, and I remember showing up at lunch time when the cafeteria was full. There were 1,200 kids enrolled at Northview, only five of which were black, and the last time any of them had seen me I looked a lot like them. Not anymore.

I strolled into school that day wearing pants five sizes too big and sagged way down low. I also wore an oversized Chicago Bulls Jacket with a backward hat, cocked to the side. Within seconds, all eyes were upon me. Teachers, students, and administrative staff stared at me like I was some exotic species. I was the first thuggish black kid many of them had seen in real life .. My mere presence had stopped the music. I was the needle being dragged across vinyl, scratching a whole new rhythm, and like hip hop itself, everybody noticed but not everyone liked what they heard. I strutted through the scene like I gave no fucks.

But that was a lie. I acted all kinds of cocky and my entrance was brash as hell, but I felt very insecure going back there. Buffalo had been like living in a blazing inferno. My early years in Brazil were a perfect incubator for post traumatic stress, and before I left I was delivered a double dose of death trauma. Moving to Indianapolis had been an opportunity to escape pity and leave all that behind. Class wasn't easy for me, but I'd made friends and developed a new style. Now, coming back, I looked different enough on the outside to perpetuate an illusion that I'd changed, but in order to change you have to work through shit. Confront it and get real. I hadn't done a shred of that hard work. I was still a dumb kid with nothing solid to lean on, and basketball tryouts ripped away any confidence I had left.

When I got to the gym, they made me suit-up in uniform rather than wear my more generic gym clothes. Back then the style was getting baggy and oversized, which Chris Webber and Jalen Rose of the Fab Five would make famous at the University of Michigan. The coaches in Brazil didn't have their fingers on that pulse. They put me in the tighty-whitey version of basketball shorts, which strangled my balls, hugged my thighs super tight, and felt all kinds of wrong. I was trapped in the coaches' preferred dream state: a Larry Bird time warp. Which made sense because Larry Legend was basically a patron saint in Brazil and all of Indiana. In fact, his daughter went to our school. We were friends. But that didn't mean I wanted to dress like him!

Then there was my etiquette. In Indianapolis the coaches let us talk shit on the court. If I made a good move or hit a shot in your face, I talked about your mama or your girlfriend. In Indy, I'd done research on my shit talking. I got good at it. I was the Draymond Green of my school, and it was all part of basketball culture in the city. Back in farm country, that cost me. When tryouts started, I handled the rock a bunch, and when I crossed some of the kids over and made them look bad I let them and the coaches know. My attitude embarrassed the coaches (who were apparently ignorant that their hero, Larry Legend, was an all-time great trash talker), and it wasn't long before they took the ball out of my hands and put me in the front court, a position I'd never played before. I was uncomfortable down low, and played like it. That shut me up good. Meanwhile, Johnny was dominating.

My only saving grace that week was getting back with Johnny Nichols. We'd stayed close while I was away and our marathon one-on-one battles were back on full swing. Though he was undersized, he was always a nice player and he was one of the best on the floor during tryouts. He was draining shots, seeing the open man, and running the court. It was no surprise when he made the varsity squad, but we were both shocked that I barely made JV.

I was crushed. And not because of basketball tryouts. To me that outcome was another symptom of something else I'd been feeling. Brazil looked the same, but shit felt different this time around. Grade school had been hard academically, but even though we were one of only a few black families in town, I didn't notice or feel any palpable racism. As a teenager I experienced it everywhere, and it wasn't because I'd become ultra sensitive. Outright racism had always been there.

Not long after moving back to Brazil, my cousin Damien and I went to a party way out in the country. We stayed out well past curfew. In fact, we were up all night long, and after daybreak we called our grandmother for a ride home.

"Excuse me?" She asked. "You disobeyed me, so you may as well start walking."

Roger that.

She lived ten miles away, down a long country road, but we joked around and enjoyed ourselves as we started to stroll.

Damien lived in Indianapolis and we were both sagging our baggy jeans and dressed in oversized Starter jackets, not exactly typical gear on Brazil's country roads. We'd walked seven miles in a few hours when a pick-up truck came bouncing down the tarmac in our direction. We edged to the side of the road to let it pass, but it slowed down, and as it crept past us, we could see two teenagers in the cab and a third standing in the bed of the truck. The passenger pointed and yelled through his open window.

"Niggers!"

We didn't overreact. We put our heads down and kept walking at the same pace, until we heard that beat-to-shit truck squeal to a stop on a patch of gravel, and kick up a dust storm. That's when I turned and saw the passenger, a scruffy looking redneck, exit the cab of the truck with a pistol in his hand. He aimed it at my head as he stalked toward me.

Where the fuck you from, and why the fuck you here in this fucking town?!"

Damien eased down the road, while I locked eyes with the gunman and said nothing. He stepped within two feet of me. The . threat of violence doesn't get much more real than that. Chills rippled my skin, but I refused to run or cower. After a few seconds he got back in the truck and they sped off.

It wasn't the first time I'd heard the word. Not long before· that I was hanging out in Pizza Hut with Johnny and a couple of girls, including a brunette I liked, named Pam. She liked me too, but we'd never acted on it. We were two innocents enjoying one another's company, but when her father arrived to take her home he caught sight of us, and when Pam saw him, her face went ghost white.

He burst into the packed restaurant and stalked toward us with all eyes on him. He never addressed me. He just locked eyes with her and said, "I don't want to ever see you sitting with this *nigger* again."

She hustled out the door after him, her face red with shame as I sat, paralyzed, staring at the floor. It was the most humiliating moment of my life, and it hurt much more than the gun incident because it happened in public, and the word had been spewed by a grown-ass man. I couldn't understand how or why he was filled with so much hate, and if he felt that way, how many other people in Brazil shared his point of view when they saw me walking down the street? It was the sort of riddle you didn't want to solve.

★ ★ ★

They won't call on me if they can't see me. That was how I operated during my sophomore year in high school in Brazil, Indiana. I would hide out in the back rows, slump low in my chair, and side-step my way through each and every class. Our high school made us take a foreign language that year, which was funny to me. Not because I couldn't see the value, but because I could barely read English, let alone understand Spanish. By then, after a good eight years of cheating, my ignorance had crystalized. I kept leveling up in school, on track, but hadn't learned a damn thing. I was one of those kids who thought he was gaming the system when, the whole time, I'd been gaming myself.

One morning, about halfway through the school year, I milled into Spanish class and grabbed my workbook from a back cupboard. There was technique involved in skating by. You didn't have to pay attention, but you did have to make it seem like you were, so I slumpe4 into my seat, opened up my workbook, and fixed my gaze on the teacher who lectured from the front of the room.

When I looked down at the page the whole room went silent.

At least to me. Her lips were still moving, but I couldn't hear because my attention had narrowed on the message left for me, and me alone.

We each had our own assigned workbook in that class, and my name was written in pencil at the top right corner of the title page. That's how they knew it was mine. Below that, someone had drawn an image of me in a noose. It looked rudimentary, like something out of the hangman game we used to play as kids. Below that were the words.

Niger we're gonna kill you!

They'd misspelled it, but I had no clue. I could barely spell myself, and they'd made their fucking point. I looked around the room as my rage gathered like a typhoon until it was literally buzzing in my ears. *I'm not supposed to be here, I thought to myself. I'm not supposed to be back in Brazil!*

I took inventory of all the incidents I'd already experienced and decided I couldn't take much more. The teacher was still talking when I rose up without warning. She called my name but I wasn't trying to hear. I left the classroom, notebook in hand, and bolted to the principal's office. I was so enraged I didn't even stop at the front desk. I walked right into his office and dropped the evidence on his desk.

"I'm tired of this shit," I said.

Kirk Freeman was the principal at that time, and to this day he still remembers looking up from his desk and seeing tears in my eyes. It wasn't some mystery why all this shit was happening in Brazil. Southern Indiana had always been a hotbed of racists, and he knew it. Four years later, in 1995, the Ku Klux Klan would march down Brazil's main drag on Independence Day, in full hooded regalia. The KKK was active in Center Point, a town located not fifteen minutes away, and kids from there went to our school. Some of them sat behind me in history class and told racist jokes for my benefit nearly every damn day. I wasn't expecting some investigation into who did it. More than anything, in that moment, I was looking for some compassion, and I could tell from the look in Principal Freeman's eyes he felt bad about what I was going through, but he was at a loss. He didn't know how to help me. Instead, he examined the drawing and the message for a long beat, then raised his eyes to mine, ready to console me with his words of wisdom.

"David, this is sheer ignorance," he said. "They don't even know how to spell *nigger*."

My life had been threatened, and that was the best he could do. The loneliness I felt leaving his office is something I'll never forget. It was scary to think that there was so much hate flowing through the halls and that someone I didn't even know wanted me dead because of the color of my skin. The same question kept looping through my mind: Who the fuck is out here who hates me like this? I had no idea who my enemy was. Was it one of the rednecks from history cJass1 or was it somebody 1 thought 1 was cool with but who really didn't like me at all? It was one thing staring down the barrel of a gun on the street or dealing with some racing patent. At least that shit was honest. Wondering who else felt that way in my school was a different kind of unnerving, and I couldn't shake it off. Even though I had plenty of friends, all of them white, I couldn't stop seeing the hidden racism scrawled all over the walls in invisible ink, which made it extremely hard to carry the weight of being the *only*.

KKK In Center Point in 1995—Center Point is fifteen minutes from my house in Brazil

Most, if not all, minorities, women, and gay people in America know that strain of loneliness well. Of walking into rooms where you are the *only* one of your kind. Most white men have no idea how hard it can be. I wish they did. Because then they'd know how it drains you. How some days, all you want to do is stay home and wallow because to go public is to be completely exposed, vulnerable to a world that tracks and judges you. At least that's how it feels. The truth is, you can't tell for sure when or if that is actually happening in a given moment. But it often feels like it, which is its own kind of mindfuck. In Brazil, I was the only everywhere I went. At my table in the cafeteria, where I chilled at lunch with Johnny and our crew. In every class I took. Even in the damn basketball gym.

By the end of that year I turned sixteen and my grandfather bought me a used, doo-doo brown Chevy Citation. One of the first mornings I ever drove it to school, someone spray painted the word "nigger" on my driver's side door. This time they spelled it correctly and Principal Freeman was again at a loss for words. The fury that churned within me that day was indescribable, but it didn't radiate out. It broke me down from within because I hadn't yet learned what to do or where to channel that much emotion.

Was I supposed to fight everybody? I'd been suspended from school three times for fighting, and by now I was almost numb. Instead, I withdrew and fell into the well of black nationalism. Malcolm X became my prophet of choice. I used to come home from school and watch the same video of one of his early speeches every damn day. I was trying to find comfort somewhere, and the way he analyzed history and spun black hopelessness into rage nourished me, though most of his political and economic philosophies went over my head. It was his anger at a system made by and for white people that I connected with because I lived in a haze of hate, trapped in my own fruitless rage and ignorance. But I wasn't Nation of Islam material. That shit took discipline, and I had none of that.

Instead, by my junior year, I went out of my way to piss people off by becoming the exact stereotype racist white people loathed and feared. I wore my pants down below my ass every day. I ghetto wired my car stereo to house speakers which filled the trunk of my Citation. I rattled windows when I cruised down Brazil's main drag blasting Snoop's *Gin and juice*. I put three of those shag carpet covers over my steering wheel and dangled a pair of fuzzy dice from the rearview. Every morning before school I stared into our bathroom mirror and came up with new ways to fuck with the racists at my school.

I even concocted wild hairdos. Once, I gave myself a reverse part—shaving away all my hair save a thin radial line on the left side of my scalp. It wasn't that I was unpopular. I was considered the cool black kid in town, but if you'd have bothered to drill down a little deeper, you'd see that I wasn't about black culture and that my antics weren't really trying to call out racism. I wasn't about anything at all.

Everything I did was to get a reaction out of the people who hated me most because everyone's opinion of me mattered to me, and that's a shallow way to live. I was full of pain, had no real purpose, and if you were watching from afar it would have looked like I'd given up on any chance of success. That I was heading for disaster. But I hadn't let go of all hope. I had one more dream left.

I wanted to join the Air Force.

My grandfather had been a cook in the Air Force for thirty-seven years, and he was so proud of his service that even after he retired he'd wear his dress uniform to church on Sundays, and his work-a-day uniform midweek just to sit on the damn porch. That level of pride inspired me to join the Civil Air Patrol, the civilian auxiliary of the Air Force. We met once a week, marched in formation, and learned about the various jobs available in the Air Force from officers, which is how I became fascinated with Pararescue—the guys who jump out of airplanes to pull downed pilots out of harm's way.

I attended a week-long course during the summer before my freshman year called PJOC, the Pararescue Jump Orientation Course. As usual, I was the only. One day a pararescuman named Scott Gearen came to speak, and he had a motherfucker of a story to tell. During a standard exercise, on a high altitude jump from 13,000 feet, Gearen deployed his chute with another sky-diver right above him. That wasn't out of the ordinary. He had the right of way, and per his training, he'd waved off the other jumper. Except the guy didn't see him, which placed Gearen in grave danger because the jumper above him was still mid freefall, hurtling through the air at over 120 mph. He went into a cannonball hoping to avoid clipping Gearen, but it didn't work. Gearen had no clue what was coming when his teammate flew through his canopy, collapsing it on contact, and slammed into Gearen's face with his knees. Gearen was knocked unconscious instantly and wobbled into another free fall, his crushed chute creating very little drag. The other skydiver was able to deploy his chute and survive with minor injuries.

Gearen didn't really land. He bounced like a fiat basketball, three times, but because he'd been unconscious, his body was limp, and he didn't come apart despite crashing into the ground at 1 0 0 mph. He died twice on the operating table, but the ER docs brought him back to life. When he woke in a hospital bed, they said he wouldn't make a full recovery and would never be a pararescuman again. Eighteen months later he 'd defied medical odds, made that full recovery, and was back on the job he loved.

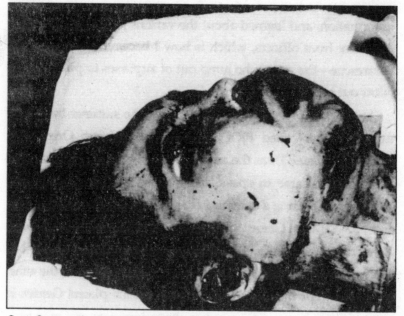

Scott Gearen after his accident

For years I was obsessed with that story because he'd survived the impossible, and I resonated with his survival. After Wilmoth's murder, with all those racist taunts raining down on my head (I won't bore you with every single episode, just know there were many more), I felt like I was free falling with no fucking chute. Gearen was living proof that it's possible to transcend anything that doesn't kill you, and from the time I heard him speak I knew I would enlist in the Air Force after graduation, which only made school seem more irrelevant.

Especially after I was cut from the varsity basketball team during my junior year. I wasn't cut because of my skills. The coaches knew I was one of the best players they had, and that I loved the game. Johnny and I played it night and day. Our entire friendship was based on basketball, but because I was angry at the coaches for how they used me on the JV team the year before, I didn't attend summer workouts, and they took that as a lack of commitment to the team. They didn't know or care that when they cut me, they'd eliminated any incentive I'd had to keep my G PA up, which I'd barely managed to do through cheating anyway. Now, I had no good reason to attend school. At least that's what I thought, because I was clueless about the emphasis that the military places on education. I figured they'd take anybody. Two incidents convinced me otherwise and inspired me to change.

The first was when I failed the Armed Services Vocational Aptitude Battery test (ASVAB) during my junior year. The ASVAB is the armed forces version of the SATs. It's a standardized test that allows the military to assess your current knowledge and future potential for learning at the same time, and I showed up for that test prepared to do what I did best: cheat. I'd been copying on every test, in every class, for years, but when I took my seat for the ASVAB I was shocked to see that the people seated to my right and left had different tests than I did. I had to go it alone and scored a 20 out of a possible 99 points. The absolute minimum standard to be admitted to the Air Force is only 36, and I couldn't even get there.

The second sign that I needed to change arrived with a postmark just before school let out for the summer after junior year. My mother was still in her emotional black hole after Wilmoth's murder, and her coping mechanism was to take on as much as possible. She worked full-time at DePauw University and taught night classes at Indiana State University because if she stopped hustling long enough to think, she would realize the reality of her life. She kept it moving, was never around, and never asked to see my grades. After the first semester of our junior year, I remember Johnny and me bringing home Fs and Ds. We spent two hours doctoring the ink. We turned Fs into Bs and Ds into Cs, and were laughing the whole damn time. I actually remember feeling a perverse pride in being able to show my fake grades to my mother, but she never even asked to see them. She took my damn word for it.

```
000940577  1992-93   GOGGINS,  DAVID
        CUM-      1.43592
     PREVIOUS  CREDITS-       21.000
GEOMETRY              D+          1.000  SM1
ENGLISH 11           D           1.000  SM1
U.S.HIST/MODERN      F                  SM1
ELECTRONICS I        D+          1.000  SM1
PHYS. SCIENCE        C-          1.000  SM1
        TOTAL  CREDITS-       25.000
        Rank:    211 OF    255
```

Junior year transcript

We lived parallel lives in the same house, and since I was more or less raising myself, I stopped listening to her. In fact, about ten days before the letter arrived, she'd kicked me out because I refused to come home from a party before curfew. She told me that if I didn't, I shouldn't come home at all.

In my mind, I had already been living by myself for several years. I made my own meals, cleaned my own clothes. I wasn't angry at her. I was cocky and figured I didn't need her anymore. I stayed out that night, and for the next week and a half I crashed at Johnny's place or with other friends. Eventually the day came when I'd spent my last dollar. By chance, she called me at Johnny's that morning and told me about a letter from school. It said I'd missed over a quarter of the year due to unexcused absences, that I had a D average, and unless I showed significant improvement in my GPA and attendance during my senior year, I would not graduate. She wasn't emotional about it. She was more exhausted than exasperated.

"I'll come home and get the note," I said.

"No need for that," she replied, " I just wanted you to know you were flunking out."

I showed up on her doorstep later that day with my stomach growling. I didn't ask for forgiveness and she didn't demand an apology. She just left the door open and walked away. I stepped into the kitchen and made myself a peanut butter and jelly sandwich. She passed me the letter without saying a word. I read it in my room where the walls were papered over with layers of Michael Jordan and special ops posters. Inspiration for twin passions slipping through my fingers.

That night, after taking a shower, I wiped the steam away from our corroded bathroom mirror and took a good look. I didn't like who I saw staring back. I was a low-budget thug with no purpose and no future. I felt so disgusted I wanted to punch that motherfucker in the face and shatter glass. Instead, I lectured him. It was time to get real.

"Look at you," I said. "Why do you think the Air Force wants your punk ass? You stand for nothing. You are an embarrassment."

I reached for the shaving cream, smoothed a thin coat over my face, unwrapped a fresh razor and kept talking as I shaved.

"You are one dumb motherfucker. You read like a third grader. You're a fucking joke! You've never tried hard at anything in your life besides basketball, and you have goals? That's fucking hilarious."

After shaving peach fuzz from my cheeks and chin, I lathered up my scalp. I was desperate for a change. I wanted to become someone new.

"You don't see people in the military sagging their pants. You need to stop talking like a wanna-be-gangster. None of this shit is gonna cut it! No more taking the easy way out! It's time to grow the fuck up! "

Steam billowed all around me. It rippled off my skin and poured from my soul. What started as a spontaneous venting session had become a solo intervention.

"It's on you," I said. "Yeah, I know shit is fucked up. I know what you've been through. I was there , bitch! Merry fucking Christmas. Nobody is coming to save your ass! Not your mommy, not Wilmoth. Nobody! It's up to you! "

By the time I was done talking, I was shaved clean. Water pearled on my scalp, streamed from my forehead, and dripped down the bridge of my nose. I looked different, and for the first time, I'd held myself accountable. A new ritual was born, one that stayed with me for years. It would help me get my grades up, whip my sorry ass into shape, and see me through graduation and into the Air Force.

The ritual was simple. I'd shave my face and scalp every night, get loud, and get real. I set goals, wrote them on Post-It notes, and tagged them to what I now call the Accountability Mirror, because each day I'd hold myself accountable to the goals I'd set. At first my goals involved shaping up my appearance and accomplishing all my chores without having to be asked.

Make your bed like You're in the military every day!

Pull up your pants!

Shave your head every morning!

Cut the grass!

Wash all dishes!

The Accountability Mirror kept me on point from then on, and though I was still young when this strategy came through me, since then I've found it useful for people at any stage in life. You could be on the cusp of retirement, looking to reinvent yourself. Maybe you're going through a bad break-up or have gained weight. Perhaps you're permanently disabled, overcoming some other injury, or are just coming to grips with how much of your life you've wasted, living without purpose. In each case, that negativity you're feeling is your internal desire for change, but change doesn't come easy, and the reason this ritual worked so well for me was because of my tone.

I wasn't fluffy. I was raw because that was the only way to get myself right. That summer between my junior and senior year in high school I was afraid. I was insecure. I wasn't a smart kid. I'd blown off all accountability for my entire teenage existence, and actually thought I was getting over on all the adults in my life, getting over on the system. I'd duped myself into a negative feedback loop of cheating and scamming that on the surface looked like advancement until I hit a brick fucking wall called reality. That night when I came home and read the letter from my school, there was no denying the truth, and I delivered it hard.

I didri't dance around and say, "Geez, David, you are not

taking your education very seriously." No, I had to own it in the raw because the only way we can change is to be real with ourselves. If you don't know shit and have never taken school seriously, then say, "I'm dumb! " Tell yourself that you need to get your ass to work because you're falling behind in life!

If you look in the mirror and you see a fat person, don't tell yourself that you need to lose a couple of pounds. Tell the truth. You're fucking fat! It's okay. Just say you're fat if you're fat. The dirty mirror that you see every day is going to tell you the truth every time, so why are you still lying to yourself? So you can feel better for a few minutes and stay the fucking same? If you're fat you need to change the fact that you're fat because it's very fucking unhealthy. I know because I've been there.

If you have worked for thirty years doing the same shit you've hated day in and day out because you were afraid to quit and take a risk, you've been living like a pussy. Period, point blank. Tell yourself the truth! That you've wasted enough time, and that you have other dreams that will take courage to realize, so you don't die a fucking pussy.

Call yourself out!

Nobody likes to hear the hard truth. Individually and as a culture, we avoid what we need to hear most. This world is fucked up, there are major problems in our society. We are still dividing ourselves up along racial and cultural lines, and people don't have the balls to hear it! The truth is racism and bigotry still fucking exist and some people are so thin-skinned they refuse to admit that. To this day, many in Brazil claim that there is no racism in their small town. That's why I have to give Kirk Freeman props. When I called him in the spring of 2018, he remembered what I went through very clearly. He's one of the few who isn't afraid of the truth.

But if you are the *only*, and you aren't stuck in some real-world genocidal twilight zone, you'd better get real too. Your life is not fucked up because of overt racists or hidden systemic racism. You aren't missing out on opportunities, making shit money, and getting evicted because of America or Donald fucking Trump or because your ancestors were slaves or because some people hate immigrants or Jews or harass women or believe gay people are going to hell. If any of that shit is stopping you from excelling in life, I've got some news. *You are stopping you!*

You are giving up instead of getting hard! Tell the truth about the real reasons for your limitations and you will turn that negativity, which is real, into jet fuel. Those odds stacked against you will become a damn runway!

There is no more time to waste. Hours and days evaporate like creeks in the desert. That's why it's okay to be cruel to yourself as long as you realize you're doing it to become better. We all need thicker skin to improve in life. Being soft when you look in the mirror isn't going to inspire the wholesale changes we need to shift our present and open up our future.

The morning after that first session with the Accountability Mirror, I trashed the shag steering wheel and the fuzzy dice. I tucked my shirt in and wore my pants with a belt, and, once school started up again, I stopped eating at my lunch table. For the first time, being liked and acting cool were a waste of my time, and instead of eating with all the popular kids, I found my own table and ate alone.

Mind you, the rest of my progress could not be described as a blink-and-you'll-miss-it metamorphosis. Lady Luck did not suddenly show up, run me a hot soapy bath, and kiss me like she loved me. In fact, the only reason I didn't become just another statistic is because, at the last possible moment, I got to work.

During my senior year in high school, all I cared about was working out, playing basketball, and studying, and it was the Accountability Mirror that kept me motivated to keep pushing toward something better. I woke up before dawn and started going to the YMCA most mornings at 5 a.m. before school to hit the weights. I ran all the damn time, usually around the local golf course after dark. One night I ran thirteen miles—the most I'd ever run in my entire life. On that run I came to a familiar intersection. It was the same street where that redneck had pulled a gun on me. I avoided it and ran on, covering a half mile in the opposite direction before something told me to turn back. When I arrived at that intersection a second time, I stopped and contemplated it. I was scared shitless of that street, my heart was leaping from my chest, which is exactly why I suddenly started charging down its fucking throat.

Within seconds, two snarling dogs got loose and chased me as the woods leaned in on both sides. It was all I could do to stay a step ahead of the beasts. I kept expecting that truck to reappear and run me the fuck down, like some scene from Mississippi circa 1965, but I kept running, faster and faster, until I was breathless. Eventually the hounds of Hell gave up and loped off, and it was just me, the rhythm and steam of my breath, and that deep country quiet. It was cleansing. By the time I turned back, my fear was gone. I owned that fucking street.

From then on, I brainwashed myself into craving discomfort. If it was raining, I would go run. Whenever it started snowing, my mind would say, *Get your fucking running shoes on.* Sometimes I wussed out and had to deal with it at the Accountability Mirror. But facing that mirror, facing myself, motivated me to fight through uncomfortable experiences, and, as a result, I became tougher. And being tough and resilient helped me meet my goals.

Nothing was as hard for me as learning. The kitchen table became my all-day, all-night study hall. After I'd failed the ASVAB a second time, my mother realized that I was serious about the Air Force, so she found me a tutor who helped me figure out a system I could use to learn. That system was memorization. I couldn't learn just by scratching a few notes and memorizing those. I had to read a text book and write each page down in my notebook. Then do it again a second and third time. That's how knowledge stuck to the mirror of my mind. Not through learning, but through transcription, memorization, and recall.

I did that for English. I did that for history. I wrote out and memorized formulas for algebra. If my tutor took an hour to teach me a lesson, I had to go back over my notes from that session for six hours to lock it in. My personal study hall schedule and goals became Post-It notes on my Accountability Mirror, and guess what happened? I developed an obsession for learning.

Over six months I went from having a fourth grade reading level to that of a senior in high school. My vocabulary mushroomed. I wrote out thousands of flash cards and went over them for hours, days, and weeks. I did the same for mathematical formulas. Part of it was survival instinct. I damn sure wasn't going to get into college based on academics, and though I was a starter on the varsity basketball team my senior year, no college scouts knew my name. All I knew was that I had to get the fuck out of Brazil, Indiana; that the military was my best chance; and to get there I had to pass the ASVAB. On my third try, I met the minimum standard for the Air Force.

Living with purpose changed everything for me—at least in the short term. During my senior year in high school, studying and working out gave my mind so much energy that hate flaked from my soul like used-up snake skin. The resentment I held toward the racists in Brazil, the emotion that had dominated me and was burning me up inside, dissipated because I'd finally considered the fucking source.

I looked at the people who were making me feel uncomfortable and realized how uncomfortable they were in their own skin. To make fun of or try to intimidate someone they didn't even know based on race alone was a clear indication that something was very wrong with them, not me. But when you have no confidence it becomes easy to value other people's opinions, and I was valuing *everyone's* opinion without considering the minds that generated them. That sounds silly, but it's an easy trap to fall into, especially when you are insecure on top of being *the only*. As soon as I made that connection, being upset with them was not worth my time. Because if I was gonna kick their ass in life, and I was, I had way too much shit to do. Each insult or dismissive gesture became more fuel for the engine revving inside me.

By the time I graduated, I knew that the confidence I'd managed to develop didn't come from a perfect family or God-given talent. It came from personal accountability which brought me self respect, and self respect will always light a way forward.

For me, it lit up a path straight out of Brazil, forever. But I didn't get away clean. When you transcend a place in time that has challenged you to the core, it can feel like you've won a war. Don't fall for that mirage. Your past, your deepest fears, have a way of going dormant before springing back to life at double strength. You must remain vigilant. For me, the Air Force revealed that I was still soft inside. I was still insecure.

I wasn't yet hard of bone and mind.

CHALLENGE #2

It's time to come eyeball to eyeball with yourself, and get raw and real. This is not a self-love tactic. You can't fluff it. Don't massage your ego. This is about abolishing the ego and taking the first step toward becoming the real you!

I tacked Post-It notes on my Accountability Mirror, and I'll ask you to do the same. Digital devices won't work. Write all your insecurities, dreams, and goals on Post-Its and tag up your mirror. If you need more education, remind yourself that you need to start working your ass off because you aren't smart enough! Period, point blank. If you look in the mirror and see someone who is obviously overweight, that means you're fucking fat! Own it! It's okay to be unkind with yourself in these moments because we need thicker skin to improve in life.j

Whether it's a career goal (quit my job, start a business), a lifestyle goal (lose weight, get more active), or an athletic one (run my first sK, 1oK, or marathon), you need to be truthful with yourself about where you are and the necessary steps it will take to achieve those goals, day by day. Each step, each necessary point of self-improvement, should be written as its own note. That means you have to do some research and break it all down. For example, if you are trying to lose forty pounds, your first Post-It may be to lose two pounds in the first week. Once that goal is achieved, remove the note and post the next goal of two to five pounds until your ultimate goal is realized.

Whatever your goal, you'll need to hold yourself accountable for the small steps it will take to get there. Self-improvement takes dedication and self-discipline. The dirty mirror you see every day is going to reveal the truth. Stop ignoring it. Use it to your advantage. If you feel it, post an image of yourself staring into your tagged-up Accountability Mirror on social media with the hashtags #canthurtme #accountabilitymirror.

CHAPTER THREE

THE IMPOSSIBLE TASK

IT WAS PAST MIDNIGHT AND THE STREETS WERE DEAD. I steered my pickup truck into another empty parking lot and killed the engine. In the quiet all I could hear were the eerie halogen hum of the street lamps and the scratch of my pen as I checked off another franchise feed trough. The latest in a never-ending series of fast food and dine-in industrial kitchens that received more nightly visitors than you'd care to know about. That's why guys like me showed up to places like this in the wee hours. I stuffed my clipboard under the armrest, grabbed my gear, and began restocking rat traps.

They're everywhere, those little green boxes. Look around almost any restaurant and you'll find them, hidden in plain sight. My job was to bait, move, or replace them. Sometimes I hit pay dirt and found a rat carcass, which never caught me by surprise. You know death when you smell it.

This wasn't the mission I signed up for when I enlisted in the Air Force with dreams of joining a Pararescue unit. Back then I was nineteen years old and weighed 175 pounds. By the time I was discharged four years later, I had ballooned to nearly 300 pounds and was on a different kind of patrol. At that weight, even bending down to bait the traps took effort. I was so damn fat I had to sew an athletic sock into the crotch of my work pants so they wouldn't split when I dropped to one knee. No bull shit. I was a sorry fucking sight.

With the exterior handled, it was time to venture indoors, which was its own wilderness. I had keys to almost every restaurant in this part of Indianapolis, and their alarm codes too. Once inside, I pumped my hand-held silver canister full of poison and placed a fumigation mask over my face. I looked like a damn space alien in that thing, with its dual filters jutting out from my mouth, protecting me from toxic fumes.

Protecting me.

If there was anything I liked about that job it was the stealth nature of working late, moving in and out of inky shadows. I loved that mask for the same reason. It was vital, and not because of any damn insecticide. I needed it because it made it impossible for anyone to see me, especially me. Even if by chance I caught my own reflection in a glass doorway or on a stainless steel countertop, it wasn't me I was seeing. It was some janky-ass, low-budget storm trooper. The kind of guy who would palm yesterday's brownies on his way out the door.

It wasn't me.

Sometimes I'd see roaches scurry for cover when I flipped the lights on to spray down the counters and the tiled floors. I'd see dead rodents stuck to sticky traps I'd laid on previous visits. I bagged and dumped them. I checked the lighting systems I'd installed to catch moths and flies and cleaned those out too. Within a half hour I was gone, rolling on to the next restaurant. I had a dozen stops every night and had to hit them all before dawn.

Maybe this kind of gig sounds disgusting to you. When I think back I'm disgusted too, but not because of the job. It was honest work. Necessary. Hell, in Air Force boot camp I got on the wrong side of my first drill sergeant and she made me the latrine queen. It was my job to keep the latrines in our barracks shining. She told me that if she found one speck of dirt in that latrine at any moment I would get recycled back to day one and join a new flight. I took my discipline. I was happy just to be in the Air Force, and I cleaned the hell out of that latrine. You could have eaten off that floor. Four years later, the guy who was so energized by opportunity that he was excited to clean latrines was gone and I didn't feel anything at all.

They say there's always light at the end of the tunnel, but not once your eyes adjust to the darkness, and that's what happened to me. I was numb. Numb to my life, miserable in my marriage, and I'd accepted that reality. I was a would-be warrior turned cockroach sniper on the graveyard shift. Just another zombie selling his time on earth, going through the motions. In fact, the only insight I had into my job at that time was that it was actually a step up.

When I was first discharged from the military I got a job at St. Vincent's Hospital. I worked security from 11 p.m. to 7 a.m. for minimum wage and cleared about $700 a month. Every now and then I'd see an Ecolab truck pull up. We were on the exterminator's regular rotation, and it was my job to unlock the hospital kitchen for him. One night we got to talking, and he mentioned that Ecolab was hiring, and that the job came with a free truck and no boss looking over your shoulder. It was also a 35 percent pay raise. I didn't think about the health risks. I didn't think at all. I was taking what was being offered. I was on that spoon-fed path of least resistance, letting dominoes fall on my head, and it was killing me slowly. But there's a difference between being numb and clueless. In the dark night there weren't a lot of distractions to get me out of my head, and I knew that I had tipped the first domino. I'd started the chain reaction that put me on Ecolab duty.

The Air Force should have been my way out. That first drill sergeant did end up recycling me into a different unit, and in my new flight I became a star recruit. I was 6 '2" and weighed about 175 pounds. I was fast and strong, our unit was the best flight in all of boot camp, and soon I was training for my dream job: Air Force Pararescue. We were guardian angels with fangs, trained to drop from the sky behind enemy lines and pull downed pilots out of harm's way. I was one of the best guys in that training. I was one of the best at push-ups, and the best at sit-ups, flutter kicks, and running. I was one point behind honor grad, but there was something they didn't talk about in the lead-up to Pararescue training: water confidence. That's a nice name for a course where they try to drown your ass for weeks, and I was uncomfortable as hell in the water.

Although my mom got us off the public dole and out of subsidized housing within three years, she still didn't have extra cash for swim lessons, and we avoided pools. It wasn't until I attended Boy Scout camp when I was twelve years old that I was finally confronted with swimming. Leaving Buffalo allowed me to join the Scouts, and camp was my best opportunity to score all the merit badges I'd need to stay on the path to becoming an Eagle Scout. One morning it was time to qualify for the swimming merit badge and that meant a one-mile swim in a lake course, marked off with buoys. All the other kids jumped in and started getting after it, and if l wanted to save face I had to pretend I knew what I was doing, so I followed them into the lake. I dog paddled the best I could, but kept swallowing water so I flipped onto my back and ended up swimming the entire mile with a fucked-up backstroke I'd improvised on the fly. Merit badge secured.

Boy Scouts

When it came time to take the swim test to get into Pararescue, I needed to be able to swim for real. This was a timed, 500-meter freestyle swim, and even at nineteen years old I didn't know how to swim freestyle. So I took my stunted ass down to Barnes & Noble, bought *Swimming for Dummies*, studied the diagrams, and practiced in the pool every day. I hated putting my face in the water, but I'd manage for one stroke, then two, and before long I could swim an entire lap.

I wasn't as buoyant as most swimmers. Whenever I stopped swimming, even for a moment, I'd start to sink, which made my heart pound with panic, and my increased tension just made it worse. Eventually, I passed that swim test, but there is a difference between being competent and comfortable in the water, another big gap from comfortable to confident, and when you can't float like most people, water confidence does not come easy. Sometimes it doesn't come at all.

In Pararescue training, water confidence is part of the ten-week program, and it's filled with specific evolutions designed to test how well we perform in the water under stress. One of the worst evolutions for me was called Bobbing. The class was divided into groups of five, lined up from gutter to gutter in the shallow end, and fully kitted up. Our backs were strapped with twin eighty-liter tanks made from galvanized steel, and we wore sixteen-pound weight belts too. We were loaded the fuck down, which would have been fine, except in this evolution we weren't allowed to breathe from those tanks. Instead, we were told to walk backward down the slope of the pool from the three-foot section to the deep end, about ten feet down, and on that slow walk into position, my mind swirled with doubt and negativity.

What the fuck are you doing here? This isn't for you! You can't swim! You're an imposter and they will find you out!

Time slowed down and those seconds seemed like minutes. My diaphragm lurched, trying to force air into my lungs. Theoretically, I knew that relaxation was the key to all the underwater evolutions, but I was too terrified to let go. My jaw clenched as tight as my fists. My head throbbed as I worked to stave off panic. Finally, we were all in position and it was time to start bobbing. That meant pushing up from the bottom to the surface (without the benefit of tinning) , getting a gulp of air, and sinking back down. It wasn't easy, getting up fully loaded, but at least I was able to breathe, and that first breath was a salvation. Oxygen flooded my system and I started to relax until the instructor yelled "Switch! " That was our cue to take our fins from our feet, place them on our hands, and use one pull with our arms to propel ourselves to the surface. We were allowed to push off the floor of the pool, but we couldn't kick. We did that for five minutes.

Shallow water and surface blackouts aren't uncommon during water confidence training. It goes along with stressing the body and limiting oxygen intake. With the flippers on my hands I'd barely get my face high enough out of the water to breathe, and in between I was working hard and burning oxygen. And when you bum too much too fast, your brain shuts down and you will black the fuck out. Our instructors called that, "meeting the wizard." As the clock ticked, I could see stars materializing in my peripheral vision and felt the wizard creeping close.

I passed that evolution, and soon, tinning with my arms or feet became easy for me. What stayed hard from beginning to end was one of our simplest tasks: treading water without our hands. We had to keep our hands and our chins high above the water, using only our legs, which we'd swirl in a blender-like motion, for three minutes. That doesn't sound like much time, and for most of the class it was easy. For me, it was damn near impossible. My chin kept hitting the water, which meant the time would start again from triple zero. All around me, my classmates were so comfortable their legs were barely moving, while mine were whirring at top speed, and I still couldn't get half as high as those white boys who looked to be defying gravity.

Every day it was another humiliation in the pool. Not that I was embarrassed publicly. I passed all the evolutions, but inside I was suffering. Each night, I'd fixate on the next day's task and become so terrified I couldn't sleep, and soon my fear morphed into resentment toward my classmates who, in my mind, had it easy, which dredged up my past.

I was *the only* black man in my unit, which reminded me of my childhood in rural Indiana, and the harder the water confidence training became, the higher those dark waters would rise until it seemed I was also being drowned from the inside out. While the rest of my class was sleeping, that potent cocktail of fear and rage thrummed through my veins and my nocturnal fixations became their own kind of self-fulfilling prophecy. One where failure you inevitable because my unchecked fear was unleashing something I couldn't control: the quitting mind.

It all came to a head six weeks into training with the "buddy breathing" exercise. We partnered up, each pair gripped one another by the forearm, and took turns breathing through just one snorkel. Meanwhile, the instructors thrashed us, trying to separate us from our snorkel. All of this was supposed to be happening at or near the surface, but I was negatively buoyant, which meant I was sinking into the middle waters of the deep end, dragging my partner down with me. He'd take a breath and pass the snorkel down to me. I'd swim to the surface, exhale and attempt to clear the water from our snorkel and get a clean breath before passing it back to him, but the instructors made that almost impossible. I'd usually only clear the tube halfway, and inhale more water than air. From the jump, I was operating from an oxygen deficit while fighting to stay near the surface.

In military training, it's the instructors' job to identify weak links and challenge them to perform or quit, and they could tell I was struggling. In the pool that day, one of them was always in my face, yelling and thrashing me, while I choked, trying and failing to gulp air through a narrow tube to stave off the wizard. I went under and remember looking up at the rest of the class, splayed out like serene starfish on the surface. C alm as can be, they passed their snorkels back and forth with ease, while I fumed. I know now that my instructor was just doing his job, but back then I thought, *This fucker's not giving me a fair shot!*

I passed that evolution too, but I still had eleven more evolutions and four more weeks of water confidence training to go. It made sense. We would be jumping out of airplanes over water. We needed it. I just didn't want to do it anymore, and the next morning, I was offered a way out I hadn't seen coming.

Weeks earlier, we'd had our blood drawn during a med check, and the doctors had just discovered I carried the Sickle Cell Trait. I didn't have the disease, Sickle Cell Anemia, but I had the trait, which was believed at the time to increase the risk of sudden, exercise-related death due to cardiac arrest. The Air Force didn't want me dropping dead in the middle of an evolution and pulled me out of training on a medical. I pretended to take the news hard, as if my dream was being ripped away. I made a big fucking act of being pissed off, but inside I was ecstatic.

Later that week the doctors reversed their decision. They didn't specifically say it was safe for me to continue, but they said the trait wasn't yet well understood and allowed me to decide for myself. When I reported back to training the Master Sergeant (MSgt) informed me that I'd missed too much time and that if I wanted to continue I would have to start over from day one, week one. Instead of less than four weeks, I'd have to endure another ten weeks of the terror, rage, and insomnia that came with water confidence.

These days, that kind of thing wouldn't even register on my radar. You tell me to run longer and harder than everyone else just to get a fair shake, I'd say, "Roger that," and keep moving, but back then I was still half-baked. Physically I was strong, but I was not even close to mastering my mind.

The MSgt stared at me, awaiting my response. I couldn't even look him in the eye when I said, "You know what, Master Sergeant, the doctor doesn't know much about this Sickle Cell thing, and it's bothering me."

He nodded, emotionless, and signed the papers pulling me out of the program for good. He cited Sickle Cell, and on paper I didn't quit, but I knew the truth. If I had been the guy I am today, I wouldn't have given two fucks about Sickle Cell. I still have the

Sickle Cell Trait. You don't just get rid of it, but back then an obstacle had appeared, and I'd folded.

I moved on to Fort Campbell, Kentucky, told my friends and family that I was forced from the program on a medical, and served out my four years in the Tactical Air Control Party (TAC-P), which works with some special operations units. I trained to liaise between ground units and air support—fast movers like F-15s and F-16s—behind enemy lines. It was challenging work with intelligent people, but sadly I was never proud of it and didn't see the opportunities offered because I knew I was a quitter who had let fear dictate my future.

I buried my shame in the gym and at the kitchen table. I got into power lifting and layered on the mass. I ate and worked out. Worked out and ate. In my last days in the Air Force I weighed 255 pounds. After my discharge I continued to bulk up with both muscle and fat until I weighed nearly 300 pounds. I wanted to be big because being big hid David Goggins. I was able to tuck this 175;.pound person into those 21-inch biceps and that flabby belly. I grew a burly mustache and was intimidating to everyone who saw me, but inside I knew I was a pussy, and that's a haunting feeling.

After Air Force Boot Camp at 175 lbs in 1994

290 lbs at the beach in 1999

★ ★ ★

The morning I began to take charge of my destiny started out like any other. When the clock struck 7 a.m., my Ecolab shift ended and I hit the Steak 'n Shake drive-thru to score a large chocolate milkshake. Next stop, 7-Eleven, for a box of Hostess mini chocolate doughnuts. I gobbled those on my forty-five-minute drive home, to a beautiful apartment on a golf course in pretty Carmel, Indiana, which I shared with my wife, Pam, and her daughter. Remember that Pizza Hut incident? I married that girl. I married a girl whose dad called me a nigger. What does that say about me?

We couldn't afford that life. Pam wasn't even working, but in those credit-card-debt-loading days, nothing made much sense. I was doing 70 mph on the highway, mainlining sugar and listening to a local classic rock station when Sound of Silence poured from the stereo. Simon & Garfunkel's words echoed like truth.

Darkness was a friend indeed. I worked in the dark, hid my true selffrom friends and strangers. Nobody would have believed how numb and afraid I was back then because I looked like a beast that no one would dare fuck with, but my mind wasn't right, and my soul was weighed down by too much trauma and failure. I had every excuse in the world to be a loser, and used them all. My life was crumbling, and Pam dealt with that by fleeing the scene. Her parents still lived in Brazil, just seventy miles away. We spent most of our time apart.

I arrived home from work around 8 a.m., and the phone rang as soon as I walked in the door. It was my mother. She knew my routine.

"Come on over for your staple," she said.

My staple was a breakfast buffet for one, the likes of which few could put down in a single sitting. Think: eight Pillsbury cinnamon rolls, a half-dozen scrambled eggs, a half-pound of bacon, and two bowls of Fruity Pebbles. Don't forget, I had just decimated a box of donuts and a chocolate shake. I didn't even have to respond. She knew I was coming. Food was my drug of choice and I always sucked up every last crumb.

I hung up, flipped on the television, and stomped down the hall to the shower, where I could hear a narrator's voice filter through the steam. I caught snippets. "Navy SEALs ...toughest... the world." I wrapped a towel around my waist and rushed back into the living room. I was so big, the towel barely covered my fat ass, but I sat down on the couch and didn't move for thirty minutes.

The show followed Basic Underwater Demolition SEAL (BUD/S) Training Class 224 through Hell Week: the most arduous series of tasks in the most physically demanding training in the military. I watched men sweat and suffer as they tore through muddy obstacle courses, ran on the soft sand holding logs overhead, and shivered in icy surf. Sweat pearled on my scalp, I was literally on the edge of my seat as I saw guys—some of the strongest of them all—ring the bell and quit. Made sense. Only one-third of the men who begin BUD/S make it through Hell Week, and in all of my time in Pararescue training, I couldn't remember feeling as awful as these men looked. They were swollen, chafed, sleep-deprived, and dead on their feet, and I was jealous of them.

The longer I watched the more certain I became that there were answers buried in all that suffering. Answers that I needed. More than once the camera panned over the endless frothing ocean, and each time I felt pathetic. The SEALs were everything I wasn't. They were about pride, dignity, and the type of excellence that came from bathing in the fire, getting beat the fuck down, and going back for more, again and again. They were the human equivalent of the hardest, sharpest sword you could imagine. They sought out the flame, took the pounding for as long as necessary, longer even, until they were fearless and deadly. They weren't motivated. They were driven. The show ended with graduation. Twenty-two proud men stood shoulder to shoulder in their dress whites before the camera pushed in on their Commanding Officer.

"In a society where mediocrity is too often the standard and too often rewarded," he said, "there is intense fascination with men who detest mediocrity, who refuse to define themselves in conventional terms, and who seek to transcend traditionally recognized human capabilities. This is exactly the type of person BUD/S is meant to find. The man who finds a way to complete each and every task to the best of his ability. The man who will adapt and overcome any and all obstacles."

In that moment it felt as though the Commanding Officer was talking directly to me, but after the show ended I walked back to the bathroom, faced the mirror, and stared myself down. I looked every bit of 300 pounds. I was everything all the haters back home said I would be: uneducated, with no real world skills, zero discipline, and a dead -end future. Mediocrity would have been a major promotion. I was at the bottom of the barrel of life, pooling in the dregs, but, for the first time in way too long, I was awake.

I barely spoke to my mother during breakfast, and only ate half my staple because my mind was on unfinished business. I 'd always wanted to join an elite special operations unit, and beneath all the rolls of flesh and layers of failure, that desire was still there. Now it was coming back to life, thanks to a chance viewing of a show that continued to work on me like a virus moving cell to cell, taking over.

It became an obsession I couldn't shake. Every morning after work for almost three weeks, I called active duty recruiters in the Navy and told them my story. I called offices all over the country. I said I was willing to move as long as they could get me to SEAL . training. Everyone turned me down. Most weren't interested in candidates with prior service. One local recruiting office was intrigued and wanted to meet in person, but when I got there they laughed in my face. I was way too heavy, and in their eyes I was just another delusional pretender. I left that meeting feeling the same way.

After calling all the active duty recruiting offices I could find, I dialed the local unit of the Naval reserves, and spoke to Petty Officer Steven Schaljo for the first time. Schaljo had worked with multiple F-14 Squadrons as an electrician and instructor at NAS Miramar for eight years before joining the recruitment staff in San Diego, where the SEALs train. He worked day and night and rose quickly in the ranks. His move to Indianapolis came with a promotion and the challenge of finding Navy recruits in the middle of the corn. He'd only been on the job in Indy for ten days by the time I called, and if I 'd reached anyone else you probably wouldn't be reading this book. But through a combination of dumb luck and stubborn persistence I found one of the finest recruiters in the Navy, a guy whose favorite task was discovering diamonds in the rough—prior service guys like me who were looking to re-enlist and hoping to land in special operations.

Our initial conversation didn't last long. He said he could help me and that I should come in to meet in person. That sounded familiar. I grabbed my keys and drove straight to his office, but didn't get my hopes too high. By the time I arrived a half-hour later he was already on the phone with BUD/S administration.

Every sailor in that office—all of them white—were surprised to see me except Schaljo. If I was a heavyweight, Schaljo was a lightweight at 5 '7 ", but he didn't seem fazed by my size, at least not at first. He was outgoing and warm, like any salesman, though I could tell he had some pit bull in him. He led me down a hall to weigh me in, and while standing on the scale I eyed a weight chart pinned to the wall. At my height, the maximum allowable weight for the Navy was 191 pounds. I held my breath, sucked in my gut as much as I could, and puffed out my chest in a sorry attempt to stave off the humiliating moment where he'd let me down easy. That moment never came.

"You're a big boy," Schaljo said, smiling and shaking his head, as he scratched 297 pounds on a chart in his ·file folder. " The Navy has a program that allows recruits in the reserves to become active duty. That's what we 'll use for this. It's being phased out at the end of the year, so we need to get you classed up before then. Point is, you have some work to do, but you knew that." I followed his eyes to the weight chart and checked it again. He nodded, smiled, patted me on the shoulder, and left me to face my truth.

I had less than three months to lose 106 pounds.

It sounded like an impossible task, which is one reason I didn't quit my job. The other was the ASVAB. That nightmare test had come back to life like Frankenstein's fucking monster. I'd passed it once before to enlist in the Air Force, but to qualify for BUD/S I 'd have to score much higher. For two weeks I studied all day and zapped pests e ach night. I wasn't working out yet. Serious weight loss would have to wait.

I took the test on a Saturday afternoon. The following Monday I called Schaljo. "Welcome to the Navy," he said. He downloaded the good news first. I 'd done exceptionally well on some sections and was now officially a reservist, but I 'd only scored a 44 on Mechanical Comprehension. To qualify for BUD/S I needed a 50. I 'd have to retake the entire test in five weeks.

These days Steven Schaljo likes to call our chance connection "fate." He said he could sense my drive the first moment we spoke, and that he believed in me from the jump, which is why my weight wasn't an issue for him, but after that ASVAB test I was full of doubt. So maybe what happened later that night was also a form of fate, or a much needed dose of divine intervention.

I'm not going to drop the name of the restaurant where it went down because if I did you'd never eat there again and I'd have to hire a lawyer. Just know, this place was a disaster. I checked the traps outside first and found a dead rat. Inside, there were more dead rodents—a mouse and two rats—on the sticky traps, and roaches in the garbage which hadn't been emptied. I shook my head, got .down on my knees under the sink, and sprayed up through a narrow gap in the wall. I didn't know it yet, but I'd found their nesting column and when the poison hit they started to scatter.

Within seconds there was a skittering across the back of my neck I brushed it off, and craned my neck to see a storm of roaches raining down to the kitchen floor from an open panel in the ceiling. I'd hit the motherlode of cockroaches and the worst infestation I ever saw on the job for Ecolab. They kept coming. Roaches landed on my shoulders and my head. The floor was writhing with them.

I left my canister in the kitchen, grabbed the sticky traps, and burst outside. I needed fresh air and more time to figure out how I was going to clear the restaurant of vermin. I considered my options on my way to the dumpster to trash the rodents, opened the lid, and found a live raccoon, hissing mad. He bared his yellow teeth and lunged at me. I slammed the dumpster shut.

What the fuck? I mean, seriously, what the fucking fuck? When was enough truly going to be enough? Was I willing to let my sorry present become a fucked-up future? How much longer would I wait, how many more years would I burn, wondering if there was some greater purpose out there waiting for me? I knew right then that if I didn't make a stand and start walking the path of most resistance, I would end up in this mental hell forever.

I didn't go back inside that restaurant. I didn't collect my gear. I started my truck, stopped for a chocolate shake—my comfort tea at that time—and drove home. It was still dark when I pulled up. I didn't care. I stripped off my work clothes, put on some sweats and laced up my running shoes. I hadn't run in over a year, but I hit the streets ready to go four miles.

I lasted·400 yards. My heart raced. I was so dizzy I had to sit down on the edge of the golf course to catch my breath before making the slow walk back to my house, where my melted shake was waiting to comfort me in yet another failure. I grabbed it, slurped, and slumped into my sofa. My eyes welled with tears.

Who the fuck did I think I was? I was born nothing, I'd proven nothing, and I still wasn't worth a damn thing. David Goggins, a Navy SEAL? Yeah, right. What a pipe dream. I couldn't even run down the block for five minutes. All my fears and insecurities I'd bottled up for my entire life started raining down on my head. I was on the ve □e of giving in and giving up for good. That's when I found my old, beat to shit VHS copy of Rocky (the one I'd had for fifteen years), slid it into the machine, and fast forwarded to my favorite scene: Round 14.

The original Rocky is still one of my all-time favorite films because it's about a know-nothing journeyman fighter living in poverty with no prospects. Even his own trainer won't work with him. Then, out of the blue, he's given a title shot with the champion, Apollo Creed, the most feared fighter in history, a man that has knocked out every opponent he's ever faced. All Rocky wants is to be the first to go the distance with Creed. That alone will make him someone he could be proud of for the first time in his life.

The fight is closer than anyone anticipated, bloody and intense, and by the middle rounds Rocky is taking on more and more punishment. He's losing the fight, and in Round 14 he gets knocked down early, but pops right back up in the center of the ring. Apollo moves in, stalking him like a lion. He throws sharp left jabs, hits a slow-footed Rocky with a staggering combination, lands a punishing right hook, and another. He backs Rocky into a comer. Rocky's legs are jelly. He can't even muster the strength to raise his arms hi defense. Apollo slams another right hook into the side of Rocky's head, then a left hook, and a vicious right handed uppercut that puts Rocky down.

Apollo retreats to the opposite comer with his arms held high, but even face down in that ring, Rocky doesn't give up. As the referee begins his ten-count, Rocky squirms toward the ropes. Mickey, his own trainer, urges him to stay down, but Rocky isn't hearing it. He pulls himself up to one knee, then all fours. The referee hits six as Rocky grabs the ropes and rises up. The crowd roars, and Apollo turns to see him still standing. Rocky waves Apollo over. The champ's shoulders slump in disbelief.

The fight isn't over yet·.

I turned off the television and thought about my own life. It was a life devoid of any drive and passion, but I knew if I continued to surrender to my fear and my feelings of inadequacy, I would be allowing them to dictate my future forever. My only other choice was to try to find the power in the emotions that had laid me low, harness and use them to empower me to rise up, which is exactly what I did.

I dumped that shake in the trash, laced up my shoes, and hit the streets again. On my first run, I felt severe pain in my legs and my lungs at a quarter mile. My heart raced and I stopped. This time I felt the same pain, my heart raced like a car running hot, but I ran through it and the pain faded. By the time I bent over to catch my breath, I'd run a full mile.

That's when I first realized that not all physical and mental limitations are real, and that I had a habit of giving up way too soon. I also knew that it would take every ounce of courage and toughness I could muster to pull off the impossible. I was staring at hours, days, and weeks of non-stop suffering. I would have to push myself to the very edge of my mortality. I had to accept the very real possibility that I might die because this time I wouldn't quit, no matter how fast my heart raced and no matter how much pain I was in. Trouble was there was no battle plan to follow, no blueprint. I had to create one from scratch.

The typical day went something like this. I'd wake up at 4:30 a.m., munch a banana, and hit the ASVAB books. Around 5 a.m., I'd take that book to my stationary bike where I'd sweat and study for two hours. Remember, my body was a mess. I couldn't run multiple miles yet, so I had to burn as many calories as I could on the bike. After that I'd drive over to Carmel High School and jump into the pool for a two-hour swim. From there I hit the gym for a circuit workout that included the bench press, the incline press, and lots of leg exercises. Bulk was the enemy. I needed reps, and I did five or six sets of 100-200 reps each. Then it was back to the stationary bike for two more hours.

I was constantly hungry. Dinner was my one true meal each day, but there wasn't much to it. I ate a grilled or sauteed chicken breast and some sauteed vegetables along with a thimble of rice. After dinner I'd do another two hours on the bike, hit the sack, wake up and do it all over again, knowing the odds were stacked sky high against me. What I was trying to achieve is like a D-student applying to Harvard, or walking into a casino and putting every single dollar you own on a number in roulette and acting as if winning is a foregone conclusion. I was betting everything I had on myself with no guarantees.

I weighed myself twice daily, and within two weeks I'd dropped twenty-five pounds. My progress only improved as I kept grinding, and the weight started peeling off. Ten days later I was at 250, light enough to begin doing push-ups, pull-ups, and to start running my ass off. I'd still wake up, hit the stationary bike, the pool, and the gym, but I also incorporated two-, three-, and four-mile runs. I ditched my running shoes and ordered a pair of Bates Lites, the same boots SEAL candidates wear in BUD/S, and started running in those.

With so much effort, you'd think my nights would have been

restful, but they were filled with anxiety. My stomach growled and my mind swirled. I'd dream of complex ASVAB questions and dread the next day's workouts. I was putting out so much, on almost no fuel, that depression became a natural side effect. My splintering marriage was veering toward divorce. Pam made it very clear that she and my stepdaughter would not be moving to San Diego with me, if by some miracle I could pull this off. They stayed in Brazil most of the time, and when I was all alone in Carmel, I was in turmoil. I felt both worthless and helpless as my endless stream of self-defeating thoughts picked up steam.

When depression smothers you, it blots out all light and leaves you with nothing to cling onto for hope. All you see is negativity. For me, the only way to make it through that was to feed off my depression. I had to flip it and convince myself that all that self-doubt and anxiety was confirmation that I was no longer living an aimless life. My task may turn out to be impossible but at least I was back on a motherfucking mission.

Some nights, when I was feeling low, I'd call Schaljo. He was always in the office early in the morning and late at night. I didn't confide in him about my depression because I didn't want him to doubt me. I used those calls to pump myself up. I told him how many pounds I dropped and how much work I was putting in, and he reminded me to keep studying for that ASVAB.

Roger that.

I had the Rocky soundtrack on cassette and I'd listen to *Going the Distance* for inspiration. On long bike rides and runs, with those horns lasting in my brain, I'd imagine myself going through BUD/S; diving into cold water, and crushing Hell Week. I was wishing, I was hoping, but by the time I was down to 250, my quest to qualify for the SEALs wasn't a daydream anymore. I had a real chance to accomplish something most people, including myself, thought was impossible. Still, there were bad days. One morning not long after I dipped below 250, I weighed in and had only lost a pound from the day before. I had so much weight to lose I could not afford to plateau. That's all I thought about while running six miles and swimming two. I was exhausted and sore when I arrived in the gym for my typical three-hour circuit.

After rocking over 100 pull-ups in a series of sets, I was back on the bar for a max set with no ceiling. Going in, my goal was to get to twelve but my hands were burning fire as I stretched my chin over the bar for the tenth time. For weeks, the temptation to pull back had been ever present, and I always refused. That day, however, the pain was too much and after my eleventh pull-up, I gave in, dropped down, and finished my workout, one pull-up shy.

That one rep stayed with me, along with that one pound. I tried to get them out of my head but they wouldn't leave me the fuck alone. They taunted me on the drive home, and at my kitchen table while I ate a sliver of grilled chicken and a bland, baked potato. I knew I wouldn't sleep that night unless I did something about it, so I grabbed my keys.

"You cut corners and you are not gonna fucking make it," I said, out loud, as I drove back to the gym. "There are no shortcuts for you, Goggins!"

I did my entire pull-up workout over again. One missed pull-up cost me an extra 250, and there would be similar episodes. Whenever I cut a run or swim short because I was hungry or tired, I'd always go back and beat myself down even harder. That was the only way I could manage the demons in my mind. Either way there would be suffering. I had to choose between physical suffering in the moment, and the mental anguish of wondering if that one missed pull-up, that last lap in the pool, the quarter mile I skipped on the road or trail, would end up costing me an opportunity of a lifetime. It was an easy choice. When it came to the SEALs, I wasn't leaving anything up to chance.

On the eve of the ASVAB, with four weeks to go before training, making weight was no longer a worry. I was already down to 215 pounds and was faster and stronger than I'd ever been. I was running six miles a day, bicycling over twenty miles, and swimming more than two. All of it in the dead of winter. My favorite run was the six-mile Monon trail, an asphalt bike and walking path that laced through the trees in Indianapolis. It was the domain of cyclists and soccer moms with jogging strollers, weekend warriors and seniors. By then Schaljo had passed along the Navy SEAL warning order. It included all the workouts I would be expected to complete during first phase of BUD/S, and I was happy to double them. I knew that 190 men usually class-up for a typical SEAL training and only about forty people make it all the way through. I didn't want to be just one of those forty. I wanted to be the best.

But I had to pass the damn ASVAB first. I'd been cramming every spare second. If I wasn't working out, I was at my kitchen table, memorizing formulas and cycling through hundreds of vocabulary words. With my physical training going well, all my anxiety stuck to the ASVAB like paper clips to a magnet. This would be my last chance to take the test before my eligibility for the SEALs expired. I wasn't very smart, and based on past academic performance there was no good reason to believe I'd pass with a score high enough to qualify for the SEALs. If I failed, my dream would die, and I'd be floating without purpose once again.

The test was held in a small classroom on Fort Benjamin Harrison in Indianapolis. There were about thirty people there, all of us young. Most were just out of high school. We were e ach assigned an old-school desktop computer. In the past month, the test had been digitized and I wasn't experienced with computers. I didn't even think I could work the damn machine let alone answer the questions, but the program proved idiot proof and I settled in.

The ASVAB has ten sections, and I was breezing through until I reached Mechanical Comprehension, my truth serum. Within the hour I would have a decent idea if I'd been lying to myself or if I had the raw stuff necessary to become a SEAL. Whenever a question stumped me, I marked my worksheet with a dash. There were about thirty questions in that section and by the time I completed the test, I'd guessed at least ten times. I needed some of them to go my way or I was out.

After completing the final section, I was prompted to send the entire bundle to the administrator's computer at the front of the room where the score would be tabulated instantly. I peeked over my monitor and saw him sitting there, waiting. I pointed, clicked, and left the room. Buzzing with nervous energy, I paced the parking lot for a few minutes before finally ducking into my Honda Accord, but I didn't start the engine. I couldn't leave.

I sat in the front seat for fifteen minutes with a thousand-yard stare. It would be at least two days before Schaljo would call with my results, but the answer to the riddle that was my future was already solved. I knew exactly where it was, and I had to know the truth. I gathered myself, walked back in, and approached the fortune teller.

"You gotta tell me what I got on this fucking test, man,, I said. He peered up at me, surprised, but he didn't buckle . .

"I'm sorry, son. This is the government. There's a system for how they do things," he said. " I didn't make the rules and I can't bend them."

"Sir, you have no idea what this test means to me, to my life. It's everything!" He looked into my glassy eyes for what felt like five minutes, then turned toward his machine.

" I 'm breaking every rule in the book right now," he said. "Goggins, rit? " I nodded and came around behind his seat as he scrolled through files. "There you are. Congratulations, you scored 6s. That's a great score." He was referencing my overall, but I didn't care about that. Everything hinged on my getting a so-spot where it counted most.

"What did I get on mechanical comprehension?" He shrugged, clicked and scrolled, and there it was. My new favorite number glowed on his screen: so.

"YES ! " I shouted. "YES! YES! "

There was still a handful of others taking the test, but this was the happiest moment in my life and I couldn't stifle it. I kept screaming "YES!" at the top of my lungs. The administrator damn near fell out of his chair and everyone in that room stared at me like I was crazy. If they only knew how crazed I'd been! For two months I'd dedicated my entire existence to this one moment, and I was damn well gonna enjoy it. I rushed to my car and screamed some more.

" FUCK YEAH! "

On my drive home I called my mom. She was the one person, aside from Schaljo, who witnessed my metamorphosis. "I fucking did it," I told her, tears in my eyes. " I fucking did it! I 'm going to be a SEAL."

When Schali o came to work the next day, he got the news and called me up. He'd sent in my recruitment package and had just heard back that I was in! I could tell he was happy for me, and proud that ·what he saw in me the first time we met turned out to be real.

But it wasn't all happy days. My wife had given me an implied ultimatum, and now I had a decision to make. Abandon the opportunity I 'd worked so hard for and stay married, or get divorced and go try to become a SEAL. In the end, my choice didn't have anything to do w:ith my feelings for Pam or her father. He'd apologized to me, by the way. It was about who I was and who I wanted to be. I was a prisoner in my own my mind and this opportunity was my only chance to break free.

I celebrated my victory the way any SEAL candidate should. I put the fuck out. The following morning and for the next three weeks I spent time in the pool, strapped with a sixteen-pound weight belt. I swam underwater for fifty meters at a time and walked the length of the pool underwater, with a brick in each hand, all on a single breath. The water would not own my ass this time.

When I was done, I'd swim a mile or two, then head to a pond near my mother's home. Remember, this was Indiana—the American Midwest—in December. The trees were naked. Icicles hung like crystals from the eaves of houses and snow blanketed the earth in all directions, but the pond wasn't completely frozen yet. I waded into the icy water, dressed in camo pants, a brown short sleeved t—shirt, and boots, laid back and looked into the gray sky. The hypothermic water washed over me, the pain was excruciating, and I fucking loved it. After a few minutes I got out and started running, water sloshing in my boots, sand in my underwear. Within seconds my t-shirt was frozen to my chest, my pants iced at the cuffs .

I hit the Monon trail. Steam poured from my nose and mouth as I grunted and slalomed speed-walkers and joggers. Civilians. Their heads turned as I picked up speed and began sprinting, like Rocky in downtown Philly. I ran as fast as I could for as long as I could, from a put that no longer defined me, toward a future undetermined. All I knew was that there would be pain and there would be purpose.

And that I was ready.

CHALLENGE #3

The first step on the journey toward a calloused mind is stepping outside your comfort zone on a regular basis. Dig out your journal again and write down all the things you don't like to do or that make you uncomfortable. Especially those things you know are good for you.

Now go do one of them, and do it again.

In the coming pages, I'll be asking you to mirror what you just read to some degree, but there is no need for you to find your own impossible task and achieve it on the fast track. This is not about changing your life instantly, it's about moving the needle bit by bit and making those changes sustainable. That means digging down to the micro level and doing something that sucks every day. Even if it's as simple as making your bed, doing the dishes, ironing your clothes, or getting up before dawn and running two miles each day. Once that becomes comfortable, take it to five, then ten miles. If you already do all those things, find something you aren't doing. We all have areas in our lives we either ignore or can improve upon. Find yours. We often choose to focus on our strengths rather than our weaknesses. Use this time to make your weaknesses your strengths.

Doing things—even small things—that make you uncomfortable will help make you strong. The more often you get uncomfortable the stronger you'll become, and soon you'll develop a more productive, can-do dialogue with yourself in stressful situations.

Take a photo or video of yourself in the discomfort zone, post it on social media describing what you're doing and why, and don't forget to include the hashtags #discomfortzone #pathofmostresistance #canthurtme #impossibletask.

CHAPTER FOUR

TAKING SOULS

THE FIRST CONCUSSION GRENADE EXPLODED AT CLOSE range, and from there everything unraveled in slow motion. One minute we were chilling in the common room, bullshitting, watching war movies, getting pumped up for the battle we knew was coming. Then that first explosion led to another, and suddenly Psycho Pete was in our faces, screaming at the top of his lungs, his cheeks flushed candy apple red, that vein in his right temple throbbing. When he screamed, his eyes bugged out and his whole body shook.

"Break! The fuck! Out! Move! Move! Move!"

My boat crew sprinted for the door single-file, just like we'd planned. Outside, Navy SEALs were firing their M6os into the darkness toward some invisible enemy. It was the bad dream we'd been waiting for our entire lives: the lucid nightmare that would define or kill us. Every impulse we had told us to hit the dirt, but at that moment, movement was our only option.

The repetitive, deep bass thud of machine-gun fire penetrated our guts, the orange halo from another explosion in the near distance provided a shock of violent beauty, and our hearts hammered as we gathered on the Grinder awaiting orders. This was war alright, but it wouldn't be fought on some foreign shore. This one, like most battles we fight in life, would be won or lost in our own minds.

Psycho Pete stomped the pocked asphalt, his brow slick with sweat, the muzzle of his rifle steaming in the foggy night. "Welcome to Hell Week, gentlemen," he said, calmly this time, in that sing-song Cali-surfer drawl of his. He looked us up and down like a predator eyeing his kill. "It will be my great pleasure to watch you suffer."

Oh, and there would be suffering. Psycho set the tempo, called out the push-ups, sit-ups, and flutter kicks, the jumping lunges and dive bombers. In between, he and his fellow instructors hosed us down with freezing water, cackling the whole damn time. There were countless reps and set after set with no end in sight.

My classmates were gathered close, each of us on our own stenciled frog footprints, overlooked by a statue of our patron saint: The Frogman, a scaly alien creature from the deep with webbed feet and hands, sharp claws, and a motherfucking six-pack. To his left was the infamous brass bell. Ever since that morning when I came home from cockroach duty and got sucked into the Navy SEAL show, it was this place that I'd sought. The Grinder: a slab of asphalt dripping with history and misery.

Basic Underwater Demolition/SEAL (BUD/S) training is six months long and divided into three phases. First Phase is all about physical training, or PT. Second Phase is dive training, where we learn how to navigate underwater and deploy stealthy, closed circuit diving systems that emit no bubbles and recycle our carbon dioxide into breathable air. Third Phase is land warfare training. But when most people picture BUD/S they think of First

Phase because those are the weeks that tenderize new recruits until the class is literally ground down from about 120 guys to the hard, gleaming spine that are the twenty-five to forty guys who are more worthy of the Trident. The emblem that tells the world we are not to be fucked with.

BUD/S instructors do that by working guys out beyond their perceived limits, by challenging their manhood, and insisting on objective physical standards of strength, stamina, and agility. Standards that are tested. In those first three weeks of training we had to, among other things, climb a vertical ten-meter rope, hammer a half-mile-long obstacle course studded with American Ninja Warrior type challenges in under ten minutes, and run four miles on the sand in under thirty-two minutes. But if you ask me, all that was child's play. It couldn't even compare to the crucible of First Phase.

Hell Week is something entirely different. It's medieval and it comes at you fast, detonating in just the third week of training. When the throbbing ache in our muscles and joints was ratcheted up high and we lived day and night with an edgy, hyperventilating feeling of our breath getting out front of our physical rhythm, of our lungs inflating and deflating like canvas bags squeezed tight in a demon's fists, for 130 hours straight. That's a test that goes way beyond the physical and reveals your heart and character. More than anything, it reveals your mindset, which is exactly what it's designed to do.

All of this happened at the Naval Special Warfare Command Center on prissy-ass Coronado Island, a Southern California tourist trap that tucks into slender Point Lorna and shelters the San Diego Marina from the open Pacific Ocean. But even Cali's golden sun couldn't pretty up the Grinder, and thank God for that. I liked it ugly. That slab of agony was everything I'd ever wanted. Not because I loved to suffer, but because I needed to know whether or not I had what it took to belong.

Thing is, most people don't.

By the time Hell Week started, at least forty guys had already quit, and when they did they were forced to walk over to the bell, ring it three times, and place their helmet on the concrete. The ringing of the bell was first brought in during the Vietnam era because so many guys were quitting during evolutions and just walking off to the barracks. The bell was a way to keep track of guys, but since then it's become a ritual that a man has to perform to own the fact that he's quitting. To the quitter, the bell is closure. To me, every clang sounded like progress.

I never liked Psycho much, but I couldn't quibble with the specifics of his job. He and his fellow instructors were there to cull the herd. Plus, he wasn't going after the runts. He was in my face plenty, and guys bigger than me too. Even the smaller dudes were studs. I was one man in a fleet of alpha specimens from back East and down South, the blue-collar and big-money surf beaches of California, a few from corn country like me, and plenty from the Texas rangeland. Every BUD/S class has their share of hard-ass backcountry Texans. No state puts more SEALs in the pipeline. Must be something in the barbecue, but Psycho didn't play favorites. No matter where we were from or who we were, he lingered like a shadow we couldn't shake. Laughing, screaming, or quietly taunting us to our face, attempting to burrow into the brain of any man he tried to break.

Despite all that, the first hour of Hell Week was actually fun. During breakout, that mad rush of explosions, shooting, and shouting, you are not even thinking about the nightmare to come. You're riding an adrenaline high because you know you're fulfilling a rite of passage within a hallowed warrior tradition. Guys are looking around the Grinder, practically giddy, thinking, "Yeah, we're in Hell Week, motherfuckers!" Ah, but reality has a way of kicking everyone in the teeth sooner or later.

"You call this putting out?" Psycho Pete asked no one in particular. "This may be the single sorriest class we ever put through our program. You men are straight up embarrassing yourselves."

He relished this part of the job. Stepping over and between us, his boot print in our pooling sweat and saliva, snot, tears, and blood. He thought he was hard. All the instructors did, and they were because they were SEALs. That fact alone placed them in rare air. "You boys couldn't have held my jock when I went through Hell Week, I'll tell you that much."

I smiled to myself and kept hammering as Psycho brushed by. He was built like a tailback, quick and strong, but was he a mortal fucking weapon during his Hell Week? Sir, I doubt that very fucking much, sir!

He caught the eye of his boss, the First Phase Officer in Charge. There was no doubt about him. He didn't talk a whole lot and didn't have to. He was 6'1", but he cast a longer shadow. Dude was jacked too. I'm talking about 225 pounds of muscle wrapped tight as steel, without an ounce of sympathy. He looked like a Silverback Gorilla (SBG), and loomed like a Godfather of pain, making silent calculations, taking mental notes.

"Sir, my dick's getting stiff just thinking about these gaping vaginas weeping and quitting like whiny little bitches this week," Psycho said. SBG offered half a nod as Psycho stared through me. "Oh, and you will quit," he said softly. "I'll make sure of that."

Psycho's threats were spookier when he delivered them in a relaxed tone like that, but there were plenty of times when his eyes went dark, his brow twisted, the blood rushed to his face, and he unleashed a scream that built from the tips of his toes to the crown of his bald head. An hour into Hell Week, he knelt down, pressed his face within an inch of my own while I finished another set of push-ups, and let loose.

"Hit the surf, you miserable fucking turds!"

We'd been in BUD/S for nearly three weeks by then, and we'd raced up and over the fifteen-foot berm that divided the beach from the cinderblock sprawl of offices, locker rooms, barracks, and classrooms that is the BUD/S compound plenty of times. Usually to lie back in the shallows, fully dressed, then roll in the sand—until we were covered in sand from head to toe—before charging back to the Grinder, dripping heavy with salt water and sand, which ramped up the degree of difficulty on the pull-up bar. That ritual was called getting wet and sandy, and they wanted sand in our ears, up our noses, and in every orifice of our body, but this time we were on the verge of something called surf torture, which is a special kind of beast.

As instructed, we charged into the surf screaming like *senseis*. Fully clothed, arms linked, we waded into the impact zone. The surf was angry that moonless night, nearly head high, and the waves were rolling thunder that barreled and foamed in sets of three and four. Cold water shriveled our balls and swiped the breath from our lungs as the waves thrashed us.

This was early May, and in the spring the ocean off Coronado ranges from 59-63 degrees. We bobbed up and down as one, a pearl strand of floating heads scanning the horizon for any hint of swell we prayed we'd see coming before it towed us under. The surfers in our crew detected doom first and called out the waves so' we could duck dive j ust in time . After ten minutes or so, Psycho ordered us back to land. On the verge of hypothermia,.we scrambled from the surf zone and stood at attention, while being checked by the doctor for hypothermia. That cycle would continue to repeat itself. The sky was smeared orange and red. The temperature dropped sharply as night loomed close.

"Say goodbye to the sun, gents," SBG said. He made us wave at the setting sun. A symbolic acknowledgement of an inconvenient truth. We were about to freeze our natural asses off.

After an hour, we fell back into our six-man boat crews, and stood nut to butt, huddling tight to get warm, but it was futile. Bones were rattling up and down that beach. Guys were jackhammering and sniffling, a physical state revealing the quaking conditions of splintering minds, which were just now coming to grips with the reality that this shit had only just begun.

Even on the hardest days of First Phase prior to Hell Week, when the sheer volume of rope climbs and push-ups, pull-ups, and flutter kicks crushes your spirit, you can find a way out. Because you know that no matter how much it sucks, you'll head home that night, meet friends for dinner, see a movie, maybe get some pussy, and sleep in your own bed. The point is, even on miserable days you can fixate on an escape from hell that's real.

Hell Week offers no such love. Especially on day one, when an hour in they had us standing, linking arms, facing the Pacific Ocean, wading in and out of the surf for hours. In between we were gifted soft sand sprints to warm up. Usually they had us carry our rigid inflatable boat or a log overhead, but the warmth, if it ever arrived, was always short-lived because every ten minutes they rotated us back into the water.

The clock ticked slowly that first night as the cold seeped in, colonizing our marrow so thoroughly the runs stopped doing any good. There would be no more bombs, no more shooting, and very little yelling. Instead, an eerie quiet expanded and deadened our spirit. In the ocean, all any of us could hear were the waves going overhead, the seawater we accidentally swallowed roiling in our guts, and our own teeth chattering.

When you're that cold and stressed, the mind cannot comprehend the next 120-plus hours. Five and a half days without sleep cannot be broken up into small pieces. There is no way to systematically attack it, which is why every single person who has ever tried to become a SEAL has asked himself one simple question during their first dose of surf torture:

"Why am I here?"

Those innocuous words bubbled up in our spinning minds each time we got sucked under a monster wave at midnight, when we were already borderline hypothermic. Because nobody *has* to become a SEAL. We weren't fucking *drafted*. Becoming a SEAL is a choice. And what that single softball question revealed in the heat of battle is that each second we remained in training was also a choice, which made the entire notion of becoming a SEAL seem like masochism. It's voluntary torture. And that makes no sense at all to the rational mind, which is why those four words unravel so many men.

The instructors know all of this, of course, which is why they stop yelling early on. Instead, as the night wore on, Psycho Pete consoled us like a concerned older brother. He offered us hot soup, a warm shower, blankets, and a ride back to the barracks. That was the bait he set for quitters to snap up, and he harvested helmets left and right. He was taking the souls of those who caved because they couldn't answer that simple question. I get it. When it's only Sunday and you know you're going to Friday and you're already far colder than you've ever been, you're tempted to believe that you can't hack it and that nobody can. Married guys were thinking, *I could be at home, cuddled up to my beautiful*

wife instead of shivering and suffering. Single guys were thinking,
I could be on the hunt for pussy right now.

It's tough to ignore that kind of glittering lure, but this was my second lap through the early stages of BUD/S. I'd tasted the evil of Hell Week as part of Class 230. I didn't make it, but I didn't quit. I was pulled out on a medical after contracting double pneumonia. I defied doctor's orders three times and tried to stay in the fight, but they eventually forced me to the barracks and rolled me back to day one, week one of Class 231.

I wasn't all the way healed up from that bout of pneumonia when my second BUD/S class kicked off. My lungs were still filled with mucus and each cough shook my chest and sounded like a rake was scraping the inside of my alveoli. Still, I liked my chances a lot better this time around because I was prepared, and because I was in a boat crew thick with bad motherfuckers.

BUD/S boat crews are sorted by height because those are the guys who will help you carry your boat everywhere you go once Hell Week begins. Size alone didn't guarantee your teammates would be tough, however, and our guys were a crew of square-peg misfits.

There was me, the exterminator who had to drop 100 pounds and take the ASV AB test twice just to get to SEAL training, only to be rolled back almost immediately. We also had the late Chris Kyle. You know him as the deadliest sniper in Navy history. He was so successful, the hajjis in Fallujah put an $80,000 bounty on his head and he became a living legend among the Marines he protected as a member of Seal Team Three. He won a Silver Star and four Bronze Stars for valor, left the military, and wrote a book, *American sniper,* that became a hit movie starring Bradley fucking Cooper. But back then he was a simple Texas hayseed rodeo cowboy who barely said a damn word.

Then there was Bill Brown, aka Freak Brown. Most people just called him Freak, and he hated it because he'd been treated like one his whole damn life. In many ways he was the white version of David Goggins. He came up tough in the river towns of South Jersey. Older kids in the neighborhood bullied him because of his cleft palate or because he was slow in class, which is how that nickname stuck. He got into enough fights over it that he eventually landed in a youth detention center for a six-month stretch. By the time he was nineteen he was living on his own in the hood, trying to make ends meet as a gas station attendant. It wasn't working. He had no coat and no car. He commuted everywhere on a rusted out ten-speed bike, literally freezing his balls off. One day after work, he stopped into a Navy recruitment office because he knew he needed structure and purpose, and some warm clothes. They told him about the SEALs, and he was intrigued, but he couldn't swim. Just like me, he taught himself, and after three attempts he finally passed the SEAL swim test.

Next thing he knew, Brown was in BUD/S, where that Freak nickname followed him. He rocked PT and sailed through First Phase, but he wasn't nearly as solid in the classroom. Navy SEAL dive training is as tough intellectually as it is physically, but he scraped by and got within two weeks of becoming a BUD/S graduate when, in one of his final land warfare evolutions, he failed re-assembling his weapon in a timed evolution known as *weapons practical*. Brown hit his targets but missed the time, and he flunked out of BUD/S at the bitter end.

But he didn't give up. No sir, Freak Brown wasn't going anywhere. I'd heard stories about him before he washed up with me in Class 231. He had two chips on his shoulders, and I liked him immediately. He was hard as hell and exactly the kind of guy I signed up to go to war with. When we carried our boat from the

Grinder to the sand for the first time, I made sure we were the two men at the front, where the boat is at its heaviest. "Freak Brown," I shouted, "we will be the pillars of Boat Crew Two!, He looked over, and I glared back.

"Don't fucking call me that, Goggins," he said with a snarl.

"Well don't you move out of position, son! You and me, up front, all fucking week!"

"Roger that," he said.

I took the lead of Boat Crew Two from the beginning, and getting all six of us through Hell Week was my singular focus. Everyone fell in line because I'd already proven myself, and not just on the Grinder. In the days before Hell Week began I got it into my head that we needed to steal the Hell Week schedule from our instructors. I told our crew as much one night when we were hanging in the classroom, which doubled as our lounge. My words fell on deaf ears. A few guys laughed but everyone else ignored me and went back to their shallow ass conversations.

I understood why. It made no sense. How were we supposed to get a copy of their shit? And even if we did, wouldn't the anticipation make it worse? And what if we got caught? Was the reward worth the risk?

I believed it was, because I'd tasted Hell Week. Brown and a few other guys had too, and we knew how easy it was to think about quitting when confronted with levels of pain and exhaustion you didn't think possible. One hundred and thirty hours of suffering may as well be a thousand when you know you can't sleep and that there will be no relief anytime soon. And we knew something else too. Hell Week was a mind game. The instructors used our suffering to pick and peel away our layers, not to find the fittest athletes. To find the strongest minds. That's something the quitters didn't understand until it was too late.

Everything in life is a mind game! Whenever we get swept under by life's dramas, large and small, we are forgetting that no matter how bad the pain gets, no matter how harrowing the torture, all bad things end. That forgetting happens the second we give control over our emotions and actions to other people, which can easily happen when pain is peaking. During Hell Week, the men who quit felt like they were running on a treadmill turned way the fuck up with no dashboard within reach. But, whether they ever figured it out or not, that was an illusion they fell for.

I went into Hell Week knowing I put myself there, that I wanted to be there, and that I had all the tools I needed to win this fucked -up game, which gave me the passion to persevere and claim ownership of the experience. It allowed me to play hard, bend rules, and look for an edge wherever and whenever I could until the horn sounded on Friday afternoon. To me this was war, and the enemies were our instructors who'd blatantly told us that they wanted to break us down and make us quit! Having their schedule in our heads would help us whittle the time down by memorizing what came next, and more than that, it would gift us a victory going in. Which would give us something to latch onto during Hell Week when those motherfuckers were beating us down.

"Yo man, I 'm not playing," I said. "We need that schedule!"

I could see Kenny Bigbee, the only other black man in Class 231, raise an eyebrow from across the room. He'd been in my first BUD/S class &, and got injured just before Hell Week. Now he was back for seconds too. "Oh shit," he said. "David Goggins is back on the log."

Kenny smiled Wide and I doubled over laughing. He'd been in the instructors' office listening in when the doctors were trying to pull me out of my first Hell Week. It was during a log PT evolution. Our boat crews were carrying logs as a unit up and down the beach, soaked, salty, and sandy as shit. I was running with a log on my shoulders, vomiting blood. Bloody snot streamed from my nose and mouth, and the instructors periodically grabbed me and sat me down nearby because they thought I might drop fucking dead. But every time they turned around I was back in the mix. Back on that log.

Kenny kept hearing the same refrain over the radio that night. "We need to get Goggins out of there," one voice said.

"Roger that, sir. Goggins is sitting down," another voice crackled. Then after a beat, Kenny would hear that radio chirp again. "Oh shit, Goggins is back on the log. I repeat, Goggins is back on the log!"

Kenny loved telling that story. At 5'10" and 170 pounds, he was smaller than I was and wasn't on our boat crew, but I knew we could trust him. In fact, there was nobody better for the job. During Class 231, Kenny was tapped to keep the instructors' office clean and tidy, which meant that he had access. That night, he tiptoed into enemy territory, liberated the schedule from a file, made a copy, and slipped it back into position before anyone ever knew it was missing. Just like that we had our first victory before the biggest mind game of our lives had even begun.

Of course, knowing something is coming is only a small part of the battle. Because torture is torture, and in Hell Week the only way to get to past it is to go through it. With a look or a few words, I made sure our guys were putting out at all times. When we stood Qn the beach holding our boat overhead, or running logs up and down that motherfucker, we went hard, and during surf torture I hummed the saddest and most epic song from *Platoon*, while we waded into the Pacific Ocean.

I've always found inspiration in film. Rocky helped motivate me to achieve my dream of being invited to SEAL training, but *Platoon* would help me and my crew find an edge during the dark nights of Hell Week, when the instructors were mocking our pain, telling us how sorry we were, and sending us into the head-high surf over and over again. Adagio in Strings was the score to one of my favorite scenes in Platoon and with bone-chilling fog wrapping all around us, I stretched my arms out like Elias when he was getting gunned down by the Viet Cong, and sang my ass off. We'd all watched that movie together during First Phase, and my antics had a dual effect of pissing off the instructors and firing up my crew. Finding moments of laughter in the pain and delirium turned the entire melodramatic experience upside down for us. It gave us some control of our emotions. Again, this was all a mind game, and I damn sure wasn't going to lose.

But the most important games within the game were the races that the instructors set up between boat crews. Damn near everything in BUD/S was a competition. We'd run boats and logs up and down the beach. We had paddle races, and we even did the damn O-Course carrying a log or a boat between obstacles. We'd carry them while balancing on narrow beams, over spinning logs, and across rope bridges. We'd send it over the high wall, and we dropped it at the foot of the thirty-foot-high cargo net while we climbed up and over that damn thing. The winning team was almost always rewarded with rest and the losing teams got extra beat downs from Psycho Pete. They were ordered to perform sets of push-ups and sit-ups in the wet sand, then do berm sprints, their bodies quivering with exhaustion, which felt like failure on top of failure. Psycho let them know it too. He laughed in their face as he hunted quitters.

"You are absolutefy pathetic," he said. "I hope to God you fucking quit because if they allow you in the field you're gonna get us all killed!"

Watching him berate my classmates gave me a dual sensation. I didn't mind him doing his job, but he was a bully, and I never liked bullies. He'd been coming at me hard since I got back to BUD/S, and early on I decided I would show him that he couldn't get to me. Between bouts of surf torture, when most guys stand nut to butt to transfer heat, body to body, I stood apart. Everyone else was shivering. I didn't even twitch, and I saw how much that bothered him.

During Hell Week

The one luxury we had during Hell Week was chow. We ate like kings. We're talking omelets, roast chicken and potatoes, steak, hot soup, pasta with meat sauce, all kinds of fruit, brownies, soda, coffee, and a lot more. The catch is we had to run the mile there and back, with that 200-pound boat on our heads. I always left chow hall with a peanut butter sandwich tucked in my wet and sandy pocket to scarf on the beach when the instructors weren't looking. One day after lunch, Psycho decided to give us a bit more than a mile. It became obvious at the quarter mile marker, when he picked up his pace, that he wasn't taking us directly back to the Grinder.

"You boys better keep the fuck up!" he yelled, as one boat crew fell back. I checked my guys.

"We are staying on this motherfucker! Fuck him!"

"Roger that," said Freak Brown. True to his word, he'd been with me on the front of that boat—the two heaviest points—since Sunday night, and he was only getting stronger.

Psycho stretched us out on the soft sand for more than four miles. He tried like hell to lose us, too, but we were his shadow. He switched up the cadence. One minute he was sprinting, then he was crouching down, wide-legged, grabbing his nuts and doing elephant walks, then he loped at a jogger's pace before breaking into another wind sprint down the beach. By then the closest boat was a quarter mile behind, but we were clipping his damn heels. We mimicked his every step and refused to let our bully gain any satisfaction at our expense. He may have smoked everybody else but he did not smoke Boat Crew Two!

Hell Week is the devil's opera, and it builds like a crescendo, peaking in torment on Wednesday and staying right there until they call it on Friday afternoon. By Wednesday we were all broke dick, chafed to holy Hell. Our whole body was one big raspberry, oozing puss and blood. Mentally we were zombies. The instructors had us doing simple boat raises and we were all dragging. Even my crew could barely lift that boat. Meanwhile, Psycho and SBG and the other instructors kept close watch, looking for weaknesses as always.

I had a real hate for the instructors. They were my enemy and I was tired of them trying to burrow into my brain. I glanced at Brown, and for the first time all week he looked shaky. The whole crew did. Shit, I felt miserable too. My knee was the size of a grapefruit and every step I took torched my nerves, which is why I was searching for something to fuel me. I locked in on Psycho Pete. I was sick of that motherfucker. The instructors looked composed and comfortable. We were desperate, and they had what we needed: energy! It was time to flip the game and own real estate in their heads.

When they clocked out that night and drove home after a pussy-ass eight hour shift while we were still going hard, I wanted them thinking about Boat Crew Two. I wanted to haunt them when they slipped into bed with their wives. I wanted to occupy so much space in their minds that they couldn't even get it up. To me that would be as powerful as putting a knife in their dick. So I deployed a process that I now call "Taking Souls."

I turned to Brown. "You know why I call you Freak?" I asked. He looked over as we lowered the boat, then lifted it up overhead like creaky robots on reserve battery power. " Because you are one of the baddest men I've ever seen in my damn life!" He cracked a smile. "And you know what I say to these motherfuckers right here?" I tipped my elbow at the nine instructors gathered on the beach, drinking coffee and talking bullshit. " I say, they can go fuck themselves!" Bill nodded and narrowed his eyes on our tor-mentors, while I turned to the rest of the crew. "Now let's throw this shit up high and show them who we are!"

" Fucking beautiful," Bill said. "Let's do it!"

Within seconds my whole team had life. We didn't just lift the boat overhead and set it down hard, we threw it up, caught it overhead, tapped the sand with it and threw it up high again. The results were immediate and undeniable. Our pain and exhaustion faded. Each rep made us stronger and faster, and each time we threw the boat up we all chanted.

"YOU CAN'T HURT BOAT CREW TWO!"

That was our *fuck* you to the instructors, and we had their full attention as we soared on a second wind. On the toughest day of the hardest week in the world's toughest training, Boat Crew Two was moving at lightning speed and making a mockery of Hell Week. The look on the instructors' faces told a story. Their mouths hung open like they were witnessing something nobody had ever seen before. Some averted their eyes, almost embarrassed. Only SBG looked satisfied.

★ ★ ★

Since that night in Hell Week, I've deployed the Taking Souls concept countless times. Taking Souls is a ticket to finding your own reserve power and riding a second wind. It's the tool you can call upon to win any competition or overcome every life obstacle. You can utilize it to win a chess match, or conquer an adversary in a game of office politics. It can help you rock a job interview or excel at school. And yes, it can be used to conquer all manner of physical challenges, but remember, this is a game you are playing within yourself. Unless you're engaged in physical competition, I'm not suggesting that you try to dominate someone or crush their spirit. In fact, they never even need to know you're playing this game. This is a tactic for you to be your best when duty calls. It's a mind game you're playing on yourself.

Taking someone's soul means you've gained a tactical advantage. Life is all about looking for tactical advantages, which is why we stole the Hell Week schedule, why we nipped Psycho's heels on that run, and why I made a show of myself in the surf, humming the *Platoon* theme song. Each of those incidents was an act of defiance that empowered us.

But defiance isn't always the best way to take someone's soul. It all depends upon your terrain. During BUD/S, the instructors didn't mind if you looked for advantages like that. They respected it as long as you were also kicking ass. You must do your own homework. Know the terrain you're operating in, when and where you can push boundaries, and when you should fall in line.

Next, take inventory of your mind and body on the eve of battle. List out your insecurities and weakness, as well as your opponent's. For instance, if you're getting bullied, and you know where you fall short or feel insecure, you can stay ahead of any insults or barbs a bully may throw your way. You can laugh at yourself along with them, which disempowers them. If you take what they do or say less personally, they no longer hold any cards. Feelings are just feelings. On the other hand, people who are secure with themselves don't bully other people. They look out for other people, so if you're getting bullied you know that you're dealing with someone who has problem areas you can exploit or soothe. Sometimes the best way to defeat a bully is to actually help them. If you can think two or three moves ahead, you will commandeer their thought process, and if you do that, you've taken their damn soul without them even realizing it.

Our SEAL instructors were our bullies, and they didn't realize the games I was playing during that week to keep Boat Crew Two sharp. And they didn't have to. I imagined that they were obsessed with our exploits during Hell Week, but I don't know that for sure. It was a ploy I used to maintain my mental edge and help our crew prevail.

In the same way, if you are up against a competitor for a promotion, and you know where you fall short, you can shape up your game ahead of your interview or evaluation. In that scenario, laughing at your weaknesses won't solve the problem. You must master them. In the. meantime, if you are aware of your competitor's vulnerabilities you can spin those to your advantage, but all of that takes research. Again, know the terrain, know yourself, and you'd better know your adversary in detail.

Once you're in the heat of battle, it comes down to staying power. If it's a difficult physical challenge you will probably have to defeat your own demons before you can take your opponent's soul. That means rehearsing answers to the simple question that is sure to rise up like a thought bubble: "Why am I here?" If you know that moment is coming and have your answer ready, you will be equipped to make the split second-decision to ignore your weakened mind and keep moving. Know why you're in the fight to stay in the fight!

And never forget that all emotional and physical anguish is finite! It all ends eventually. Smile at pain and watch it fade for at least a second or two. If you can do that, you can string those seconds together and last longer than your opponent thinks you can, and that may be enough to catch a second wind. There is no scientific consensus on second wind. Some scientists think it's the result of endorphins flooding your nervous system, others think it's a burst of oxygen that can help break down lactic acid, as well as the glycogen and triglycerides muscles need to perform. Some say its purely psychological. All I know is that by going hard when we felt defeated we were able to ride a second wind through the worst night in Hell Week. And once you have that second wind behind you it's easy to break your opponent down and snatch a soul. The hard part is getting to that point, because the ticket to victory often comes down to bringing your very best when you feel your worst.

★ ★ ★

After rocking boat presses,. the whole class was gifted an hour of sleep in a big green army tent they'd set up on the beach and outfitted with military cots. Those motherfuckers had no mattresses, but may as well have been a cotton topped cloud of luxury because once we were horizontal we all went limp

Oh, but Psycho wasn't done with me. He let me sleep for a solitary minute, then woke me up and led me back onto the beach for some one-on-one time. He saw an opportunity to get in my head, at last, and I was disoriented as I staggered toward the water all alone, but the cold woke me the fuck up. I decided to savor my extra hour of private surf torture. When the water was chest high I began humming *Adagio in Strings* once more. Louder this time. Loud enough for that motherfucker to hear me over the crash of the surf. That song gave me life!

I'd come to SEAL training to see if I was hard enough to belong and found an inner beast within that I never knew existed. A beast that I would tap into from then on whenever life went wrong. By the time I emerged from that ocean, I considered myself unbreakable.

If only.

Hell Week takes its toll on everybody, and later that night, with forty-eight hours to go, I went to med check to get a Toradol shot in my knee to bring the swelling down. By the time I was back on the beach, the boat crews were out at sea in the midst of a paddling drill. The surf was pounding, the wind swirling. Psycho looked over at SBG. "What the fuck are we gonna do with him?"

For the first time, he was hesitant, and tired of trying to beat me down. I was good to go, ready for any challenge, but Psycho was over it. He was ready to give my ass a spa vacation. That's when I knew I'd outlasted him; that I had his soul. SBG had other ideas. He handed me a life jacket and attached a chem light to the back of my hat.

"Follow me," he said as he charged up the beach. I caught

up and we ran north for a good mile. By then we could barely see the boats and their bobbing lights through the mist and over the waves. "All right, Goggins. Now go swim out and find your fucking boat!"

He'd landed a hollow point on my deepest insecurity, pierced my confidence, and I was stunned silent. I gave him a look that said, "Are you fucking kidding me?" I was a decent swimmer by then, and surf torture didn't scare me because we weren't that far from shore, but an open water, hypothermic swim a thousand yards off shore in a storm, to a boat that had no fucking idea I was heading their way? That sounded like a death sentence, and I hadn't prepared for anything like it. But sometimes the unexpected descends like chaos, and without warning even the bravest among us must be ready to take on risks and tasks that seem beyond our capabilities.

For me, in that moment, it came down to how I wanted to be remembered. I could have refused the order, and I wouldn't have gotten in trouble because I had no swim buddy (in SEAL training you always have to be with a swim buddy), and it was obvious that he was asking me to do something that was extremely unsafe. But I also knew that my objective coming into SEAL training was more than making it through to the other side with a Trident. For me it was the opportunity to go up against the best of the best and distance myself from the pack. So even though I couldn't see the boats out past the thrashing waves there was no time to dwell on fear. There was no choice to make at all.

"What are you waiting on Goggins? Get your fucking ass out there, and do not fuck this up!"

"Roger that!" I shouted and sprinted into the surf. Trouble was, strapped with a buoyancy vest, nursing a wounded knee, wearing boots, I couldn't swim for shit and it was almost impossible to duck dive through the waves. I had to flail over the white wash, and with my mind managing so many variables, the ocean seemed colder than ever. I swallowed water by the gallon. It was as if the sea was prying open my jaws and flooding my system, and with each gulp, my fear magnified.

I had no idea that back on land, SBG was preparing for a worst-case scenario rescue. I didn't know he'd never put another man in that position before. I didn't realize that he saw something special in me and like any strong leader wanted to see how far I could take it, as he watched my light bob on the surface, nervous as hell. He told me all of that during a recent conversation. At the time I was just trying to survive.

I finally made it through the surf and swam another half-mile off-shore only to realize I had six boats bearing down on my head, teeter tottering in and out of view thanks to a four-foot wind swell. They didn't know I was there! My light was faint, and in the trench I couldn't see a damn thing. I kept waiting for one of them to come barreling down from the peak of a swell and mow me the fuck down. All I could do was bark into the darkness like a hoarse sea lion.

"Boat Crew Two! Boat Crew Two! "

It was a minor miracle that my guys heard me. They wheeled our boat around, and Freak Brown grabbed me with his big ass hooks and hauled me in like a prized catch. I lay back in the middle of the boat, my eyes closed, and jackhammered for the first time all week. I was so cold I couldn't hide it.

"Damn, Goggins," Brown said, "you must be insane ! You okay?" I nodded once and got a hold of myself. I was the leader of that crew and couldn't allow myself to show weakness. I tensed every muscle in my body, and my shiver slowed to a stop in real time.

"That's how you lead from the motherfucking front," I said, coughing up saltwater like a wounded bird. I couldn't keep a straight face for long. Neither could my crew. They knew damn well that crazy-ass swim wasn't my idea.

As the clock ran down on Hell Week, we were in the demo pit, just off Coronado's famous Silver Strand. The pit was filled with cold mud and topped off with icy water. There was a rope bridge—two separate lines, one for the feet and one for the hands—stretching across it from end to end. One by one, each man had to navigate their way across while the instructors shook the shit out of it, trying to make us fall. To maintain that kind of balance takes tremendous core strength, and we were all cooked and at our wits end. Plus, my knee was still fucked. In fact, it had gotten worse and required a pain shot every twelve hours. But when my name was called, I climbed onto that rope, and when the instructors went to work, I flexed my core and held on with all I had left.

Nine months earlier, I had topped out at 297 pounds and couldn't even run a quarter mile. Back then, when I was dreaming of a different life, I remember thinking that just getting through Hell Week would be the biggest honor of my life so far. Even if I never graduated from BUD/S, surviving Hell Week alone would have meant something. But I didn't just survive. I was about to finish Hell Week at the top of my class, and for the first time, I knew I was a bad motherfucker.

Once, I was so focused on failing, I was afraid to entry. Now I would take on any challenge. All my life, I was terrified of water, and especially cold water, but standing there in the final hour, I wished the ocean, wind, and mud were even colder! I was completely transformed physically, which was a big part of my success in BUD/S, but what saw me through Hell Week was my mind, and I was just starting to tap into its power.

That's what I was thinking about as the instructors did their best to throw me off that rope bridge like a mechanical bull. I hung tough and got as far as anyone else in Class 231 before nature won out and I was sent spinning into the freezing mud. I wiped it from my eyes and mouth and laughed like mad as Freak Brown helped me up. Not long after that, SBG stepped to the edge of the pit.

"Hell Week secure ! " He shouted to the thirty guys still left, quivering in the shallows. All of us chafed and bleeding, bloated and stiff. "You guys did an amazing job ! "

Some guys screamed with joy. Others collapsed to their knees with tears in their eyes and thanked God. I stared into the heavens too, pulled Freak Brown in for a hug, and high-fived my team. Every other boat crew had lost men, but not Boat Crew Two! We lost no men and won every single race!

We continued to celebrate as we boarded a bus to the Grinder. Once we arrived, there was a large pizza for each guy along with a sixty-four-ounce bottle of Gatorade and the coveted brown t-shirt. That pizza tasted like motherfucking manna from heaven, but the shirts meant something more significant. When you first arrive at BUD/S you wear white t-shirts every day. Once you survive Hell Week, you get to swap them out for brown shirts. It was a symbol that we'd advanced to a higher level, and after a lifetime of mostly failure, I definitely felt like I was someplace new.

I tried to enjoy the moment like everyone else, but my knee hadn't felt right in two days and I decided to leave and see the medics. On my way off the Grinder, I looked to my right and saw nearly a hundred helmets lined up. They belonged to the men who'd rung the bell, and they stretched past the statue, all the way to the quarterdeck. I read some of the names—guys who I liked. I knew how they felt because I was there when my Pararescue class graduated without me. That memory had dominated me for years, but after 130 hours of Hell, it no longer defined me.

Every man was required to see the medics that evening, but our bodies were so swollen they had a hard time discerning injuries from general soreness. All I knew was my right knee was thrice fucked and I needed crutches to get around. Freak Brown left med check bruised and battered. Kenny came out clean and barely limped, but he was plenty sore. Thankfully, our next evolution was walk week. We had seven days to eat, drink, and heal up before shit got real once again. It wasn't much, but enough time for most of the insane motherfuckers that managed to remain in Class 231 to get well.

Me, on the other hand? My swollen knee hadn't gotten any better by the time they snatched my crutches away. But there was no time for boo-hoo-ing. First Phase fun wasn't over yet. After walk week came *knot tying*, which may not sound like much but was way worse than I expected because that particular drill took place at the bottom of the pool, where those same instructors would do their best to drown my one-legged ass.

It was as if the Devil had been watching the whole show, waited out intermission, and now his favorite part was coming right up. The night before BUD/S kicked back up in intensity I could hear his words ringing in my stressed-out brain as I tossed and turned all night long.

They say you like suffering, Goggins. That you think you're a bad motherfucker. Enjoy your extended stay in Hell!

CHALLENGE #4

Choose any competitive situation that you're in right now. Who is your opponent? Is it your teacher or coach, your boss, an unruly client? No matter how they're treating you there is one way to not only earn their respect, but turn the tables. Excellence.

That may mean acing an exam, or crafting an ideal proposal, or smashing a sales goal. Whatever it is, I want you to work harder on that project or in that class than you ever have before. Do everything exactly as they ask, and whatever standard they set as an ideal outcome, you should be aiming to surpass that.

If your coach doesn't give you time in the games, dominate practice. Check the best guy on your squad and show the fuck out. That means putting time in off the field. Watching film so you can study your opponent's tendencies, memorizing plays, and training in the gym. You need to make that coach pay attention.

If it's your teacher, then start doing work of high quality. Spend extra time on your assignments. Write papers for her that she didn't even assign! Come early to class. Ask questions. Pay attention. Show her who you are and want to be.

If it's a boss, work around the clock. Get to work before them. Leave after they go home. Make sure they see that shit, and when it's time to deliver, surpass their maximum expectations.

Whoever you're dealing with, your goal is to make them watch you achieve what they could never have done themselves. You want them thinking how amazing you are. Take their negativity and use it to dominate their task with everything you've got. Take their motherfucking soul ! Afterward, post about it on social and add the hashtag # canthurtme # takingsouls.

CHAPTER FIVE

ARMORED MIND

" YOUR KNEE LOOKS PRETTY BAD, GOGGINS ."

No fucking shit, doc. With two days to go in walk week, I'd come by medical for a follow-up. The doctor rolled up my camo pants and when he gave my right kneecap a gentle squeeze, pain seized my brain, but I couldn't show it. I was playing a role. I was the beat up but otherwise healthy BUD/S student ready for the fight, and I couldn't so much as grimace to pull it off. I already knew the knee was fucked, and that the odds of getting through another five months of training on one leg were low, but accepting another roll back meant enduring another Hell Week, and that was way too much to process.

"The swelling hasn't gone down much. How's it feel?"

The doctor was playing a role too. SEAL candidates had a don't ask, don't tell agreement with most of the medical staff at Naval Special Warfare Command. I wasn't about to make the doctor's job easier by revealing anything to him, and he wasn't gonna take caution's side and pull the rip cord on a man's dream. He lifted his hand and my pain faded. I coughed and pneumonia once again rattled in my lungs until I felt the cold truth of his stethoscope on my skin.

Ever since Hell Week was called, I'd been coughing up brown knots of mucus. For the first two days I lay in bed, day and night, spitting them into a Gatorade bottle, where I stored them like so many nickels. I could barely breathe, and couldn't move much either. I may have been a bad motherfucker in Hell Week, but that shit was over, and I had to deal with the fact that the Devil (and those instructors) branded me too.

" It's all right, doc," I said. "A little stiff is all."

Time is what I needed. I knew how to push through pain, and my body had almost always responded with performance. I wasn't going to quit just because my knee was barking. It would come around eventually. The doc prescribed medicine to reduce the congestion in my lungs and sinuses, and gave me some Motrin for my knee. Within two days my breathing improved, but I still couldn't bend my right leg.

This would be a problem.

Of all the moments in BUD/S that I thought could break me, a knot-tying exercise never registered on my radar. Then again, this wasn't the fucking Boy Scouts. This was an underwater knot-tying drill held in the fifteen-foot section of the pool. And while the pool didn't strike mortal fear into me like it once did, being negatively buoyant, I knew that any pool evolution could be my undoing, especially those that demanded treading water.

Even before Hell Week, we'd been tested in the pool. We had to perform mock rescues on the instructors and do a fifty-meter underwater swim without fins on a single breath. That swim started with a giant stride into the water followed by a full somersault to siphon off any momentum whatsoever. Then without kicking off the side, we swam along the lane lines to the end of our twenty-five-meter pool. On the far side we were allowed to kick off the wall then swim back. When I arrived at the fifty-meter mark I rose up and gasped for air. My heart hammered until my breath smoothed, and I grasped that I'd actually passed the first of a series of complicated underwater evolutions that were supposed to teach us to be calm, cool, and collected underwater on a breath hold.

The knot-tying evolution was next in the series and it wasn't about our ability to tie various knots or a way to time our max breath hold. Sure, both skills come in handy on amphibian operations, but this drill was more about our capacity to juggle multiple stressors in an environment that's not sustainable for human life. Despite my health, I was heading into the drill with some confidence. Things changed when I started treading water.

That's how the drill began, with eight students strung out across the pool, moving our hands and legs like egg beaters. That's hard enough for me on two good legs, but because my right knee didn't work, I was forced to tread water with just my left. That spiked the degree of difficulty, and my heart rate, which sapped my energy.

Each student had an instructor assigned to them for this evolution and Psycho Pete specifically requested me. It was obvious I was struggling, and Psycho, and his bruised pride, were hungry for a little payback. With each revolution of my right leg, shockwaves of pain exploded like fireworks. Even with Psycho eyeballing me, I couldn't hide it. When I grimaced, he smiled like a kid on Christmas morning.

"Tie a square knot! Then a bowline!" He shouted. I was working so hard it was difficult to catch my breath, but Psycho didn't give two fucks. "Now, dammit!" I gulped air, bent from the waist and kicked down.

There were five knots in the drill altogether and each student was told to grab their eight-inch slice of rope, and tie them off one at a time at the bottom of the pool. We were allotted a breath in between, but could do as many as all five knots on a single breath. The instructor called out the knots, but the pacing was up to each student. We weren't allowed to use a mask or goggles to complete the evolution, and the instructor. had to approve each knot with a thumbs up before we were permitted to surface. If they flashed a thumb down instead, we had to re-tie that knot correctly, and if we surfaced before a given knot was approved, that meant failure and a ticket home.

Once back at the surface, there was no resting or relaxing between tasks. Treading water was the constant refrain, which meant soaring heart rates and the continual burning up of oxygen in the bloodstream for the one-legged man. Translation: the dives were uncomfortable as hell, and blacking out was a real possibility.

Psycho glared at me through his mask as I worked my knots. After about thirty seconds he'd approved both and we surfaced. He breathed free and easy, but I was gasping and panting like a wet, tired dog. The pain in my knee was so bad I felt sweat bead up on my forehead. When you're sweating in an unheated pool, you know shit's fucked up. I was breathless, low on energy, and wanted to quit, but quitting this evolution meant quitting BUD/S altogether, and that wasn't happening.

"Oh no, are you hurt, Goggins? Do you have some sand in your pussy?" Psycho asked. " I 'll bet you can't do the last three knots on one breath."

He said it with a smirk, like he was daring me. I knew the rules. I didn't have to accept his challenge, but that would have made Psycho just a little too happy and I couldn't allow that. I nodded and kept treading water, delaying my dive until my pulse evened out and I could score one deep, nourishing breath. Psycho wasn't having it. Whenever I opened my mouth he splashed water in my face to stress me out even more, a tactic used when trainees started to panic. That made breathing impossible.

"Go under now or you fail! "

I'd run out o f time. I tried t o gulp some air before my duck dive, and tasted a mouthful of Psycho's splash water instead as I dove to the bottom of the pool on a negative breath hold. My lungs were damn near empty which meant I was in pain from the jump, but I knocked the first one out in a few seconds. Psycho took his sweet time examining my work. My heart was thrumming like high alert Morse code. I felt it flip flop in my chest, like it was trying to break through my rib cage and fly to freedom. Psycho stared at the twine, flipped it over and perused it with his eyes and fingers, before offering a thumb's up in slow motion. I shook my head, untied the rope and hit the next one. Again he gave it a close inspection while my chest burned and diaphragm contracted, trying to force air into my empty lungs. The pain level in my knee was at a ten. Stars gathered in my peripheral vision. Those multiple stressors had me teetering like a Jenga tower, and I felt like I was about to black out. If that happened, I 'd have to depend on Psycho to swim me to the surface and bring me around. Did I really trust this man to do that? He hated me. What if he failed to execute? What if my body was too burned -out that even a rescue breath couldn't rouse me?

My mind was spun with those simple toxic questions that never go away. Why was I here? Why suffer when I could quit and be comfortable again? Why risk passing out or even death for a fucking knot drill? I knew that if I succumbed and bolted to the surface my SEAL career would have ended then and there, but in that moment I couldn't figure out why I ever gave a fuck.

I looked over at Psycho. He held both thumbs up and sported a big goofy smile on his face like he was watching a damn comedy show. His split second of pleasure in my pain, reminded me of all the bullying and taunts I felt as a teenager, but instead of playing the victim and letting negative emotions sap my energy and force me to the surface, a failure, it was as if a new light blazed in my brain that allowed me to flip the script.

Time stood still as I realized for the first time that I'd always looked at my entire life, everything I'd been through, from the wrong perspective. Yes, all the abuse I'd experienced and the negativity I had to push through challenged me to the core, but in that moment I stopped seeing myself as the victim of bad circumstance, and saw my life as the ultimate training ground instead. My disadvantages had been callousing my mind all along and had prepared me for that moment in that pool with Psycho Pete.

I remember my very first day in the gym back in Indiana. My palms were soft and quickly got torn up on the bars because they weren't accustomed to gripping steel. But over time, after thousands of reps, my palms built up a thick callous as protection. The same principle works when it comes to mind set. Until you experience hardships like abuse and bullying, failures and disappointments, your mind will remain soft and exposed. Life experience, especially negative experiences, help callous the mind. But it's up to you where that callous lines up. If you choose to see yourself as a victim of circumstance into adulthood, that callous will become resentment that protects you from the unfamiliar. It will make you too cautious and untrusting, and possibly too angry at the world. It will make you fearful of change and hard to reach, but not hard of mind. That's where I was as a teenager, but after my second Hell Week, I'd become someone new. I'd fought through so many horrible situations by then and remained open and ready for more. My ability to stay open represented a willingness to fight for my own life, which allowed me to withstand hail storms of pain and use it to callous over my victim's mentality. That shit was gone, buried under layers of sweat and hard fucking flesh, and I was starting to callous over my fears too. That realization gave me the mental edge I needed to outlast Psycho Pete one more time.

To show him he couldn't hurt me anymore I smiled back, and the feeling of being on the edge of a blackout went away. Suddenly, I was energized. The pain faded and I felt like I could stay under all day. Psycho saw that in my eyes. I tied off the last knot at leisurely pace, glaring at him the whole time. He gestured with his hands for me to hurry up as his diaphragm contracted. I finally finished, he gave me a quick affirmative and kicked to the surface, desperate for a breath. I took my time, joined him topside and found him gasping, while I felt strangely relaxed. When the chips were down at the pool during Air Force pararescue training, I'd buckled. This time I won a major battle in the water. It was a big victory, but the war wasn't over.

After I passed the knot-tying evolution, we had two minutes to climb out on to the deck, get dressed, and head back to the classroom. During First Phase, that's usually plenty of time, but a lot of us—not just me—were still healing from Hell Week and not moving at our typical lightning pace. On top of that, once we got through Hell Week, Class 231 went through a bit of an attitude adjustment.

Hell Week is designed to show you that a human is capable of much more than you know. It opens your mind to the true possibilities of human potential, and with that comes a change in your mentality. You no longer fear cold water or doing push-ups all day. You realize that no matter what they do to you, they will never break you, so you don't rush as much to make their arbitrary deadlines. You know if you don't make it, the instructors will beat you down. Meaning push-ups, getting wet and sandy, anything to up the pain and discomfort quotient, but for those of us knuckle draggers still in the mix, our attitude was, *So the fuck be it!* None of us feared the instructors anymore, and we weren't about to rush. They didn't like that one damn bit.

I had seen a lot of beat downs while at BUD/S, but the one we received that day will go down as one of the worst in history. We did push-ups until we couldn't pick ourselves up off the deck, then they turned us on our backs and demanded flutter kicks. Each kick was torture for me. I kept putting my legs down because of the pain. I was showing weakness and if you show weakness, IT IS ON!

Psycho and SBG descended and took turns on me. I went from push-ups to flutter kicks to bear crawls until *they* got tired. I could feel the moving parts of my knee shifting, floating, and grabbing every time I bent it to do those bear crawls, and it was agonizing. I moved slower than normal and knew I was broken. That simple question bubbled up again. Why? What was I trying to prove? Quitting seemed the sane choice. The comfort of mediocrity sounded like sweet relief until Psycho screamed in my ear.

"Move faster, motherfucker!"

Once again, an amazing feeling washed over me. I wasn't focused on outdoing him this time. I was in the worst pain of my life, but my victory in the pool minutes before came rushing back. I'd finally proved to myself that I was a decent enough waterman to belong in the Navy SEALs. Heady stuff for a negatively buoyant kid that never took a swim lesson in his entire life. And the reason I got there was because I'd put in the work. The pool had been my kryptonite. Even though I was a far better swimmer as a

SEAL candidate, I was still so stressed about water evolutions that I used to hit the pool after a day of training at least three times a week. I scaled the fifteen-foot fence just to gain after-hours access. Other than the academic aspect, nothing scared me as much about the prospects of BUD/S like the swimming drills, and by dedicating time I was aple to callous over that fear and hit new levels underwater when the pressure was on.

I thought about the incredible power of a calloused mind on task, as Psycho and SBG beat me down, and that thought became a feeling that took over my body and made me move as fast as a bear around that pool. I couldn't believe what I was doing. The intense pain was gone, and so were those nagging questions. I was putting out harder than ever, breaking through the limitations of injury and pain tolerance, and riding a second wind delivered by a calloused mind.

After the bear crawls, I went back to doing flutter kicks, and I still had no pain! As we were leaving the pool a half-hour later, SBG asked, "Goggins, what got into your ass to make you Superman?" I just smiled and left the pool. I didn't want to say anything because I didn't yet understand what I now know.

Similar to using an opponent's energy to gain an advantage, leaning on your calloused mind in the heat of battle can shift your thinking as well. Remembering what you've been through and how that has strengthened your mindset can lift you out of a negative brain loop and help you bypass those weak, one-second impulses to give in so you can power through obstacles. And when you leverage a calloused mind like I did around the pool that day and keep fighting through pain, it can help you push your limits because if you accept the pain as a natural process and refuse to give in and give up, you will engage the sympathetic nervous system which shifts your hormonal flow.

The sympathetic nervous system is your fight or flight reflex. It's bubbling .just below the surface, and when you are lost, stressed out, or struggling, like I was when I was a down and out kid, that's the part of your mind that's driving the bus. We've all tasted this feeling before. Those mornings when going on a run is the last thing you want to do, but then twenty minutes into it you feel energized, that's the work of the sympathetic nervous system. What I've found is that you can tap into it on-call as long as you know how to manage your own mind.

When you indulge in negative self-talk, the gifts of a sympathetic response will remain out of reach. However, if you can manage those moments of pain that come with maximum effort, by remembering what you've been through to get to that point in your life, you will be in a better position to persevere and choose fight over flight. That will allow you to use the adrenaline that comes with a sympathetic response to go even harder.

Obstacles at work and school can also be overcome with your calloused mind. In those cases, pushing through a given flashpoint isn't likely to lead to a sympathetic response, but it will keep you motivated to push through any doubt you feel about your own abilities. No matter the task at hand, there is always opportunity for self-doubt. Whenever you decide to follow a dream or set a goal, you are just as likely to come up with all the reasons why the likelihood of success is low. Blame it on the fucked-up evolutionary wiring of the human mind. But you don't have to let your doubt into the cockpit! You can tolerate doubt as a backseat driver, but if you put doubt in the pilot's seat, defeat is guaranteed. Remembering that you've been through difficulties before and have always survived to fight again shifts the conversation in your head. It will allow you to control and manage doubt, and keep you focused on taking each and every step necessary to achieve the task at hand.

Sounds simple, right? It isn't. Very few people even bother to try to control the way their thoughts and doubts bubble up. The vast majority of us are slaves to our minds. Most don't even make the first effort when it comes to mastering their thought process because it's a never-ending chore and impossible to get right every time. The average person thinks 2,000-3,000 thoughts per hour. That's thirty to fifty per minute! Some of those shots will slip by the goalie. It's inevitable. Especially if you coast through life.

Physical training is the perfect crucible to learn how to manage your thought process because when you're working out, your focus is more likely to be single pointed, and your response to stress and pain is immediate and measurable. Do you hammer hard and snag that personal best like you said you would, or do you crumble? That decision rarely comes down to physical ability, it's almost always a test of how well you are managing your own mind. If you push yourself through each split and use that energy to maintain a strong pace, you have a great chance of recording a faster time. Granted, some days it's easier to do that than others. And the clock, or the score, doesn't matter anyway. The reason it's important to push hardest when you want to quit the most is because it helps you callous your mind. It's the same reason why you have to do your best work when you are the least motivated. That's why I loved PT in BUD/S and why I still love it today. Physical challenges strengthen my mind so I'm ready for whatever life throws at me, and it will do the same for you.

But no matter how well you deploy it, a calloused mind can't heal broken bones. On the mile-long hike back to the BUD/S compound, the feeling of victory evaporated, and I could feel the damage I'd done. I had twenty weeks of training in front of me, dozens of evolutions ahead, and I could barely walk. While I wanted to deny the pain in my knee, I knew I was fucked so I limped straight to medical.

When he saw my knee, the doc didn't say a damn thing. He just shook his head and sent me to get an x-ray that revealed a fractured kneecap. In BUD/S when reservists sustain injuries that take a long time to heal, they're sent home, and that's what happened to me.

I crutched my ass back to the barracks, demoralized, and while checking out, I saw some of the guys that quit during Hell Week. When I first glimpsed their helmets lined up beneath the bell, I felt sorry for them because I knew the empty feeling of giving up, but seeing them face to face reminded me that failure is a part of life and now we all had to press on.

I hadn't quit, so I knew I'd be invited back, but I had no idea if that meant a third Hell Week or not. Or if after getting rolled twice I still had the burning desire to fight through another hurricane of pain with no guarantee of success. Given my injury record, how could I ? I left the BUD/S compound with more self awareness and more mastery over my mind than I'd ever had before, but my future was just as uncertain.

★ ★ ★

Airplanes have always made me claustrophobic, so I decided to take the train from San Diego to Chicago, which gave me three full days to think, and my mind was all fucked up. On the first day I didn't know if I wanted to be a SEAL anymore. I had overcome a lot. I beat Hell Week, realized the power of a calloused mind and conquered my fear of the water. Perhaps I'd already learned enough about myself? What else did I need to prove? On day two I thought about all the other jobs I could sign up for. Maybe

I should move on and become a firefighter? That's a bad-ass job, and it would be an opportunity to become a different sort of hero. But on day three, as the train veered into Chicago, I slipped into a bathroom the size of a phone booth and checked in with the Accountability Mirror. *Is that really how you feel? Are you sure you're ready to give up on the SEALs and become a civilian fireman?* I stared at myself for five minutes before I shook my head. I couldn't lie. I had to tell myself the truth, out loud.

"I'm afraid. I'm afraid of going through all of that shit again. I'm afraid of day one, week one."

I was divorced by then, but my ex-wife, Pam, met me at the train station to drive me home to my mother's place in Indianapolis. Pam was still living in Brazil. We'd been in touch while I was in San Diego, and after seeing each other through the crowd on the train platform, we fell back on our habits, and later that night we fell into bed.

That whole summer, from May to November, I stayed in the Midwest, healing up then rehabbing my knee. I was still a reservist but remained undecided about going back to Navy SEAL training. I looked into the Marine Corps. I explored the application process for a handful of fire fighting units but finally picked up the phone, ready to call into the BUD/S compound. They needed my final answer.

I sat there, holding the telephone, and thought about the misery of SEAL training. Shit, you run six miles a day just to eat, not including your training runs. I visualized all the swimming and paddling, carrying heavy-ass boats and Ags on our heads, over the berm all day. I flashed onto hours of sit-ups, push-ups, flutter kicks, and the O-Course. I remembered the feeling of rolling around in the sand, of being chafed all fucking day and night. My memories were a mind-body experience, and I felt the cold deep in my bones. A normal person would give up. They'd say, fuck it, it's just not meant to be, and refuse to torture themselves one minute more.

But I wasn't wired normal.

As I dialed the number, negativity rose up like an angry shadow. I couldn't help but think that I was put on this earth to suffer. Why wouldn't my own personal demons, the fates, God, or Satan, just leave me the fuck alone? I was tired of trying to prove myself. Tired of callousing my mind. Mentally, I was worn to the nub. At the same time, being worn the fuck down is the price of being hard and I knew if I quit, those feelings and thoughts wouldn't just go away. The cost of quitting would be lifelong purgatory. I'd be trapped in the knowing that I didn't stay in the fight to the bitter end. There is no shame in getting knocked out. The shame comes when you throw in the motherfucking towel, and if I was born to suffer, then I may as well take my medicine.

The training officer welcomed me back and confirmed that I was starting from day one, week one. As expected, my brown shirt would have to be swapped out for a white one, and he had one more sliver of sunshine to share. "Just so you know, Goggins," he said, "this will be the last time we will allow you to go through BUD/S training. If you get injured, that's it. We will not allow you to come back again."

" Roger that," I said.

Class 235 would muster in just four weeks. My knee still wasn't all the way right, but I'd better be ready because the ultimate test was about to begin.

Within seconds of hanging up the phone, Pam called and said she needed to see me. It was good timing. I was leaving town again, hopefully for good this time, and I needed to level with her. We'd been enjoying one another, but it was always a temporary thing for me. We'd been married once and we were still different people with totally different worldviews. That hadn't changed and obviously neither had some of my insecurities, as they kept me going back to what was familiar. Insanity is doing the same thing over and over again and expecting a different result. We would never work and it was time to say so.

She got to her news first.

"I'm late," she said, as she burst through the door, clutching a brown paper bag. "Like *late* late." She seemed excited and nervous as she disappeared into the bathroom. I could hear that bag crinkle and the tearing open of a package as I lay on my bed staring at the ceiling. Minutes later, she opened the bathroom door, a pregnancy test in her fist and a big smile on her face. " I knew it," she said, biting her lower lip. "Look, David, we're pregnant! "

I stood up slow, she hugged me with everything she had, and her excitement broke my heart. It wasn't supposed to go like this. I wasn't ready. My body was still broken, I was $30,000 in credit card debt, and still only a reservist. I had no address of my own and no car. I was unstable, and that made me very insecure. Plus, I wasn't even in love with this woman. That's what I said to myself while I stared into that Accountability Mirror over her shoulder. The mirror that never lies.

I averted my eyes.

Pam went home to share the news with her parents. I walked her to the door of my mother's place, then slumped into the couch. In Coronado, I felt like I 'd come to terms with my fucked up past and found some power there, and here I was sucked under once again. Now it wasn't just about me and my dreams of becoming a SEAL. I had a family to think about, which raised the stakes that much higher. If I failed this time, it wouldn't mean that I was just going back to ground zero, emotionally and financially, but I would be bringing my new family there with me. When my mother got home I told her everything, and as we talked the dam broke and my fear, sadness, and struggle came bursting out of me. I put my head in my hands and sobbed.

"Mom, my life from the time I was born until now has been a nightmare. A nightmare that keeps getting worse," I said. "The harder I try, the harder my life becomes."

"I can't argue with that, David," she said. My mom knew hell and she wasn't trying to baby me. She never had. "But I also know you well enough to know that you will find a way to get through this."

"I have to," I said as I wiped the tears from my eyes. "I don't have a choice."

She left me alone, and I sat on that couch all night. I felt like I'd been stripped of everything, but I was still breathing, which meant I had to find a way to keep going. I had to compartmentalize doubt and find the strength to believe that I was born to be more than some tired-ass Navy SEAL reject. After Hell Week I'd felt I had become unbreakable, yet within a week I'd been zeroed out. I hadn't levelled up after all. I still wasn't shit, and if I was going to fix my broke-down life, I would have to become more!

On that sofa, I found a way.

By then I'd learned how to hold myself accountable, and I knew I could take a man's soul in the heat of battle. I had overcome many obstacles, and realized that each of those experiences had calloused my mind so thick, I could take on any challenge. All of that that made me feel like I'd dealt with my past demons, but I hadn't. I'd been ignoring them. My memories of abuse at the hands of my father, of all those people who called me nigger, didn't vaporize after a few victories. Those moments were anchored deep in my subconscious, and as a result, my foundation was cracked. In a human being your character is your foundation, and when you build a bunch of successes and pile up even more failures on a fucked-up foundation, the structure that is the self won't be sound. To develop an armored mind—a mindset so calloused and hard that it becomes bulletproof—you need to go to the source of all your fears and insecurities.

Most of us sweep our failures and evil secrets under the rug, but when we run into problems, that rug gets lifted up, and our darkness re-emerges, foods our soul, and influences the decisions which determine our character. My fears were never just about the water, and my anxieties toward Class 235 weren't about the pain of First Phase. They were seeping from the infected wounds I'd been walking around with my entire life, and my denial of them amounted to a denial of myself. I was my own worst enemy! It wasn't the world, or God, or the Devil that was out to get me. It was me!

I was rejecting my past and therefore rejecting myself. My foundation, my character was defined by self-rejection. All my fears came from that deep-seated uneasiness I carried with being David Goggins because of what I'd gone through. Even after I'd reached a point where I no longer cared about what others thought of me, I still had trouble accepting *me*.

Anyone who is of sound mind and body c an sit down and think of twenty things in their life that could have gone differently. Where maybe they didn't get a fair shake and where they took the path of least resistance. If you're one of the few who acknowledge that, want to callous those wounds, and strengthen your character, its up to you to go back through your past and make peace with yourself by facing those incidents and all of your negative influences, and accepting them as weak spots in your own character. Only when you identify and accept your weaknesses will you finally stop running from your past. Then those incidents can be used more efficiently as fuel to become better and grow stronger.

Right there on mom's couch, as the moon burned its arc in the night sky, I faced down my demons. I faced myself. I couldn't run from my dad anymore. I had to accept that he was part of me and that his lying, cheating character influenced me more than I cared to admit. Before that night, I used to tell people that my father had died rather than tell the truth about where I came from. Even in the SEALs I trotted out that lie. I knew why. When you get beat up, you don't want to acknowledge getting your ass kicked. It doesn't make you feel very manly, so the easiest thing to do is forget about it and move on. Pretend it never happened.

Not anymore.

Going forward it became very important for me to rehash my life, because when you examine your experiences with a fine-toothed comb and see where your issues come from, you can find strength in enduring pain and abuse. By accepting Trunnis Goggins as part of me, I was free to use where I came from as fuel. I realized that each episode of child abuse that could have killed me made me tough as hell and as sharp as a Samurai's blade.

True, I had been dealt a fucked-up hand, but that night I started thinking of it as running a 100-mile race with a fifty-pound ruck on my back. Could I still compete in that race even if everyone else was running free and easy, weighing 130 pounds? How fast would I be able to run once I 'd shed that dead weight? I wasn't even thinking about ultras yet. To me the race was life itself, and the more I took inventory, the more I realized how prepared I was for the fucked-up events yet to come. Life had put me in the fire, taken me out, and hammered me repeatedly, and diving back into the BUD/S cauldron, feeling a third Hell Week in a calendar year, would decorate me with a PhD in pain. I was about to become the sharpest sword ever made!

★ ★ ★

I showed up to Class 235 on a mission and kept to myself throughout much of First Phase. There were 156 men in that class on day one. I still led from the front, but I wasn't about shepherding anyone through Hell Week t}J.is time. My knee was still sore and I needed to put every ounce of energy into getting my ass through BUD/S. I had everything riding on the next six months, and I had no illusions about how difficult it would be to make it through.

Case in point: Shawn Dobbs.

Dobbs grew up poor in Jacksonville, Florida. He battled some of the same demons I did, and he came into class with a chip on his shoulder. Right away, I could see he was an elite, natural athlete. He was at or near the front on all the runs, he blitzed the 0-Course in 8:30 after just a few reps, and he knew he was a bad motherfucker. Then again, like the Taoists say, those that know don't speak, and those who speak, well, they don't know jack shit.

On the night before Hell Week began he talked a lot of noise about the guys in Class 235. There were already fifty-five helmets on the Grinder, and he was sure he'd be one of a handful of graduates at the end. He mentioned the guys he *knew* would make it through Hell Week and also talked a lot of nonsense about the guys he knew would quit.

He had no clue that he was making the classic mistake of measuring himself against others in his class. When he beat them in an evolution or outperformed them during PT, he took a lot of pride in that. It boosted his self-confidence and his performance. In BUD/S, it's common and natural to do some of that. It's all part of the competitive nature of the alpha males who are drawn to the SEALs, but he didn't realize that during Hell Week you need a solid boat crew to survive, which means depending upon your classmates, not defeating them. While he talked and talked, I took notice. He had no idea what was in store for him and how bad sleep deprivation and being cold fucks you up. He was about to find out. In the early hours of Hell Week, he performed well, but that same drive to defeat his classmates in evolutions and on timed runs came out on the beach.

At 5 '4" and 188 pounds, Dobbs was built like a fire hydrant, but since he was short he was assigned to a boat crew of smaller guys referred to as Smurfs by the instructors. In fact, Psycho Pete made them draw a picture of Papa Smurf on the front of their boat just to fuck with them. That's the kind of thing our instructors did. They looked for any way to break you, and with Dobbs it worked. He didn't like being grouped up with guys he considered smaller and weaker, and took it out on his team-mates. Over the next day he would grind his own crew down before our eyes. He took up the position at the front of the boat or the log and set a blistering pace on the runs. Instead of checking in with his crew and holding something back in reserve, he went all out from the jump. I reached out to him recently and he said he remembered BUD/S like it happened last week.

"I was grinding an axe on my own people," he said. "I was purposely beating them down, almost like if I made guys quit, it was a checkmark on my helmet."

By Monday morning he'd done a decent job of it. Two of his guys had quit and that meant four smaller guys had to carry their boat and log by themselves. He admitted he was fighting his own demons on that beach. That his foundation was cracked.

"I was an insecure person with low self esteem trying to grind an axe," he said, "and my own ego, arrogance, and insecurity made my own life more difficult."

Translation: his mind broke down in ways he'd never experienced before or since.

On Monday afternoon we did a bay swim, and when he emerged from the water, he was hurting. Watching him it was obvious he could barely walk and that his mind was teetering on the brink. We locked eyes ·and I saw that he was asking himself those simple questions and couldn't find an answer. He looked a lot like I did when I was in Pararescue, searching for a way out. From then on Dobbs was one of the worst performers on the whole beach, and that fucked him up bad.

"All the people I'd categorized as lower than worms were kicking my butt," he said. Soon his crew was down to two men, and he got moved to another boat crew with taller guys. When they lifted the boat head high, he wasn't even able to reach that motherfucker, and all of his insecurities about his size and his past started caving in on him.

"I started to believe that I didn't belong there," he said. "That I was genetically inferior. It was like I had superpowers, and I'd lost them. I was in a place in my mind I'd never been, and I didn't have a road map."

Think about where he was at that time. This man had excelled through the first few weeks of BUD/S. He'd come from nothing and was a phenomenal athlete. He had so many experiences along the way he could have leaned on. He'd calloused his mind plenty, but because his foundation was cracked, when shit got real he lost control of his mindset and became a slave to his self doubt.

On Monday night, Dobbs reported to medical complaining about his feet. He was sure he had stress fractures, but when he took off his boots they weren't swollen or black and blue like he'd imagined. They looked perfectly healthy. I know that because I was at med check too, sitting right beside him. I saw his blank stare and knew the inevitable was near. It was the look that comes over a man's face after he surrenders his soul. I had the same look in my eyes when I quit Pararescue. What will forever bond me and Shawn Dobbs is the fact that I knew he was going to quit before he did.

The docs offered him Motrin and sent him back into the suffering. I remember watching Shawn lace his boots, wondering at what point he would finally break. That's when SBG pulled up in his truck and yelled, "This will be the coldest night that you will ever experience in your entire lives!"

I was under my boat with my crew headed toward the infamous Steel Pier when I glanced behind me and saw Shawn in the back ofSBG's warm truck. He'd surrendered. Within minutes he would toll the bell three times, and place his helmet down.

In Dobbs' defense, this was one nightmare of a Hell Week. It rained all day and all night, which meant you never got warm and never got dry. Plus, somebody in command had the brilliant idea that the class shouldn't be fed and watered like kings at chow. Instead, we were supplied cold MREs for almost every meal. They thought that would test us even more. Make it more like a real-world battlefield situation. It also meant there was absolutely no relief, and without abundant calories to burn it was hard for anybody to find the energy to push through pain and exhaustion, let alone keep warm.

Yes, it was miserable, but I fucking loved it. I thrived off of the barbaric beauty of seeing the soul of a man destroyed, only to rise again and overcome every obstacle in his path. By my third go 'round, I knew what the human body could take. I knew what I could take, and I was feeding off that shit. At the same time, my legs didn't feel right and my knee had been barking since day one. So far, the pain was something I could handle for at least a couple more days, but the thought of injury was a whole different piece of fuck-you pie that I had to block out of my mind. I went into a dark place where there was just me and the pain and suffering. I didn't focus on my classmates or my instructors. I went full caveman. I was willing to die to make it through that motherfucker.

I wasn't the only one. Late on Wednesday night, with thirty-six hours to go before the end of Hell Week, tragedy hit Class 235 We were in the pool for an evolution called the caterpillar swim, in which each boat crew swam on their backs, legs locked around torsos, in a chain. We had to use our hands in concert to swim.

We mustered up at the pool. There were just twenty-six guys left and one of them was named John Skop. Mr. Skop was a specimen at 6 '2" and 225 pounds, but he'd been sick from breakout and had been in and out of med check all week. While twenty-five of us stood at attention on the pool deck, swollen, chafed, and bleeding, he sat on the stairs by the pool, jackhammering in the cold. He looked like he was freezing, but waves of heat poured offhis skin. His body was a radiator on full blast. I could feel him from ten feet away.

I'd had double pneumonia during my first Hell Week and knew what it looked and felt like. His alveoli, or air sacs, were filling with fluid. He couldn't clear them so he could barely breathe, which exacerbated his problem. When pneumonia goes uncontrolled, it can lead to pulmonary edema, which can be deadly, and he was halfway there.

Sure enough, during the caterpillar swim, his legs went limp and he darted to the bottom of the pool like a doll stuffed with lead. Two instructors jumped in after him and from there it was chaos. They ordered us out of the water and lined us up along the fence with our backs facing the pool as medics worked to revive Mr. Skop. We heard everything and knew his chances were slipping. Five minutes later, he still wasn't breathing, and they ordered us to the locker room. Mr. Skop was transported to the hospital and we were told to run back to the BUD/S classroom. We didn't know it yet, but Hell Week was already over. Minutes later, SBG walked in and delivered the news cold.

"Mr. Skop is dead," he said. He took stock of the room. His words had been a collective gut punch to men who were already on the knife's edge after nearly a week with no sleep and no relief. SBG didn't give a fuck. " This is the world you live in. He's not the first and he won't be the last to die in your line of work." He looked over at Mr. Skop's roommate and said, "Mr. Moore, don't steal any of his shit." Then he left the room like it was just another fucked-up day.

I felt torn between grief, nausea, and relief. I was sad and sick to my stomach that Mr. Skop had died, but we were all relieved to have survived Hell Week, plus the way SBG handled it was straight ahead, no bullshit, and I remember thinking if all SEALs were like him, this would definitely be the world for me. Talk about mixed emotions.

See, most civilians don't understand that you need a certain level of callousness to do the job we were being trained to do. To live in a brutal world, you have to accept cold-blooded truths. I'm not saying it's good. I'm not necessarily proud of it. But special ops is a calloused .world and .it demands a calloused mind.

Hell Week had ended thirty-six hours early. There was no pizza or brown shirt ceremony on the Grinder, but twenty-five men out of a possible 156 had made it. Once again, I was one of the few, and once again I was swollen like a Pillsbury dough-boy and on crutches with twenty-one weeks of training still to come. My patella was intact, but both of my shins were slivered with small fractures. It gets worse. The instructors were surly because they'd been forced to c all Hell Week prematurely, so they ended walk week after just forty-eight hours. By every conceivable metric I was fucked. When I moved my ankle, my shins were activated and I felt searing pain, which was a monumental problem because a typical week in BUD/S demands up to sixty miles of running. Imagine doing that on two broken shins.

Most of the guys in Class 235 lived on base at Naval Special Warfare Command in Coronado. I lived about twenty miles away in a $700 a month studio apartment with a mold problem in Chula Vista, which I shared with my pregnant wife and stepdaughter. After she got pregnant, Pam and I remarried, I financed a new Honda Passport—which put me roughly $60,000 in debt—and the three of us drove out from Indiana to San Diego to restart our family. I'd just cleared Hell Week for the second time in a calendar year and she was set to deliver our baby right around graduation, but there was no happiness in my head or my soul. How could there be? We lived in a shithole that was at the edge of atfordability, and my body was broken once again. If I couldn't make it through I wouldn't even be able to afford rent, would have to start all over, and find a new line of work. I could not and would not let that happen.

The night before First Phase kicked back up in intensity, I shaved my head and stared into my reflection. For almost two years straight I'd been taking pain to the extreme and coming back for more. I'd succeeded in spurts only to be buried alive in failure. That night, the only thing that allowed me to continue pushing forward was the knowledge that everything I'd been through had helped callous my mind. The question was, how thick was the callous? How much pain could one man take? Did I have it in me to run on broken legs?

I woke up at 3:30 the next morning and drove to the base. I limped to the BUD/S cage where we kept our gear and slumped onto a bench, dropping my backpack at my feet. It was dark as hell inside and out, and I was all alone. I could hear the rolling surf in the distance as I dug through my dive bag. Buried beneath my dive gear were two rolls of d'-;lct tape. I could only shake my head and smile in disbelief as I grabbed them, knowing how insane my plan was.

I carefully pulled a thick black tube sock over my right foot. The shin was tender to the touch and even the slightest twitch of the ankle joint registered high on the suffering scale. From there I looped the tape around my heel then up over my ankle and back down to my heel, eventually moving both down the foot and up my calf until my entire lower leg and foot were wrapped tight. That was just the first coat. Then I put another black tube sock on and taped my foot and ankle the same way. By the time I was done, I had two sock layers and two tape layers, and once my foot was laced up in the boot, my ankle and shin were protected and immobilized. Satisfied, I did up my left foot, and an hour later, it was as though both my lower legs were sunk into soft casts. It still hurt to walk, but the torture that I'd felt when my ankle moved was more tolerable. Or at least I thought so. I'd find out for sure when we started to run.

Our first training run that day was my trial by fire, and I did the best I could to run with my hip flexors. Usually we let our feet and lower legs drive the rhythm. I had to reverse that. It took intense focus to isolate each movement and generate motion and power in my legs from the hip down, and for the first thirty minutes the pain was the worst I'd ever felt in my life. The tape cut into my skin, while the pounding sent shockwaves of agony up my slivered shins.

And this was just the first run in what promised to be five months of continual pain. Was it possible to survive this, day after day? I thought about quitting. If failure was my future and I'd have to rethink my life completely, what was the point of this exercise? Why delay the inevitable? Was I fucked in the head ? Each and every thought boiled down to the same old simple question: why?

"The only way to guarantee failure is to quit right now, motherfucker!" I was talking to myself now. Silently screaming over the din of anguish that was crushing my mind and soul. "Take the pain, or it won't just be your failure. It will be your family's failure! "

I imagined the feeling I would have if I could actually pull this off. If I could endure the pain required to complete this mission. That bought me another half mile before more pain rained down and swirled within me like a typhoon.

"People have a hard time going through BUD/S healthy, and you're going through it on broken legs! Who else would even think of this?" I asked. "Who else would be able to run even one minute on one broken leg, let alone two? Only Goggins! You are twenty minutes in the business, Goggins ! You are a fucking machine ! Each step you run from now until the end will only make you harder! "

That last message cracked the code like a password. My calloused mind was my ticket forward, and at the forty-minute mark something remarkable happened. The pain receded to low tide. The tape had loosened so it wasn't cutting into my skin, and my muscles and bones were warm enough to take some pounding. The pain would come and go throughout the day, but it became much more manageable, and when the pain did show up, I told myself it was proof of how tough I was and how much tougher I was becoming.

Day after day the same ritual played itself out. I showed up early, duct taped my feet, endured thirty minutes of extreme pain, talked myself through it, and survived. This was no fake-it-till-you-make-it bullshit. To me, the fact that I showed up every day willing to put myself through something like that was truly amazing. The instructors rewarded me for it too. They offered to bind my hands and feet and throw .me in the pool to see if I could swim four fucking laps. In fact, they didn't offer. They insisted. This was one part of an evolution they liked to call Drown Proofing. I preferred to call it controlled drowning!

With our hands bound behind us and feet tied behind our back, all we could do is dolphin kick, and unlike some of the experienced swimmers in our class, who looked like they'd been pulled from the Michael Phelps gene pool, my dolphin kick was that of a stationary rocking horse and provided about the same propulsion. I was continually out of breath, fighting to stay near the surface, chicken necking my head above the water to get a breath, only to sink down and kick hard, trying in vain to find momentum. I'd practiced for this. For weeks, I'd hit the pool and even experimented with wetsuit shorts to see if I could hide them under my uniform to provide some buoyancy. They made it look like I was wearing a diaper under the tight-ass-nut-hugging UDT shorts, and they didn't help, but all that practice did get me comfortable enough with the feeling of drowning that I was able to endure and pass that test.

We had another brutal underwater evolution in Second Phase, aka dive phase. Again, it involved treading water, which always sounds basic as hell whenever I write it, but for this drill we were fitted with fully-charged, twin eighty-liter tanks and a sixteen-pound weight belt. We had fins, but kicking with fins increased the pain quotient and stress on my ankles and shins. I couldn't tape up for the water. I had to suck up the pain.

After that we had to swim on our backs for fifty meters without sinking. Then flip over and swim fifty meters on our stomach, once again staying on the surface, all while being fully loaded! We weren't allowed to use any flotation devices whatsoever, and keeping our heads up caused intense pain in our necks, shoulders, hips, and lower backs.

The noises coming out of the pool that day are something I'll never forget. Our desperate attempts to stay afloat and breathe conjured an audible mixture of terror, frustration, and exertion. We were gurgling, grunting, and gasping. I heard guttural screams and high-pitched squeals. Several guys sank to the bottom, took off their weight belts, and slipped free of their tanks, letting them crash to the floor of the pool, then jetted to the surface.

Only one man passed that evolution on the first try. We only got three chances to pass any given evolution and it took me all three to pass that one. On my last attempt I focused on long, fluid scissor kicks, again using my overworked hip flexors. I barely made it.

By the time we got to Third Phase, the land warfare training module on San Clemente Island, my legs were healed up, and I knew I'd make it through to graduation, but just because it was the last lap doesn't mean it was easy. At the main BUD/S compound on The Strand, you get lots of looky-loos coming through. Officers of all stripes stop in to watch training, which means there are people peering over the instructors' shoulders. On the island, it's just you and them. They are free to get nasty, and they show no mercy. Which is exactly why I loved the island!

One afternoon we split into teams of two and three guys tobuild hide sites that blend in with the vegetation. We were coming down to the end by then, and everyone was in killer shape and unafraid. Guys were getting sloppy with their attention to detail and the instructors were pissed off, so they called everyone down into a valley to give us a classic beat down.

There would be push-ups, sit-ups, flutter kicks, and eight-count bodybuilders (advanced burpees) galore. But first they told us to kneel down and dig holes with our hands, large enough to bury ourselves up to the neck for some unspecified length of time. I was smiling rny ass off and digging deep when one of the instructors came up with a new, creative way to torture me.

"Goggins, get up. You like this shit too much." I laughed and kept digging, but he was serious. "I said get up, Goggins. You're getting way too much pleasure."

I stood up, stepped to the side, and watched my classmates suffer for the next thirty minutes without me. From then on the instructors stopped including me in their beat downs. When the class was ordered to do push-ups, sit-ups, or get wet and sandy, they'd always exclude me. I took it as a point of pride that I'd finally broken the will of the entire BUD/S staff, but I also missed the beat downs. Because I saw them as opportunities to callous my mind. Now, they were over for me.

Considering that the Grinder was center stage for a lot of Navy SEAL training, it makes sense that's where BUD/S graduation is held . Families fly in. Fathers and brothers puff their chests out; mothers, wives, and girlfriends are all done up and drop dead gorgeous. Instead of pain and misery, it was all smiles on that patch of asphalt as the graduates of Class 235 mustered up in our dress whites beneath a huge American flag billowing in the sea breeze. To our right was the infamous bell that 130 of our classmates tolled in order to quit what is arguably the most challenging training in the military. Each of us was introduced and acknowledged individually. My mother had tears of joy in her eyes when my name was called, but strangely, I didn't feel much of anything, except sadness.

Mom and I at BUD/S graduation

On the Grinder and later at McP's—the SEAL pub of choice in downtown Coronado—my teammates beamed with pride as they gathered to take photos with their families. At the bar, music blared while everyone got drunk and raised hell like they'd just won something. And to be honest, that shit annoyed me. Because I was sorry to see BUD/S go.

When I first locked in on the SEALs,. I was looking for an arena that would either destroy me completely or make me unbreakable. BUD/S provided that. It showed me what the human mind is capable of, and how to harness it to take more pain than I'd ever felt before, so I could learn to achieve things I never even knew were possible. Like running on broken legs. After graduation it would be up to me to continue to hunt impossible tasks because though it was an accomplishment to become just the thirty-sixth African American BUD/S graduate in Navy SEAL history, rriy quest to defy the odds had only just begun!

CHALLENGE #5

It's time to visualize! Again, the average person thinks 2,000-3,000 thoughts per hour. Rather than focusing on bullshit you cannot change, imagine visualizing the things you can. Choose any obstacle in your way, or set a new goal, and visualize overcoming or achieving it. Before I engage in any challenging activity, I start by painting a picture of what my success looks and feels like. I'll think about it every day and that feeling propels me forward when I'm training, competing, or taking on any task I choose.

But visualization isn't simply about daydreaming of some trophy ceremony—real or metaphorical. You must also visualize the challenges that are likely to arise and determine how you will attack those problems when they do. That way you can be as prepared as possible on the journey. When I show up for a foot race now, ·I drive the entire course first, visualizing success but also potential challenges, which helps me control my thought process. You can't prepare for everything but if you engage in strategic visualization ahead of time, you'll be as prepared as you possibly can be.

That also means being prepared to answer the simple questions. Why are you doing this? What is driving you toward this achievement? Where does the darkness you're using as fuel come from? What has calloused your mind? You'll need to have those answers at your fingertips when you hit a wall of pain and doubt. To push through, you'll need to channel your darkness, feed off it, and lean on your calloused mind.

Remember, visualization will never compensate for work undone. You cannot visualize lies. All the strategies I employ to answer the simple questions and win the mind game are only effective because I put in work. It's a lot more than mind over matter. It takes relentless self-discipline to schedule suffering into your day, every day, but if you do, you'll find that at the other end of that suffering is a whole other life just waiting for you.

This challenge doesn't have to be physical, and victory doesn't always mean you came in first place. It can mean you've finally overcome a lifelong fear or any other obstacle that made you surrender in the past. Whatever it is, tell the world your story about how you created your #armoredmind and where it's taken you.

CHAPTER SIX

IT'S NOT ABOUT A TROPHY

EVERYTHING ABOUT THE RACE WAS GOING BETTER THAN I could have hoped. There were enough clouds in the sky to blunt the heat of the sun, my rhythm was as steady as the mellow tide that sloshed against the hulls of sailboats docked in the nearby San Diego Marina, and though my legs felt heavy, that was to be expected considering my "tapering" plan the night before. Besides, they seemed to be loosening up as I rounded a bend to complete my ninth lap—my ninth mile—just an hour and change into a twenty-four-hour race.

That's when I saw John Metz, race director of the San Diego One Day, eyeballing me at the start-finish line. He was holding up his white board to inform each competitor of their time and position in the overall field. I was in fifth place, which evidently confused him. I offered a crisp nod to reassure him that I knew what I was doing, that I was right where I was supposed to be.

He saw through that shit.

Metz was a veteran. Always polite and soft-spoken. It didn't look like there was much that could faze him, but he was also a seasoned ultra-marathoner with three fifty-mile races in his saddlebag. He'd either reached or topped a hundred miles, seven times, and he'd achieved his personal best of 144 miles in twenty-four hours when he was fifty years old! Which is why it meant something to me that he looked concerned.

I checked my watch, synced to a heart rate monitor I wore around my chest. My pulse straddled my magic number line: 145 A few days earlier I'd run into my old BUD/S instructor, SBG, at Naval Special Warfare Command. Most SEALs do rotations as instructors between deployments, and SBG and I worked together. When I told him about the San Diego One Day he insisted I wear a heart rate monitor to pace myself. SBG was a big geek when it came to performance and recovery, and I watched as he scratched out a few formulas, then turned to me and said, "Keep your pulse steady between 140 and 145 and you'll be golden." The next day he handed me a heart rate monitor as a race day gift.

If you set out to mark a course that could crack open a Navy SEAL like a walnut, chew him up, and spit him the fuck out, San Diego's Hospitality Point would not make the cut. We're talking about terrain so vanilla it's downright serene. Tourists descend year-round for views of San Diego's stunning marina, which spills into Mission Bay. The road is almost entirely smooth asphalt and perfectly flat, save a brief seven-foot incline with the pitch of a standard suburban driveway. There are manicured lawns, palm trees, and shade trees. Hospitality Point is so inviting that disabled and convalescing folks head there with their walkers for an afternoon's rehab stroll, all the time. But the day after John Metz chalked his easy, one-mile course, it became the scene of my total destruction.

I should have known that a breakdown was coming. By the time I started running at 10 a.m. on November 12, 2005, I hadn't run more than a mile in six months, but I looked like I was fit because I'd never stopped hitting the gym. While I was stationed in Iraq, on my second deployment with SEAL Team Five earlier that year, I'd gotten back into serious power lifting, and my only dose of cardio was twenty minutes on the elliptical once a week. The point is, my cardiovascular fitness was an absolute joke, and still I thought it was a brilliant idea to try and run a hundred miles in twenty-four hours.

Okay, it was always a fucked-up idea, but I considered it doable because a hundred miles in twenty-four hours demands a pace of just under fifteen minutes a mile. If it came to it, I figured I could walk that fast. Only, I didn't walk. When that horn sounded at the start of the race, I took off hot and zoomed to the front of the pack. Exactly the right move if your race-day goal is to blow the fuck up.

Also, I didn't exactly come in well-rested. The night before the race, I passed by the SEAL Team Five gym on my way off base after work, and peeked in like I always did, just to see who was getting after it. SBG was inside warming up, and called out.

"Goggins," he said, "let's jack some fucking steel!" I laughed. He stared me down. "You know, Goggins," he said, stepping closer, "when the Vikings were getting ready to raid a fucking village, and they were camped out in the fucking woods in their goddam tents made out of fucking deer hides and shit, sitting around a campfire, do you think they said, *Hey, let's have some herbal fucking tea and call it an early night? Or were they more like, Fuck that, we are going to drink some vodka made out of some mushrooms and get all drunked up,* so the next morning when they were all hung-over and pissed off they would be in the ideal mood to slaughter the shit out of some people?"

SBG could be a funny motherfucker when he wanted to be, and he could see me wavering, considering my options. On the one hand, that man would always be my BUD/S instructor and he was one of the few instructors who was still hard, putting out, and living the SEAL ethos every day. I'll always want to impress him. Jacking weights the night before my first 100 mile race would definitely impress that masochistic motherfucker. Plus, his logic made some fucked-up sense to me. I needed to get my mind ready to go to war, and lifting heavy would be my way of saying, bring on all your pain and misery, I'm ready to go! But, honestly, who does that before running a hundred fucking miles?

I shook my head in disbelief, threw my bag to the ground and started racking weights. With heavy metal blaring from the speakers, two knuckle draggers came together to put the fuck out. Most of our work focused on the legs, including long sets of squats and dead lifts at 315 pounds. In between we bench pressed 225. This was a real deal power-lifting session, and afterwards we sat on the bench next to one another and watched our quads and hamstrings quiver. It was fucking funny ... until it wasn't.

Ultra running has gone at least somewhat mainstream since then, but in 2005, most ultra races—especially the San Diego One Day—were pretty obscure, and it was all new to me. When the majority of people think of ultras they picture trail runs through remote wilderness and don't often imagine circuit races, but there were some serious runners in the field at the San Diego One Day.

This was the American National 24-Hour Championship and athletes descended from all over the country hoping for a trophy, a place on the podium, and the modest winner take-all cash prize of, ahem, $2,000. No, this was not a gilded event, basking in corporate sponsorship, but it was the site for a team comp between the U.S. ultra—distance national team and a team from Japan. Each side fielded teams of four men and four women who each ran for twenty-four hours. One of the top individual athletes in the field was also from Japan. Her name was Ms. Inagaki, and early on she and I kept pace.

Ms. Inagaki and I during San Diego 100

SBG turned up to cheer me on that morning with his wife and two-year-old son. They huddled up on the sidelines with my new wife, Kate, who I 'd married a few months before, a little over two years after my second divorce from Pam was finalized. When they saw me, they couldn't help but double over in laughter. Not just because SBG was still beat up from our workout the night before, and here I was trying to run a hundred miles, but because of how out of place I looked. When I spoke to SBG about it not long ago, the scene still made him laugh.

"So ultra marathoners are a little weird, right," SBG said, "and that morning it was like there were all these skinny ass, college professor looking, fucking granola e ating weirdoes, and then there is this one big black dude who looks like a fucking linebacker from the Raiders, running around this track jacked the fuck up with no shirt on, and I'm thinking of that song we had in kindergarten ... *one of these things is not like the other.* That was the song going through my head when I saw this fucking NFL linebacker running around this damn track with all these skinny little nerds. I mean they were some hard motherfuckers, those runners. I am not taking that away from them, but they were all super clinical about nutrition and shit, and you just put a pair of shoes on and said, let's go! "

He's not wrong. I didn't put much thought into my race plan at all. I hatched it at Walmart the night before, where I bought a fold-out lawn chair for Kate and me to use during the race and my fuel for the entire day: one box of Ritz crackers and two four-packs of Myoplex. I didn't drink much water. I didn't even consider my electrolyte or potassium levels or eat any fresh fruit. SBG brought me a pack of Hostess chocolate donuts when he showed up, and I gobbled those in a few seconds. I mean, I was winging it for real. Yet, at mile fifteen I was still in fifth place, still keeping pace with Ms. Inagaki, while Metz was getting more and more nervous. He ran up to me and tagged along.

"You should slow down, David," he said, "Pace yourself a bit more."

I shrugged. "I got this."

It's true that I felt okay in that moment, but my bravado was also a defense mechanism. I knew if I were to start planning my race at that point, the bigness of it would become too much to comprehend. It would feel like I was supposed to run the length of the damn sky. It would feel impossible. In my mind, strategy was the enemy of the moment, which is where I needed to be. Translation: when it came to ultras, I was green as fuck. Metz didn't press me, but he kept a close watch.

I finished mile twenty-five at about the four-hour mark and I was still in fifth place, still running with my new Japanese friend. SBG was long gone, and Kate was my only support crew. I'd see her every mile, posted up in that lawn chair, offering a sip of Myoplex and an encouraging smile.

I'd run a marathon only once before, while I was stationed in Guam. It was unofficial, and I ran it with a fellow SEAL on a course we made up on the spot, but back then I was in excellent cardiovascular shape. Now, here I was bearing down on 26.2 miles for just the second time in my entire life, this time without training, and once I got there I realized that I'd run beyond known territory. I had twenty more hours and nearly *three more marathons to go.* Those were incomprehensible metrics, with no traditional milestone in between to focus on. I was running across the sky. That's when I started thinking that this could end badly.

Metz didn't stop trying to help. Each mile he'd run alongside and check on me, and me being who I am, I told him that I had everything under control and had it all figured out. Which was true. I'd figured out that John Metz knew what the fuck he was talking about.

Oh yes, the pain was becoming real. My quads throbbed, my feet were chafed and bleeding, and that simple question was once again bubbling up in my frontal lobe. *Why? Why run a hundred fucking miles without training? Why was I doing this to myself?* Fair questions, especially since I hadn't even heard of the San Diego One Day until three days before race day, but this time my answer was different. I wasn't on Hospitality Point to deal with my own demons or to prove anything at all. I came with a purpose bigger than David Goggins. This fight was about my once and future fallen teammates, and the families they leave behind when shit goes wrong.

Or at least that's what I told myself at mile twenty-seven.

★ ★ ★

I had gotten the news about Operation Red Wings, a doomed operation in the remote mountains of Afghanistan, on my last day of U.S. Army Free fall school in Yuma, Arizona, in June. Operation Red Wings was a four-man reconnaissance mission tasked with gathering intelligence on a growing pro-Tali ban force in a region called Sawtalo Sar. If successful, what they learned would help define strategy for a larger offe nsive in the coming weeks. I knew all four guys.

Danny Dietz was in BUD/S Class 231 with me. He got injured and rolled just like I did. Michael Murphy, the OIC of the mission, was with me in Class 235 before he got rolled. Matthew Axelson was in my Hooyah Class when I graduated (more on the Hooyah Class tradition in a moment) , and Marcus Luttrell was one of the first people I met on my original lap through BUD/S.

Before training begins, each incoming BUD/S class throws a party, and the guys from previous classes who are still in BUD/S training are always invited. The idea is to juice as much information from brown shirts as possible, because you never know what might help get you through a crucial evolution that could make all the difference between graduation and fai lure. Marcus was 6'4", 2 25 pounds, and he stuck out in that crowd like I did. I was a bigger guy too, back up to 210 by then, and he sought me out. In some ways we were an odd pair. He was a hard-ass axe handle from the Texas rangeland, and I was a self-made masochist from the Indiana cornfields, but he'd heard I was a good runner, and running was his main weakness.

"Goggins, do you have any tips for me?" he asked. "Because I can't run for shit."

I knew Marcus was a badass, but his humility made him real.

When he graduated a few days later, we were his Hooyah Class, which meant we were the first people they were allowed to order around. They embraced that SEAL tradition and told us to go get wet and sandy. It was a SEAL's rite of passage, and an honor to share that with him. After that I didn't see him for a long time.

I thought I ran into him again when I was about to graduate with Class 235, but it was his twin brother, Morgan Luttrell, who was part of my Hooyah Class, Class 237, along with Matthew Axelson. We could have ordered up some poetic justice, but after we graduated, instead of telling their class to go get wet and sandy, we put ourselves in the surf, in our dress whites!

I had something to do with that.

In the Navy SEALs, you are either deployed and operating in the field, instructing other SEALs, or in school yourself, learning or perfecting skills. We cycle through more military schools than most because we are trained to do it all, but when I went through BUD/S we didn't learn to freefall. We jumped by static lines, which deployed our chutes automatically. Back then you had to be chosen to attend U.S. Army Freefall School. After my second platoon, I was picked up for Green Team which is one of the training phases to get accepted into the Naval Special Warfare Development Group (DEVGRU), an elite unit within the SEALs. That required me to get freefall qualified. It also required that I face my fear of heights in the most confrontational way possible.

We started off in the classrooms and wind tunnels of Fort Bragg, North Carolina, which is where I reconnected with Morgan in 2005. Floating on a bed of compressed air in a fifteen-foot-high wind tunnel, we learned correct body position, how to shift left and right, and push forward and back. It takes very small movements with your palm to move and it's easy to start spinning out of control, which is never good. Not everyone could master those subtleties but these of us who could left Fort Bragg after that first week of training and headed to an airstrip in the cactus fields of Yuma to start jumping for real.

Morgan and I trained and hung out together for four weeks in the 127-degree desert heat of summer. We did dozens of jumps out of C130 transport jets from altitudes ranging from 12,500 to 19,000 feet, and there is no rush like the surge of adrenaline and paranoia that comes with plummeting to earth from high altitude at terminal velocity. Each time we jumped I couldn't help but think of Scott Gearen, the Pararescuman who survived a botched jump from high altitude and inspired me on this path when I met him as a high school student. He was a constant presence for me in that desert, and a cautionary tale. Proof that something can go horribly wrong on any given jump.

When I jumped out of an airplane for the first time from high altitude, all I felt was extreme fear, and I couldn't pry my eyes from my altimeter. I wasn't able to embrace the jump because fear had clogged my mind. All I could think about was whether or not my canopy would open. I was missing the unbelievable thrill-ride of the freefall, the beauty of the mountains painted against the horizon, and the wide-open sky. But as I became conditioned to the risk, my tolerance for that same fear increased. It was always there, but I was used to the discomfort and before long I was able to handle multiple tasks on a jump and appreciate the moment too. Seven years earlier I had been rooting around fast food kitchens and open dumpsters zapping vermin. Now I was fucking flying!

The final task in Yuma was a midnight jump in full kit. We were weighed down with a fifty-pound rucksack, strapped with a rifle and an oxygen mask for the free fall. We were also equipped with chem lights, which were a necessity because when the back ramp of the C-130 opened up, it was pitch black.

We couldn't see any damn thing, but still we leapt into that moonless sky, eight of us in a line, one after another. We were supposed to form an arrow, and as I maneuvered through the real-world wind tunnel to take my place in the grand design, all I could see were swerving lights streaking like comets in an inkwell sky. My goggles fogged up as the wind ripped through me. We fell for a full minute, and when we deployed our chutes at around 4,000 feet, the overpowering sound went from full tornado to eerie silence. It was so quiet I could hear my heart beat through my chest. It was fucking bliss, and when we all landed safely, we were freefall qualified! We had no idea that at that moment, in the mountains of Afghanistan, Marcus and his team were locked into an all-out battle for their lives, at the center of what would become the worst incident in SEAL history.

One of the best things about Yuma is that you have horrible cell service. I'm not big on texting or talking on the phone so this gave me four weeks of peace. When you graduate any military school, the last thing you do is clean all the areas your class used until it's like you were never there. My cleaning detail was in charge of the bathrooms, which happened to be one of the only places in Yuma that has cell service, and as soon as I walked in I could hear my phone blow up. Text messages about Operation Red Wings going bad flooded in, and as I read them my soul broke. Morgan hadn't heard anything about it yet, so I walked outside, found him, and told him the news. I had to. Marcus and his crew were all MIA and presumed KIA. He nodded, considered it for a second, and said, "My brother's not dead."

Morgan is one minute older than Marcus. They were inseparable as kids, and the first time they'd ever been apart for longer than a day was when Marcus joined the Navy. Morgan opted for college before joining up, and during Marcus' Hell Week, he tried to stay up the whole time in solidarity. He wanted and needed to share that feeling, but there is no such thing as a Hell Week simulation. You have to go through it to know it, and those that survive are forever changed. In fact, the period after Marcus survived Hell Week and before Morgan became a SEAL himself was the only time there was any emotional distance between the brothers, which speaks to the power of those 130 hours and their emotional toll. Once Morgan went through it for real, everything was right again. They each have half a Trident tattooed on their back. The picture is only complete when they stand side by side.

Morgan took off immediately to drive to San Diego and figure out what the hell was going on. He still hadn't heard anything about the operation directly, but once he reached civilization and his service hit, a tide of messages flooded his phone too. He floored his rental car to 120 mph and zoomed directly to the base in Coronado.

Morgan knew all the guys in his brother's unit well. Axelson was his classmate in BUD/S, and as facts trickled in it was obvious to most that his brother wouldn't be found alive. I thought he was gone too, but you know what they say about twins.

"I knew my brother was out there, alive," Morgan told me when we connected again in April 2018. " I said that the whole time."

I'd called Morgan to talk about old times and asked him about the hardest week in his life. From San Diego, he flew out to his family's ranch in Huntsville, Texas, where they were getting updates twice a day. Dozens of fellow SEALs turned up to show support, Morgan said, and for five long days, he and his family cried themselves to sleep at night. To them it was torture knowing that Marcus might be alive and alone in hostile territory. When officials from the Pentagon arrived, Morgan made himself clear as cut glass, " [Marcus] may be hurt and fucked up, but he's *alive* and either you go out there and find him, or I will! "

Operation Red Wings went horribly wrong because there were many more pro-Taliban hajjis active in those mountains than had been expected, and once Marcus and his team were discovered by villager$ there, it was four guys against a well-armed militia of somewhere between 30-200 men (reports on the size of the pro-Taliban force vary). Our guys took RPG and machine gun fire, and fought hard. Four SEALs can put on a hell of a show. Each one of us can usually do as much damage as five regular troops, and they made their presence felt.

The battle played out along a ridgeline above 9,000 feet in elevation, where they had communication troubles. When they finally broke through and the situation was made plain to their commanding officer back at special operations headquarters, a quick reaction force of Navy SEALs, marines, and aviators from 16oth Special Operations Aviation Regiment was assembled, but they were delayed for hours because of lack of transport capacity. One thing about the SEAL teams is we don't have our own transport. In Afghanistan we hitch rides with the Army, and that delayed relief.

They eventually loaded up into two Chinook transport choppers and four attack helicopters (two Black Hawks and two Apaches) and took off for Sawtalo Sar. The Chinooks took the lead, and as they closed in on the ridge, they were hit by small arms fire. Despite the onslaught, the first Chinook hovered, attempting to unload eight Navy SEALs on a mountain top, but they made a fat target, lingered too long, and were hit with a rocket propelled grenade. The bird spun, crashed into the mountain, and exploded. Everyone aboard was killed. The remaining choppers bailed out, and by the time they could return with ground assets, everyone who was left behind, including Marcus' three teammates on Operation Red Wings, was found dead. Everyone, that is, except for Marcus.

Marcus was hit multiple times by enemy fire and went missing for five days. He was saved by Afghan villagers who nursed and sheltered him, and was finally found alive by U.S. troops on July 3, 2005, when he became the lone survivor of a mission that took the lives of nineteen special operations warriors, including eleven Navy SEALs.

No doubt, you've heard this story before. Marcus wrote a best-selling book about it, *Lone Survivor*, which became a hit movie starring Mark Wahlberg. But in 2005, that was all years away, and in the aftermath of the worst battlefield loss ever to hit the SEALs, I was looking for a way to contribute to the families of the men who were killed. It's not like bills stop rolling in after a tragedy like that. There were wives and kids out there with basic needs to fulfill, and eventually they'd need their college educations covered too. I wanted to help in any way I could.

A few weeks before all of this, Itd spent an evening Googling around for the world's toughest foot races and landed on a race called Bad water 135. I'd never even heard of ultra marathons before, and Badwater was an ultra marathoner's ultra marathon. It started below sea level in Death Valley and finished at the end of the road at Mount Whitney Portal, a trailhead located at 8,374 feet. Oh, and the race takes place in late July, when Death Valley isn't just the lowest place on Earth. It's also the hottest.

Seeing images from that race materialize on my monitor terrified and thrilled me. The terrain looked all kinds of harsh, and the expressions on tortured runners' faces reminded me of the kind of thing I saw in Hell Week. Until then, I'd always considered the marathon to be to pinnacle of endurance racing, and now I was seeing there were several levels beyond it. I filed the information away and figured I'd come back to it someday.

Then Operation Red Wings happened, and I vowed to run

Badwater 135 to raise money for the Special Operations Warrior Foundation, a non-profit founded as a battlefield promise in 1980, when eight special operations warriors died in a helicopter crash during the famous hostage rescue operation in Iran and left seventeen children behind. The surviving servicemen promised to make sure each one of those kids had the money to go to college. Their work continues. Within thirty days of a fatality, like those that occurred during Operation Red Wings, the foundation's hardworking staff reach out to surviving family members.

"We are the interfering aunt," said Executive Director Edie Rosenthal. "We become a part of our students' lives."

They pay for preschool and private tutoring during grade school. They arrange college visits and host peer support groups. They help with applications, buy books, laptop computers, and printers, and cover tuition at whichever school one of their students manages to gain acceptance, not to mention room and board. They also send students to vocational schools. It's all up to the kids. As I write this, the foundation has 1,280 kids in their program.

They are an amazing organization, and with them in mind, I called Chris Kostman, Race Director of Bad water 135, at 7 a.m. in mid-November, 2005. I tried to introduce myself, but he cut me off, sharp. "Do you know what time it is?!" he snapped.

I took the phone away from my ear and stared at it for a second. In those days, by 7 a.m. on a typical weekday I'd have already rocked a two-hour gym workout and was ready for a day's work. This dude was half asleep. " Roger that ," I said. " I'll call you back at 0900."

My second call didn't go much better, but at least he knew who I was .. SBG and I had already discussed Badwater and he'd emailed Kostman a letter of recommendation. SBG has raced triathlons, captained a team through the Ec-Challenge, and watched several Olympic qualifiers attempt BUD/S. In his email to Kostman, he wrote that I was the "best endurance athlete with the greatest mental toughness" he'd ever seen. To put me, a kid who came from nothing, at the top of his list meant the world to me and still does.

It didn't mean shit to Chris. Kostman. He was the definition of unimpressed. The kind of unimpressed that can only come from real-world experience. When he was twenty years old he'd competed in the Race Across America bicycle race, and before taking over as Badwater race director, he'd run three 100-mile races in winter in Alaska and completed a triple Ironman triathlon, which ends with a seventy-eight-mile run. Along the way, he'd seen dozens of supposedly great athletes crumble beneath the anvil of ultra.

Weekend warriors sign up for and complete marathons after a few months' training all the time, but the gap between marathon running and becoming an ultra athlete is much wider, and Bad water was the absolute apex of the ultra universe. In 2005, there were approximately twenty-two 100-mile races held in the United States, and none had the combination of the elevation gain and unforgiving heat that Bad water 135 brought to the table. Just to put on the race, Kostman had to wrangle permissions and assistance from five government agencies, including the National Forest Service, the National Park Service, and the California Highway Patrol, and he knew that if he allowed some greenhorn into the most difficult race ever conceived, in the middle of summer, that motherfucker might die, and his race would vaporize overnight. No, if he was going to let me compete in Bad water, I was going to have to earn it. Because earning my way in would provide him at least some comfort that I probably wouldn't collapse into a steaming pile of road kill somewhere between Death Valley and Mount Whitney.

In his email, SBG attempted to make a case that because I was busy working as a SEAL, the prerequisites required to compete at Bad water—the completion of at least one too-mile race or one twenty-four-hour race; while covering at least one hundred miles—should be waived. If I was allowed in, SBG guaranteed him that I'd finish in the top ten. Kostman wasn't having any of it. He'd had accomplished athletes beg him to waive his standards over the years, including a champion marathoner and a champion sumo wrestler (yeah, no shit), and he'd never budged.

"One thing about me is, I'm the same with everyone," Kostman said when I called him back. "We have certain standards for getting into our race, and that's the way it is. But hey, there's this twenty-four-hour race in San Diego coming up this weekend," he continued, his voice dripping with sarcasm. "Go run one hundred miles and get back to me."

Chris Kostman had made me. I was as unprepared as he suspected. The fact that I wanted to run Bad water was no lie, and I planned to train for it, but to even have a chance to do that I'd have to run one hundred miles at the drop of a damn hat. If I chose not to, after all that Navy SEAL bluster, what would that prove? That I was just another pretender ringing his bell way too early on a Wednesday morning. Which is how and why I wound up running the .San Diego One Day with three days' notice.

★ ★ ★

After surpassing the fifty-mile mark, I could no longer keep up with Ms. Inagaki, who bounded ahead like a damn rabbit. I soldiered on in a fugue state. Pain washed through me in waves. My thighs felt like they were loaded with lead. The heavier they got the more twisted my stride became. I torqued my hips to keep my legs moving and fought gravity to lift my feet a mere millimeter from the earth. Ah, yes, my feet. My bones were becoming more brittle by the second, and my toes h ad banged the tips of my shoes for nearly ten hours. Still, I fucking ran. Not fast. Not with much style. But I kept going.

My shins were the next domino to fall. Each subtle rotation of the ankle joint felt like shock therapy—like venom flowing through the marrow of my tibia . Vhrought back memories of my duct tape days from Class 235, but I didn't bring any tape with me this time. Besides, if I stopped for even a few seconds, starting up again would be near impossible.

A few miles later, my lungs seized, and my chest rattled as I hocked up knots of brown mucus. It got cold. I became short of breath. Fog gathered around the halogen street lights, ringing the lamps with electric rainbows, which lent the whole event an otherworldly feel. Or maybe it was just me in that other world. One in which pain was the mother tongue, a language synced to memory.

With every lung-scraping cough I flashed to my first BUD/S class. I was back on the motherfucking log, staggering ahead, my lungs bleeding. I could fee l and see it happening all over again. Was I asleep? Was I dreaming? I opened my eyes wide, pulled my ears and slapped my face to wake up. I felt my lips and chin for fresh blood, and found a translucent slick of saliva, sweat, and mucus dribbling from my nose. SBG's hard-ass nerds were all around me now, running in circles, pointing, mocking *the only;* the only black man in the mix. Or were they? I took another look. Everyone who passed me was focused. Each in their own pain zone. They didn't even see me.

I was losing touch with reality in small doses, because my

mind was folding over on itself, loading tremendous physical pain with dark emotional garbage it had dredged up from the depths of my soul. Translation: I was suffering on an unholy level reserved for dumb fucks who thought the laws of physics and physiology did not apply to them. Cocky bastards like me who felt like they could push the limits safely because they'd done a couple of Hell Weeks.

Right, well, I hadn't done this. I hadn't run one hundred miles with zero training. Had anybody in the history of mankind even attempted something so fucking foolish? Could this even be done at all? Iterations of that one simple question slid by like a digital ticker on my brain screen. Bloody thought bubbles floated from my skin and soul.

Whyr Whyr Why the fuck are you still doing this to yourselfr?!

I hit the incline at mile sixty—nine-that seven-foot ramp, the pitch of a shallow driveway—which would make any seasoned trail runner laugh out loud. It buckled my knees and sent me reeling backward like a delivery truck in neutral. I staggered, reached for the ground with the tips of my fingers, and nearly capsized. It took ten seconds to cover the distance. Each one dragged out like an elastic thread, sending shockwaves of pain from my toes to the space behind my eyeballs. I hacked and coughed, my gut twisted. Collapse was imminent. Collapse is what the fuck I deserved.

At the seventy-mile mark I couldn't take another step forward. Kate had set up our lawn chair on the grass near the start/finish line and when I teetered toward her I saw her in triplicate, six hands roping toward me, guiding me into that folding chair. I was dizzy and dehydrated, starved of potassium and sodium.

Kate was a nurse; I had EMT training, and went through my own mental checklist. I knew my blood pressure was probably dangerously low. She removed my shoes. My foot pain was no

Shawn Dobbs illusion. My white tube socks were caked in blood from cracked toenails and broken blisters. I asked Kate to grab some Motrin and anything she thought might be helpful from John Metz. And when she was gone, my body continued to decline. My stomach rumbled and when I looked down I saw bloody piss leak down my leg. I shit myself too. Liquefied diarrhea rose in the space between my ass and a lawn chair that would never be quite the same again. Worse, I had to hide it because I knew if Kate saw how bad off I really was she would beg me to pull out of the race.

I'd run seventy miles in twelve hours with no training, and this was my reward. To my left on the lawn was another four-pack of Myoplex. Only a muscle head like me would choose that thick-ass protein drink as my hydrating agent of choice. Next to it was half a box of Ritz crackers, the other half now congealing and churning in my stomach and intestinal tract like an orange blob.

I sat there with my head in my hands for twenty minutes. Runners shuffled, glided, or staggered past me, as I felt time tick down on my hastily imagined, ill-conceived dream. Kate returned, knelt down, and helped me lace back up. She didn't know the extent of my breakdown and hadn't quit on me yet. That was something, at least, and in her hands were a welcome reprieve from more Myoplex and more Ritz crackers. She handed me Motrin, then some cookies and two peanut butter and jelly sandwiches, which I washed down with Gatorade. Then she helped me stand.

The world wobbled on its axis. Again she split into two, then three, but she held me there as my world stabilized and I took a single, solitary step. Cue the ungodly pain. I didn't know it yet, but my feet were slivered with stress fractures. The toll of hubris is heavy on the ultra circuit, and my bill had come due. I took another step. And another .. I winced .. My eyes watered. Another step. She let go .. l walked on.

Slowly.

Way too fucking slow.

When I stopped at the seventy-mile mark, I was well ahead of the pace I needed to run one hundred miles in twenty four hours, but now I was walking at a twenty-minute -a-mile clip, which was as fast as I could possibly move . Ms. Inagaki breezed by me and glanced over. There was pain in her eyes too, but she still looked the part of an athlete. I was a motherfucking zombie, giving away all the precious time I stored up, watching my margin for error burn to ash. *Why?* Again the same boring question. *Why?* Four hours later, at nearly 2 a.m., I hit the eighty-one-mile mark and Kate broke some news.

"I don't believe you're gonna make the time at this pace," she said, walking with me, encouraging me to drink more Myoplex. She didn't cushion the blow. She was matter-of-fact about it. I stared over at her, mucus and Myoplex dripping down my chin, all the life drained from my eyes. For four hours, each agonizing step had demanded maximum focus and effort, but it wasn't enough and unless I could find more, my philanthropic dream was dead. I choked and coughed. Took another sip.

"Roger that," I said softly. I knew that she was right. My pace continued to slow and was only getting worse.

That's when I finally realized that this fight wasn't about Operation Red Wings or the families of the fallen. It was to a point, but none of that would help me run nineteen more miles before to a.m. No, this run, Badwater, my entire desire to push myself to the brink of destruction, was about me. It was about how much I was willing to suffer, how much more I could take, and how much I had to give. If I was gonna make it, this shit would have to get personal.

I stared down at my legs. I could still see a trail of dried piss and blood stuck to my inner thigh and thought to myself, who in this entire fucked-up world would still be in this fight? *Only you, Goggins! You haven't trained, you don't know dick about hydration and performance—all you know is you refuse to quit.*

Why?

It's funny, humans tend to hatch our most challenging goals and dreams, the ones that demand our greatest effort yet promise absolutely nothing, when we are tucked into our comfort zones. I was at work when Kostman laid out his challenge for me. I'd just had a warm shower. I was fed and watered. I was comfortable. And looking back, every single time I've been inspired to do something difficult, I was in a soft environment, because it all sounds doable when you're chilling on your fucking couch, with a glass of lemonade or a chocolate shake in your hand. When we're comfortable we can't answer those simple questions that are bound to arise in the heat of battle because we don't even realize they're coming.

But those answers are very important when you are no longer in your air-conditioned room or under your fluffy blanket. When your body is broken and beaten, when you're confronted with agonizing pain and staring into the unknown, your mind will spin, and that's when those questions become toxic. If you aren't prepared in advance, if you allow your mind to remain undisciplined in an environment of intense suffering (it won't feel like it, but it is very much a choice you are making), the only answer you are likely to find is the one that will make it stop as fast as possible.

I don't know.

Hell Week changed everything for me. It allowed me to have the mindset to sign up for that twenty-four-hour race with less than a week's notice because during Hell Week you live all the emotions of life, all the highs and lows, in six days. In

130 hours, you earn decades of wisdom. That's why there was a schism between the twins after Marcus went through BUD/S. He'd gained the kind of self-knowledge that can only come from being broken down to nothing and finding more within. Morgan couldn't speak that language until he endured it for himself.

After surviving two Hell Weeks and participating in three, I was a native speaker. Hell Week was home. It was the fairest place I've ever been in this world. There were no timed evolutions. There was nothing graded, and there were no trophies. It was an all-out war of me against me, and that's exactly where I found myself again when I was reduced to my absolute lowest on Hospitality Point.

Why?! Why are you still doing this to yourself, Goggins?!

"Because you are one hard motherfucker," I screamed.

The voices in my head were so penetrating, I had to bite back out loud. I was onto something. I felt an energy build immediately, as I realized that still being in the fight was a miracle in itself. Except it wasn't a miracle. God didn't come down and bless my ass. I did this! I kept going when I should have quit five hours ago. I am the reason I still have a chance. And I remembered something else too. This wasn't the first time I'd taken on a seemingly impossible task. I picked up my pace. I was still walking, but I wasn't sleepwalking anymore. I had life! I kept digging into my past, into my own imaginary Cookie Jar.

I remembered as a kid, no matter how fucked up our life was, my mother always figured out a way to stock our damn cookie jar. She'd buy wafers and Oreos, Pepperidge Farm Milanos and Chips Ahoy!, and whenever she showed up with a new batch of cookies, she dumped them into one jar. With her permission we'd get to pick one or two out at a time. It was like a mini treasure hunt. I remember the joy of dropping my fist into that jar, wondering what I'd find, and before I crammed the cookie in my mouth I always took the time to admire it first, especially when we were broke in Brazil. I'd turn it around in my hand and say my own little prayer of thanks. The feeling of being that kid, locked in a moment of gratitude for a simple gift like a cookie, came back to me. I felt it viscerally, and I used that concept to stuff a new kind of Cookie Jar. Inside it were all my past victories.

Like the time when I had to study three times as hard as anybody else during my senior year in high school just to graduate. That was a cookie. Or when I passed the ASVAB test as a senior and then again to get into BUD/S. Two more cookies. I remembered dropping over a hundred pounds in under three months, conquering my fear of water, graduating BUD/S at the top of my class, and being named Enlisted Honor Man in Army Ranger School (more on that soon) . All those were cookies loaded with chocolate chunks.

These weren't mere flashbacks. I wasn't just floating through my memory files, I actually tapped into the emotional state I felt during those victories, and in so doing accessed my sympathetic nervous system once again. My adrenaline took over, the pain started to fade just enough, and my pace picked up. I began swinging my arms and lengthening my stride. My fractured feet were still a bloody mess, full of blisters, the toenails peeling olf almost every toe, but I kept pounding, and soon it was me who was slaloming runners with pained expressions as I raced the clock.

From then on, the Cookie Jar became a concept I've employed whenever I need a reminder of who I am and what I'm capable of. We all have a cookie jar inside us, because life, being what it is, has always tested us. Even if you're feeling low and beat down by life right now, I guarantee you can think of a time or two when you overcame odds and tasted success. It doesn't have to be a big victory either. It can be something small.

I know we all want the whole victory today, but when I was teaching myself to read I would be happy when I could understand every word in a single paragraph. I knew I still had a long way to go to move from a third-grade reading level to that of a senior in high school, but even a small win like that was enough to keep me interested in iearning and finding more within myself. You don't drop one hundred pounds in less than three months without losing five pounds in a week first. Those first five pounds I lost were a small accomplishment, and it doesn't sound like a lot, but at the time it was proof that I could lose weight and that my goal, however improbable, was not impossible !

The engine in a rocket ship does not fire without a small spark first. We all need small sparks, small accomplishments in our lives to fuel the big ones. Think of your small accomplishments as kindling. When you want a bonfire, you don't start by lighting a big log. You collect some witch's hair—a small pile of hay or some dry, dead grass. You light that, and then add small sticks and bigger sticks before you feed your tree stump into the blaze. Because it's the small sparks, which start small fires, that eventually build enough heat to burn the whole fucking forest down.

If you don't have any big accomplishments to draw on yet, so be it. Your small victories are your cookies to savor, and make sure you do savor them. Yeah, I was hard on myself when I looked in the Accountability Mirror, but I also praised myself whenever I could claim a small victory, because we all need that, and very few of us take the time to celebrate our successes. Sure, in the moment, we might enjoy them, but do we ever look back on them and feel that win again and again? Maybe that sounds narcissistic to you. But I'm not talking about bullshitting about the glory days here. I'm not suggesting you crawl up your own ass and bore your friends with all your stories about what a badass you *used to be*. Nobody wants to hear that shit. I'm talking about utilizing past successes to fuel you to new and bigger ones. Because in the heat of battle, when shit gets real, we need to draw inspiration to push through our own exhaustion, depression, pain, and misery. We need to spark a bunch of small fires to become the motherfucking inferno.

But digging into the Cookie Jar when things are going south takes focus and determination because at first the brain doesn't want to go there. It wants to remind you that you're suffering and that your goal is impossible. It wants to stop you so it can stop the pain. That night in San Diego was the most difficult night of my life, physically. I'd never felt so broken, and there were no souls to take. I wasn't competing for a trophy. There was no one standing in my way. All I had to draw on to keep myself going was me.

The Cookie Jar became my energy bank. Whenever the pain got to be too much, I dug into it and took a bite. The pain was never gone, but I only felt it in waves because my brain was otherwise occupied, which allowed me to drown out the simple questions and shrink time. Each lap became a victory lap, celebrating a different cookie, another small fire. Mile eighty-one became eighty-two, and an hour and a half later, I was in the nineties. I'd run ninety fucking miles with no training! Who does that shit? An hour later I was at ninety-five, and after nearly nineteen hours of running almost non-stop, I 'd done it! I'd hit one hundred miles! Or had I? I couldn't remember, so I ran one more lap just to make sure.

After running 101 miles, my race finally over, I staggered to my lawn chair and Kate placed a camouflaged poncho liner over my body as I shivered in the fog. Steam poured off me. My vision was blurred. I remember feeling something warm on my leg, looked down and saw I was pissing blood again. I knew what was coming next, but the port-a-potties were about forty feet away, which may as well have been forty miles, or 4,000. I tried to get up but I was way too dizzy and collapsed back into that chair, an immovable object ready to accept the inevitable truth that I was about to shit myself. It was much worse this time. My entire backside and lower back were smeared with warm feces.

Kate knew what an emergency looked like. She sprinted to our Toyota Camry and backed the car up on the grassy knoll beside me. My legs were stiff as fossils frozen in stone, and I leaned on her to slide into the backseat. She was frantic behind the wheel and wanted to take me directly to the ER, but I wanted to go home.

We lived on the second deck of an apartment complex in Chula Vista, and I leaned on her back with my arms around her neck as she led me up that staircase. She balanced me up against the stucco as she opened the door to our apartment. I took a few steps inside before blacking out.

I came to, on the kitchen floor, a few minutes later. My back was still smeared with shit, my thighs caked in blood and urine. My feet were blistered up and bleeding in twelve places. Seven of my ten toenails were dangling loose, connected only by tabs of dead skin. We had a combination tub and shower and she got the shower going before helping me crawl toward the bathroom and climb into the tub. I remember lying there, naked, with the shower pouring down upon me. I shivered, felt and looked like death, and then I started peeing again. But instead of blood or urine, what came out of me looked like thick brown bile.

Petrified, Kate stepped into the hall to dial my mom. She'd been to the race with a friend of hers who happened to be a doctor. When he heard my symptoms, the doctor suggested that I might be in kidney failure and that I needed to go to the ER immediately. Kate hung up, stormed into the bathroom, and found me lying on my left side, in the fetal position.

"We need to get you to the ER now, David! "

She kept talking, shouting, crying, trying to reach me through the haze, and I heard most of what she said, but I knew if we went to the hospital they'd give me pain killers and I didn't want to mask this pain. I'd just accomplished the most amazing feat in my entire life. It was harder than Hell Week, more significant to me than becoming a SEAL, and more challenging than my deployment to Iraq because this time I had done something I'm not sure anyone had ever done before. I ran 101 miles with zero preparation.

I knew then that I'd been selling myself short. That there was a whole new level of performance out there to tap into. That the human body can withstand and accomplish a hell of a lot more than most of us think possible, and that it all begins and ends in the mind. This wasn't a theory. It wasn't something I'd read in a damn book. I'd experienced it first hand on Hospitality Point.

This last part. This pain and suffering. This was my trophy ceremony. I'd earned this. This was confirmation that I'd mastered my own mind—at least for a little while—and that what I'd just accomplished was something special. As I lay there, curled up in the tub, shivering in the fetal position, relishing the pain, I thought of something else too. If I could run 101 miles with zero training, imagine what I could do with a little preparation.

CHALLENGE #6

Take inventory o f your Cookie Jar. Crack your journal open again. Write it all out. Remember, this is not some breezy stroll through your personal trophy room. Don't just write down your achievement hit list. Include life obstacles you've overcome as well, like quitting smoking ot: overcoming depression or a stutter. Add in those minor tasks you failed earlier in life, but tried again a second or third time and ultimately succeeded at. Feel what it was like to overcome those struggles, those opponents, and win. Then get to work.

Set ambitious goals before each workout and let those past victories carry you to new personal bests. If it's a run or bike ride, include some time to do interval work and challenge yourself to beat your best mile split. Or simply maintain a maximum heart rate for a full minute, then two minutes. If you're at home, focus on pull-ups or push-ups. Do as many as possible in two minutes. Then try to beat your best. When the pain hits and tries to stop you short of your goal, dunk your fist in, pull out a cookie, and let it fuel you!

If you're more focused on intellectual growth, train yourself to study harder and longer than ever before, or read a record number of books in a given month. Your Cookie Jar can help there too. Because if you perform this challenge correctly and truly challenge yourself, you'll come to a point in any exercise where pain, boredom, or self-doubt kicks in, and you'll need to push back to get through it. The Cookie Jar is your shortcut to taking control of your own thought process. Use it that way! The point here □n't to make yourself feel like a hero for the fuck of it. It's not a hooray-for-me session. It's to remember what a badass you are so you can use that energy to succeed again in the heat of battle!

Post your memories and the new successes they fueled on social media, and include the hashtags: #canthurtme #cookiejar.

CHAPTER SEVEN

THE MOST POWERFUL WEAPON

TWENTY-SEVEN HOURS AFTERS AVORING IN TENSE, gratifying p ain and basking i n the afterglow of my greatest achievement so far, I was back at my desk on a Monday morning. SBG was my commanding officer, and I had his permission, and every known excuse, to take a few days off. Instead, swollen, sore, and miserable, I pulled myself out of bed, hobbled into work, and later that morning called Chris Kostman.

I'd bee n looking forward to this. I imagined the sweet note of surprise in his voice, after hearing that I'd taken his challenge and run 101 miles in less than twenty-four hours. Perhaps there'd even be some overdue respect as he made my entry to Bad water official. Instead, my call went to voicemail. I left him a polite message he never returned, and two days later I dropped him an email.

```
Sir, how are you doing? Iran the one hundred
miles needed to qualify in 18 hours and 56
minute... I would like to know now what I need
to do to  get into Badwater...so  we can  begin
```

raising money for the [Special Operations
Warrior] foundation. Thanks again...

His reply came in the next day, and it threw me way the
fuck off.

Congrats on your hundred-mile finish. But did
you actuallys top then? The point of a twenty-
four-hour event is to run for twenty-four
hours...Anyway...stay tuned for the an noun cement
that you can apply... The race will be July 24-26.

Best regards,

Chris Kostman

I couldn't help but take his response personally. On a Wednesday he suggested I run one hundred miles in twenty-four hours
that Saturday. I got it done in less time than he required, and he
still wasn't impressed? Kostman was a veteran of ultra races, so
he knew that strewn behind me were a dozen performance barriers
and pain thresholds I'd shattered. Obviously, none of that
meant much to him.

I cooled off for a week before I wrote him back, and in the
meantime looked into other races to bolster my resume. There
were very few available that late in the year. I found a fifty-miler
on Catalina, but. only triple digits would impress a guy like Kostman. Plus, it had been a full week since the San Diego One Day
and my body was still monumentally fucked. I hadn't run three
feet since finishing mile 101. My frustration flashed with the
cursor as I crafted my rebuttal.

Thanks for emailing me back. I see that you
enjoy talking about as much as I do. The only
reason why I'm still bugging you is because
this race and the cause behind it is important...
If you have any you her qualifying races that
you think I should do, please let me know...
Thanks for letting me know I'm supposed to run
the full twenty-four hours. Next time I 'll be
sure to do that.

It took him another full week to respond, and he didn't offer
a hell of a lot more hope, but at least he salted it with sarcasm.

Hi David,

If you can do some more ultras between now
and Jan 3-24,the applic ation period, great.
If not, subm it the best possible application
during the Jan 3-24 window and cross
your fingers.

Thanks for your enthusiasm,

Chris

At this point I was starting to like Chris Kostman a lot better
than my chances of getting into Bad water. What I didn't know,
because he never mentioned it, is that Kostman was one of five
people on the Bad water admissions committee, which reviews
upwards of 1,000 applications a year. Each judge scores every
application, and based on their cumulative scores, the top ninety

applicants get in on merit. From the sounds of it, my resume was thin and wouldn't crack the top ninety. On the other hand, Kostman held ten wild cards in his back pocket. He could have already guaranteed me a spot, but for some reason he kept pushing me. Once again I'd have to prove myself beyond a minimum standard to get a fair shake. To become a SEAL, I had to deal three Hell Weeks, and now, if I really wanted to run Bad water and raise money for families in need, I was going to have to find a way to make my application bulletproof.

Based on a link he sent along with his reply, I found one more ultra race scheduled before the Badwater application was due. It was called the Hurt 100, and the name did not lie. One of the toughest 100-mile trail races in the world, it was set in a triple canopy rainforest on the island of Oahu. To cross the finish line, I'd have to run up and down 24,500 vertical feet. That's some Himalayan shit. I stared at the race profile. It was all sharp spikes and deep dives. It looked like an arrhythmic EKG. I couldn't do this race cold. There 's no way I could finish it without at least some training, but by early December I was still in so much agony that walking up the stairs to my apartment was pure torture.

The following weekend I zoomed up Interstate 15 to Vegas for the Las Vegas Marathon. It wasn't spur of the moment. Months before I 'd ever heard the words "San Diego One Day," Kate, my mom, and I had circled December 5th on our calendars. It was 2005, the first year that the Las Vegas Marathon started on the Strip, and we wanted to be part of that shit. Except I never trained for it, then the San Diego One Day happened, and by the time we got to Vegas I had no illusions about my fitness level. I tried to run the morning before we left, but I still had stress fractures in my feet, my medial tendons were wobbly, and even while wrapped with a special bandage I'd found that could stabilize my ankles,

I couldn't last longer than a quarter mile. So I didn't plan on running as we rocked up to the Mandalay Bay Casino & Resort on race day.

It was a beautiful morning. Music was pumping, there we thousands of smiling faces in the street, the clean desert air had a chill to it, and the sun was shining. Running conditions don't get much better, and Kate was ready to go. Her goal was to break five hours, and for once, I was satisfied being a cheerleader. My mom had always planned on walking it, and I figured I'd stroll with her for as long as I could, then hail a cab to the finish line and cheer my ladies to the tape.

The three of us toed up with the masses as the clock struck 7 a.m., and someone got on the mic to begin the official count down. "Ten... nine... eight... " When he hit one, a horn sounded, and like Pavlov's dog something clicked inside me. I still don't know what it was. Perhaps I underestimated my competitive spirit. Maybe it was because I knew Navy SEALs were supposed to be the hardest motherfuckers in the world. We were supposed to run on broken legs and fractured feet. Or so went the legend I'd bought into long ago. Whatever it was, something triggered and the last thing I remember seeing as the horn echoed down the street was shock and real concern on the faces of Kate and my mother as I charged down the boulevard and out of sight.

The pain was serious for the first quarter mile, but after that adrenaline took over. I hit the first mile marker at 7:10 and kept running like the asphalt was melting behind me. Ten kilometers into the race, my time was around forty-three minutes. That's solid, but I wasn't focused on the clock because considering how I'd felt the day before, I was still in total disbelief that I'd actually run 6.2 miles! My body was broken. How was this happening?

Most people in my condition would have both feet in soft casts, and here I was running a marathon!

I got to mile thirteen, the halfway point, and saw the offiti.at clock. It read, "1:35:55." I did the math and realized that I was in the hunt to qualify for the Boston marathon, but was right on the cusp. In order to qualify in my age group, I had to finish in under 3:10:59. I laughed in disbelief and slammed a paper cup of Gatorade. In less than two hours the game had flipped, and I might never get this chance again. I'd seen so much death by then—in my personal life and on the battlefield—that I knew tomorrow was not guaranteed. Before me was an opportunity, and if you give me an opportunity, I will break that motherfucker off!

It wasn't easy. I'd surfed an adrenaline wave for the first thirteen miles, but I felt every inch of the second half, and at mile eighteen, I hit a wall. That's a common theme in marathon running, because mile eighteen is usually when a runner's glycogen levels run low, and I was bonking, my lungs heaving. My legs felt like I was running in deep Saharan sand. I needed to stop and take a break, but I refused, and two hard miles later I felt rejuvenated. I reached the next clock at mile twenty-two. I was still in the hunt for Boston, though I'd fallen thirty seconds off the pace, and to qualify, the final four miles would have to be my very best.

I dug deep, kicked my thighs up high, and lengthened my stride. I was a man possessed as I turned the final corner and charged toward the finish line at the Mandalay Bay. Thousands of people had assembled on the sidewalk, cheering. It was all a beautiful blur to me as I sprinted home.

I ran my last two miles at a sub-seven-minute pace, finished the race in just over 3:08, and qualified for Boston. Somewhere on the streets of Las Vegas,. my wife and mother would deal with their own struggles and overcome them to finish too, and as I sat on a patch of grass, waiting for them, I contemplated another simple question I couldn't shake. It was a new one, and wasn't fear-based, pain-spiked, or self-limiting. This one felt open.

What am I capable of?

SEAL training had pushed me to the brink several times, mit whenever it beat me down I popped up to take another pounding. That experience made me hard, but it also left me wanting more of the same, and day-to-day Navy SEAL life just wasn't like that. Then came the San Diego One Day, and now this. I'd finished a marathon at an elite pace (for a weekend warrior) when I had no business even walking a mile. Both were incredible physical feats that didn't seem possible. But they'd happened.

What am I capable of?

I couldn't answer that question, but as I looked around the finish line that day and considered what I'd accomplished, it became clear that we are all leaving a lot of money on the table without realizing it. We habitually settle for less than our best; at work, in school, in our relationships, and on the playing field or race course. We settle as individuals, and we teach our children to settle for less than their best, and all of that ripples out, merges, and multiplies within our communities and society as a whole. We're not talking some bad weekend in Vegas, no more cash at the ATM kind of loss either. In that moment, the cost of missing out on so much excellence in this eternally fucked-up world felt incalculable to me, and it still does. I haven't stopped thinking about it since.

★ ★ ★

Physically, I bounced back from Vegas within a few days. Meaning I was back to my new normal: dealing with the same serious yet tolerable pain I'd come home to after the San Diego One Day.

The aches were still there by the following Saturday, but I was done convalescing. I needed to start training or I'd burn out on the trail during the Hurt 100, and there would be no Badwater. I'd been reading up on how to prepare for ultras and knew it was vital to get in some hundred-mile weeks. I only had about a month to build my strength and endurance before race day on January 14th.

My feet and shins weren't even close to right, so I came up with a new method to stabilize both the bones in my feet and my tendons. I bought high performance inserts, cut them down to fit flush with the soles of my feet, and taped my ankles, heels, and " lower shins with compression tape. I also slid a small heel wedge into my shoes to correct my running posture and ease pressure. After what I'd endured, it took a lot of props to get me running (nearly) pain free.

Getting hundred-mile weeks in while holding down a steady job isn't easy, but that was no excuse. My sixteen-mile commute to work from Chula Vista to Coronado became my go-to run. Chula Vista had a split personality when I lived there. There was the nicer, newer, middle class section, where we lived, which was surrounded by a concrete jungle of gritty, dangerous streets. That's the part I ran through at dawn, beneath freeway overpasses, and alongside Home Depot shipping bays. This was not your tourist brochure's version of sunny San Diego.

I sniffed car exhaust and rotting garbage, spotted skittering rats, and dodged sleepless homeless camps before reaching Imperial Beach, where I picked up the seven-mile Silver Strand bike path. It banked south past Coronado's landmark hotel, the turn of the century Hotel Del Coronado, and a crop of luxury condo towers which overlooked the same wide strip of sand shared by Naval Special Warfare Command, where I spent the day jumping out of airplanes and shooting guns. I was living the Navy SEAL legend, trying to keep it real!

I ran that sixteen-mile stretch at least three times a week. Some days I ran home too, and on Fridays I added a ruck run. Inside the radio pouch of my standard issue ruck sack, I slid two twenty-five-pound weights and ran fully loaded for as many as twenty miles to build quad strength. I loved waking up at 5 a.m. and starting work with three hours of cardio already in the bank while most of my teammates hadn't even finished their coffee. It gave me a mental edge, a better sense of self-awareness, and a ton of self-confidence, which made me a better SEAL instructor. That's what getting up at the ass crack of dawn and putting out will do for you. It makes you better in all facets of your life.

During my first real deal week of training, I ran seventy-seven miles. The following week, I ran 109 miles, including a twelve-mile run on Christmas Day. The next week I pushed it to 111.5, including a nineteen-mile run on New Year's Day, and .. the following week I backed off to taper my legs, but still got 56.5 miles in. All of those were road miles, but what I had coming up was a trail run, and I had never run on a trail before. I'd bush-whacked a bunch, but I hadn't run distance on single track with a clock running. The Hurt 100 was a twenty-mile circuit course, and I'd heard that only a slim slice of those who start the race finish all five laps. This was my last chance to pad my Bad water resume. I had a lot riding on a successful outcome, and there was so much about the race, and about ultra running, that I still didn't know.

	AM	NOON	PM
WEEK 3 TOTAL=1115 WEEK 3			
MON 26 DEC	15 miles		
TOTAL: 15m			
TUE 27 DEC	20.0 miles	FIRST DAY NEW SHOES	
TOTAL: 20m			
WED 28 DEC		14.0 miles	
TOTAL: 14m			
THU 29 DEC		11.0 miles	
TOTAL: 11m			
FRI 30 DEC		16.5 miles	
TOTAL: 16.5m			
SAT 31 DEC	11.4 miles	4.6 miles	
TOTAL: 16m			
SUN 1 JAN	17.0 miles		2.0 mi
TOTAL: 19.0m			
WEEK 3 TOTAL = 111.5 miles			

Hurt 100 Week 3 training log

I flew into Honolulu a few days early and checked into the Halekoa, a military hotel where active duty and veterans stay with their families when they come through town. I'd studied the maps and knew the basics when it came to the terrain, but I hadn't seen it up close, so I drove over to the Hawaii Nature Center the day before the race and stared into the velvety, jade mountains. All I could see was a steep cut of red earth disappearing into the dense green. I walked up the trail for a half mile, but there was only so far I could hike. I was tapering, and the first mile was straight uphill. Everything beyond that would have to remain a mystery for a little longer.

There were just three aid stations on the twenty-mile course, and most athletes were self-reliant and dialed in their own nutritional regimen. I was still a neophyte, and had no clue what I needed when it came to fuel. I met a woman at the hotel at 5:30 a.m. on race day morning as we were about to leave. She knew I was a rookie and asked what I'd brought with me to keep myself going. I showed her my meager stash of flavored energy gels, and my CamelBak.

"You didn't bring salt pills?" she asked, shocked. I shrugged. I didn't know what the fuck a salt pill was. She poured a hundred of them into my palm. "Take two of these, e very hour. They'll keep you from cramping."

"Roger that." She smiled and shook her head like she could see my fucked-up future.

I had a strong start and felt great, but not long after the race began I knew I was facing a monster course. I'm not talking about the grade and elevation variance. I expected that. It was all the rocks and roots that took me by surprise. I was lucky that it hadn't rained in a couple of days because all I had to wear were my standard running shoes, which had precious little tread. Then my CamelBak broke at mile six.

I shook it off and kept hammering, but without a water source, I'd have to rely on the ·aid stations to hydrate, and they were spaced miles apart. I didn't even have my support crew (of one) yet. Kate was chilling on the beach and didn't plan on showing up until later in the race, which was was my own fault. I enticed her to come along by promising a vacation, and early that morning I insisted she enjoy Hawaii and leave the suffering to me. With or without a CamelBak, my mind set was to make it from aid station to aid station and see what happens.

Before the race started I heard people talking about Karl Meltzer. I'd seen him stretching out and warming up. His nickname was the Speedgoat, and he was trying to become the first person ever to complete the race in less than twenty-four hours. For the rest of us there was a thirty-six hour time limit. My first lap took four and a half hours, and I felt okay afterwards, which was to be expected considering all the long days I'd done in preparation, but I was also concerned because each lap demanded an ascent and descent of around 5,000 vertical feet, and the amount of focus it took to pay attention to every step so I didn't turn an ankle amped up my mental fatigue. Each time my medial tendon twinged it felt like a raw nerve exposed to the wind, and I knew one stumble could fold my wobbly ankle and end my race. I felt that pressure every single moment, and as a result, I burned more calories than expected. Which was a problem because I had very little fuel, and without a water source, I couldn't hydrate effectively.

Between laps, I guzzled water, and with my belly sloshing started my second loop, with a slow jog up that one-mile-long, 800-foot climb into the mountains (basically straight uphill) . That's when it started to rain. Our red earth trail became mud within minutes. The soles of my shoes were coated with it and slick as skis. I sloshed through shin deep puddles, skidded down descents, and slipped on ascents. It was a full-body sport. But at least there was water. Whenever I was dry I tipped my head back, opened wide, and tasted the rain, which filtered through a triple canopy jungle that smelled of leaf rot and shit. The feral funk of fertility invaded my nostrils, and all I could think of was the fact that I had to run four more fucking laps!

At mile thirty, my body reported some positive news. Or maybe it was the physical manifestation of a backhanded compliment? The tendon pain in my ankles had vanished... because my feet had swollen enough to stabilize those tendons. Was this a good thing long-term? Probably not, but you take what you can get on the ultra circuit, where you have to roll with whatever gets you from mile to mile. Meanwhile, my quads and calves ached like they'd been thumped with a sledgehammer. Yeah, I had done a lot of running, but most of it—including my ruck runs—on pancake fiat terrain in San Diego, not on slick jungle trails.

Kate was waiting for me by the time I completed my second lap, and after spending a relaxing morning on Waikiki beach, she watched in horror as I materialized from the mist like a zombie from the Walking Dead. I sat and guzzled as much water as I could. By then, word had gotten out that it was my first trail race.

Have you ever had a very public fuck-up, or were in the midst of a shitty day/week/month/year, yet people around you felt obliged to comment on the source of your humiliation? Maybe they reminded you of all the ways you could have ensured a very different outcome? Now imagine consuming that negativity, but having to run sixty more miles in the sweaty, jungle rain on top of it. Does that sound like fun? Yeah, I was the talk of the race. Well, me and Karl Meltzer. Nobody could believe he was gunning for a sub-twenty-four-hour experience, and it was equally baffling that I showed up to one of the most treacherous trail races on the planet, undersupplied and unprepared, with no .trail races under my belt. By the time I began my third loop there were only forty athletes, out of nearly a hundred, left in the race, and I started running with a guy named Luis Escobar. For the tenth time I heard the following words:

"So it's your first trail race?" he asked. I nodded. "You really picked the wrong ... "

"I know," I said.

"It's just such a technical..."

"Right. I'm a fucking idiot. I've heard that a lot today."

"That's okay," he said, "we're all of bunch of idiots out here, man." He handed ine a water bottle. He was carrying three of them. "Take this. I heard about your CamelBak."

This being my second race, I was starting to understand the rhythm of ultra. It's a constant dance between competition and camaraderie, which reminded me of BUD/S. Luis and I were both racing the clock and each other, but we wanted one another to make it. We were in it alone, together, and he was right. We were a couple of fucking idiots.

Darkness descended and left us with a pitch-black jungle night. Running side by side, the glow of our headlamps merged and shed a wider light, but once we separated all I could see was a yellow ball bouncing on the trail ahead of me. Countless trip wires—..,shin-high logs, slick roots, lichen-wrapped rocks— remained out of sight. I slipped, stumbled, fell, and cursed. Jungle noises were everywhere. It wasn't just the insect world that had my attention. In Hawaii, on all the islands, bow hunting for wild pig in the mountains is a major pastime, and master hunters often leave their pit bulls chained up in the jungle to develop a nose for swine. I heard every one of those hungry bulls snapping and growling, and I heard some pigs squealing too. I smelled their fear and rage, their piss and shit, their sour fucking breath.

With each nearby bark or yelp, my heart skipped and I jumped on terrain so slick that injury was a real possibility. One wrong step could roll my ass out of the race and out of contention for Bad water. I could picture Kostman hearing the news and nodding like he figured that shit would happen all along. I know him pretty well now, and he was never out to get me, but that's how my mind worked back then. And in the steep, dark mountains of Oahu, my exhaustion magnified my stress. I felt close to my absolute limit, but still had more than forty miles to go!

On the backside of the course, after a long technical descent into the dark, dank forest I saw another headlamp circling ahead of me in a cutout on the trail. The runner was moving in curlicues and when I caught up to him I could see it was a Hungarian runner I'd met in San Diego named Akos Konya. He was one of the best runners in the field on Hospitality Point, where he covered 134 miles in twenty-four hours. I liked Akos and had mad respect for him. I stopped and watched him move in conjoining circles, covering the same terrain over and over again. Was he looking for something? Was he hallucinating?

"Akos," I asked, "you o ay, man? Do you need some help?"

"David, no! I ... no, I'm fine," he said. His eyes were full-moon flying saucers. He was in delirium, but I was barely hanging on myself and wasn't sure what I could do for him other than tell staff at the next aid station he was wandering in a daze. Like I said, there's camaraderie and there's competition on the ultra circuit, and since he wasn't in obvious pain and refused my help, I had to go into barbarian mode. With two full laps to go, I had no choice but to keep moving.

I staggered back to the start line and slumped into my chair, dazed. It was dark as space, the temperature was dropping, and rain was still pissing down. I was at the very edge of my capability, and wasn't sure that I could take one more step. I felt like I'd drained 99 percent from my tank, at least. My gas light was on, my engine shuddering, yet I knew I had to find more if I was going to finish this race and get myself into Bad water.

But how do you push yourself when pain is all you feel with every step? When agony is the feedback loop that permeates each cell in your body, begging you to stop? That's tricky because the threshold for suffering is different for everybody. What's universal is the impulse to succumb. To feel like you've given everything you can, and that you are justified in leaving a job undone.

By now, I'm sure you can tell that it doesn't take much for me to become obsessed. Some criticize my level of passion, but I'm not down with the prevailing mentalities that tend to dominate American society these days; the ones that tell us to go with the flow or invite us to learn how to get more with less effort. Fuck that shortcut bullshit. The reason I embrace my own obsessions and demand and desire more of myself is because I've learned that it's only when I push beyond pain and suffering, past my perceived limitations, that I'm capable of accomplishing more, physically and mentally—in endurance races but also in life as a whole.

And I believe the same is true for you.

The human body is like a stock car. We may look different on the outside, but under the hood we all have huge reservoirs of potential and a governor impeding us from reaching our maximum velocity. In a car, the governor limits the flow of fuel and air so it doesn't burn too hot, which places a ceiling on performance. It's a hardware issue; the governor can easily be removed, and if you disable yours, watch your car rocket beyond 130 mph.

It's a subtler process in the human animal.

Our governor is buried deep in our minds, intertwined with our very identity. It knows what and who we love and hate; it's read our whole life story and forms the way we see ourselves and how we'd like to be seen. It's the software that delivers personalized feedback—in the form of pain and exhaustion, but also fear and insecurity, and it uses all of that to encourage us to stop before we risk it all . But, here's the thing, it doesn't have absolute control. Unlike the governor in an engine, ours can't stop us unless we buy into its bullshit and agree to quit.

Sadly, most of us give up when we've only given around 40 percent of our maximum effort. Even when we feel like we've reached our absolute limit, we still have 60 percent more to give! That's the governor in action! Once you know that to be true, it's simply a matter of stretching your pain tolerance, letting go of your identity and all your self-limiting stories, so you can get to 60 percent, then 80 percent and beyond without giving up. I call this The 40% Rule, and the reason it's so powerful is that if you follow it, you will unlock your mind to new levels of performance and excellence in sports and in life, and your rewards will run far deeper than mere material success.

The 40% Rule can be applied to everything we do. Because in life almost nothing will turn out exactly as we hope. There are always challenges, and whether we are at work or school, or feeling tested within our most intimate or important relationships, we will all be tempted to walk away from commitments, give up on our goals and dreams, and sell our own happiness short at some point. Because we will feel empty, like we have no more to give, when we haven't tapped even half of the treasure buried deep in our minds, hearts, and souls.

I know how it feels to be approaching an energetic dead end. I've been there too many times to count. I understand the temptation to sell short, but I also know that impulse is driven by your mind's desire for comfort, and it's not telling you the truth. It's your identity trying to find sanctuary, not help you grow. It's looking for status quo, not reaching for greatness or seeking wholeness. But the software update that you need to shut your governor down is no supersonic download. It takes twenty years to gain twenty years of experience, and the only way to move beyond your 40 percent is to callous your mind, day after day. Which means you'll have to chase pain like it's your damn job!

Imagine you're a boxer, and on your first day in the ring you take one on your chin. It's gonna hurt like fucking hell, but at year · ten of being a boxer, you won't be stopped by one punch. You'll be able to absorb twelve rounds of getting beat the fuck down and come back the very next day and fight again. It's not that the punch has lost power. Your opponents will be even stronger. The change has happened within your brain. You've calloused your mind. Over a period of time, your tolerance for mental and physical suffering will have expanded because your software will have learned that you can take a hell of a lot more than one punch, and if you stay with any task that is trying to beat you down, you will reap rewards.

Not a fighter? Say you like to run but have a broken pinky toe. I'll bet if you continue running on it, pretty soon you'll be able to run on broken legs. Sounds impossible, right? I know it's true, because I've run on broken legs, and that knowledge helped me endure all manner of agonies on the ultra circuit, which has revealed a clear spring of self confidence that I drink from whenever my tank is dry.

But nobody taps their reserve 60 percent right away or all at once. The first step is to remember that your initial blast of pain and fatigue is your governor talking. Once you do that, you are in control of the dialogue in your mind, and you can remind yourself that you are not as drained as you think. That you haven't given it your all. Not even close. Buying into that will keep you in the fight, and that's worth an extra 5 percent. Of course, that's easier read than done.

It wasn't easy to begin the fourth lap of the Hurt 100 because I knew how much it would hurt, and when you are feeling dead and buried, dehydrated, wrung out, and torn the fuck up at 40 percent, finding that extra 60 percent feels impossible. I didn't want my suffering to continue. Nobody does! That's why the line "fatigue makes cowards of us all" is true as shit.

Mind you, I didn't know anything about The 40% Rule that day. The Hurt 100 is when I first started to contemplate it, but

I had hit the wall many times before, and I had learned to stay present and open minded enough to recalibrate my goals even at my lowest. I knew that staying in the fight is always the hardest, and most rewarding, first step.

Of course, it's easy to be open minded when you leave yoga class and are taking a stroll by the beach, but when you're suffering, keeping an open mind is hard work. The same is true if you are facing a daunting challenge on the job or at school. Maybe you are tackling a hundred-question test and know that you've bricked the first fifty. At that point, it's extremely difficult to maintain the necessary discipline to force yourself to keep taking the test seriously. It's also imperative that you find it because in every· failure there is something to be gained, even if it's only practice for the next test you'll have to take. Because that next test is coming. That's a guarantee.

I didn't start my fourth lap with any sort of conviction. I was in wait-and-see mode, and halfway up that first climb I became· so dizzy I had to sit under a tree for a while. Two runners passed me, one at a time. They checked in but I waved them on. Told them I was just fine.

Yeah, I was doing great. I was a regular Akos Konya.

From my vantage point I could see the crest of the hill above and encouraged myself to walk at least that far. If I still wanted to quit after that, I told myself that I would be willing to sign off, and that there is no shame in not finishing the Hurt 100. I said that to myself again and again because that's how our governor works. It massages your ego even as it stops you short of your goals. But once I got to the top of the climb, the higher ground gave me a new perspective and I saw another place off in the dista.nce and decided to cover that small stretch of mud, rock, and root too-you know, before quitting for good.

Once I got there I was staring down a long descent and even though the footing was troubling, it still looked much easier than going uphill. Without realizing it, I'd gotten to a point where I was able to strategize. On the first climb, I was so dizzy and weak I was swept into a moment offuck, which clogged my brain. There was no room for strategy. I just wanted to quit, but by moving a little bit further I'd reset my brain. I'd calmed down and realized I could chunk the race down to size, and staying in the game like that gave me hope, and hope is addictive.

I chunked the race out that way, collecting 5 percent chips, unlocking more energy, then burning it up as time bled into the wee hours. I became so tired I damn near fell asleep on my feet, and that's dangerous on a trail with so many switchbacks and drop offs. Any runner could have easily sleepwalked into oblivion. The one thing keeping me awake was the piss-poor trail condition. I fell on my ass dozens of times. My street shoes were out of their element. It felt like I was running on ice, and the inevitable fall was always jarring, but at least it woke me up.

By running a little while, then walking a stretch, I was able to forge ahead to mile seventy-seven, the toughest descent of them ·all, which is when I saw Karl Meltzer, the Speedgoat, crest the hill behind me. He wore a lamp on his head and another on his wrist, and a hip pack with two big water bottles. Silhouetted in pink dawn light he charged down slope, navigating a section that had me stumbling and groping for tree branches to stay upright. He was about to lap me, three miles from the finish line, on pace for a course record, twenty-two hours and sixteen minutes, but what I remember most is how graceful he looked running at an incredible 6:30 per mile pace. He was levitating over the mud, riding a whole different Zen. His feet barely touched the ground, and it was a beautiful fucking sight. The Speedgoat was the living, breathing answer to the question that colonized my mind after the Las Vegas marathon.

What am I capable of?

Watching that bad man glide across the most challenging terrain made me realize that there is a whole other level of athlete out there in the world, and that some of that was inside me too. In fact, it's in all of us. I'm not saying that genetics don't play a role in athletic performance, or that everyone has an undiscovered ability to run a four-minute mile, dunk like LeBron James, shoot like Steph Curry, or run the Hurt 100 in twenty-two hours. We don't all have the same floor or ceiling, but we each have a lot more in us than we know, and when it comes to endurance sports like ultra running, everyone can achieve feats they once thought impossible. In order to do that we must change our minds, be willing to scrap our identity, and make the extra effort to always find more in order to become more.

We must remove our governor.

That day on the Hurt 100 circuit, after seeing Meltzer run like a superhero, I finished my fourth lap in all kinds of pain and took time to watch him celebrate, surrounded by his team. He'd just achieved something nobody had ever done before and here I was with another full lap to go. My legs were rubber, my feet swollen. I did not want to go on, but I also knew that was my pain talking. My true potential was still undetermined. Looking back, I'd say I'd given 60 percent, which meant my tank was just shy of half-full.

I'd like to sit here and tell you I went all-out and drained that fucker on lap five, but I was still a mere tourist on planet ultra. I wasn't the master of my mind. I was in the laboratory, still in discovery mode, and I walked every single step of my fifth and final lap. It took me eight hours, but the rain had stopped, the tropical glow of the warm Hawaiian sun felt phenomenal, and I got the job done. I finished Hurt 100 in thirty-three hours and twenty-three minutes, just shy of the thirty-six-hour cut off, good enough for ninth place. Only twenty-three athletes finished the entire race, and I was one of them.

I was so thrashed afterward, two people carried me to the car, and Kate had to spin me up to my room in a damn wheelchair. When we got there, we had more work to do. I wanted to get my B ad water application done ASAP, so without so much as a cat nap, we polished that shit up.

Within a matter of days, Kostman em ailed me to let me know that I had been accepted into Bad water. It was a great feeling. It also meant that for the next six months I had two full-time jobs. I was a Navy SEAL in full preparation mode for Bad water. This time I would get strategic and specific because I knew that in order to unleash my best performance—if I wanted to blow past 40 percent, drain my tank, and tap my full potential—! had to first give myself an opportunity.

I didn't research or prepare for the Hurt 100 well enough. I hadn't anticipated the rough terrain, I had no support crew for the first part of the race, and I had no back-up water source. I didn't bring two headlamps, which would have helped during the long, bleak night, and though I sure felt like I had given everything I had, l never even had a chance to access my true 100 percent.

Badwater was going to be different. I researched day and night. I studied the course, noted temperature and elevation variances, and charted them out. I wasn't just interested in the air temperature. I drilled down deeper so I knew how hot the pavement would be on the hottest Death Valley day ever. I Googled videos of the race and watched them for hours. I read blogs from runners who completed it, noted their pitfalls and training techniques. I drove north to Death Valley and explored the entire course.

Seeing the terrain up close revealed its brutality. The first forty-two miles were dead flat—a run through God's blast furnace cranked up high. That would be my best opportunity to make great time, but to survive it, I'd need two crew vehicles to leap frog one another and set up cooling stations every third of a mile. The thought of it thrilled me, but then again, I wasn't living it yet. I was listening to music, windows down on a spring day in a blooming desert. I was comfortable as hell! It was all still a fucked-up fantasy!

I marked off the best spots to set up my cooling stations. I noted wherever the shoulder was wide, and where stopping would have to be avoided. I also took note of gas stations and other places to fill up on water and buy ice. There weren't many of them, but they were all mapped. After running the desert gauntlet I'd earn some relief from the heat and pay for it with altitude. The next stage of the race was an eighteen-mile climb to Towne Pass at 4,800 feet. The sun would be setting by then and after driving that section, I pulled over, closed my eyes, and visualized it all.

Research is one part of preparation; visualization is another. Following that Towne Pass climb, I would face a bone-crushing, nine-mile descent. I could see it unfurl from the top of the pass. One thing I learned from the Hurt 100 is that running downhill fucks you up bad, and this time I'd be doing it on asphalt. I closed my eyes, opened my mind, and tried to feel the pain in my quads and calves, knees and shins. I knew my quads would bear the brunt of that descent, so I made a note to add muscle. My thighs would n'eed to be plated in steel.

The eighteen-mile climb up Darwin Pass from mile seventy-two would be pure hell. I'd have to run-walk that section, but the sun would be down, I'd welcome the chill in Lone Pine, and from there I could make up some time because that's where the road flattened out again before the final thirteen-mile climb up Whitney Portal Road, to the finish line at 8,374 feet.

Then again, it's easy to write "make up time" in your note-pad, and another to execute it when you get there in real life, but at least I had notes. Together with my annotated maps, they made up my Badwater file; which I studied like I was preparing for another ASVAB test. I sat at my kitchen table, read and re-read them, and visualized each mile the best I could, but I also knew that my body still hadn't recovered from Hawaii, which hampered the other, even more important aspect of my Bad water prep: physical training.

I was in dire need of PT, but my tendons still hurt so bad I couldn't run for months. Pages were flying off the calendar. I needed to get harder and become the strongest runner possible, and the fact that I couldn't train like I'd hoped sapped my confidence. Plus, word had gotten out at work about what I was getting myself into, and while I had some support from fellow SEALs, I got my share of negativity too, especially when they found out I still couldn't run. But that was nothing new. Who hasn't dreamed up a possibility for themselves only to have friends, colleagues, or family shit all over it? Most of us are motivated as hell to do anything to pursue our dreams until those around us remind us of the danger, the downside, our own limitations, and all the people before us that didn't make it. Sometimes the advice comes from a well-intentioned place. They really believe they are doing it for our own good but if you let them, these same people will talk you out of your dreams, and your governor will help them do it. That's one reason I invented the Cookie Jar. We must create a system that constantly reminds us who the fuck we are when we are at our best, because life is not going to pick us up when we fall. There will be forks in the road, knives in your fucking back, mountains to climb, and we are only capable of living up to the image we create for ourselves.

Prepare yourself!

We know life can be hard, and yet we feel sorry for ourselves when it isn't fair. From this point forward, accept the following as Goggins' laws of nature:

- You will be made fun of.
- You will feel insecure.
- You may not be the best all the time.
- You may be the only black, white, Asian, Latino, female, male, gay, lesbian or [fill in your identity here] in a given situation.
- There will be times when you feel alone.

Get over it!

Our minds are fucking strong, they are our most powerful weapon, but we have stopped using them. We have access to so many more resources today than ever before and yet we are so much less capable than those who came before us. If you want to be one of the few to defy those trends in our ever-softening society, you will have to be willing to go to war with yourself and create a whole new identity, which requires an open mind. It's funny, being open minded is often tagged as new age or soft. Fuck that. Being open minded enough to find a way is old school. It's what knuckle draggers do. And that's exactly what I did.

I borrowed my friend Stokes' bike (he also graduated in Class 235), and instead of running to work, I rode there and back every day. There was an elliptical trainer in the brand-new SEAL Team Five gym, and I hit it once and sometimes twice a day, with five layers of clothes on! Death Valley heat scared the shit out of me, so I simulated it. I suited up in three or four pairs of sweatpants, a few pul over sweatshirts, a hoodie, and a fleece hat, all sealed up in a Gore-Tex shell. After two minutes on the elliptical my heart rate was at 170, and I stayed at it for two hours at a time. Before or after that I'd hop on the rowing machine and bang out 30,000 meters—which is nearly twenty miles. I never did anything for ten or twenty minutes. My entire mind set was ultra. It had to be. Afterward I could be seen wringing my clothes out, like I'd just soaked them in a river. Most of the guys thought I was whacked out, but my old BUD/S instructor, SBG, fucking loved it.

That spring I was tasked as a land warfare instructor for SEALs at our base in Niland, California; a sorry scrap of Southern California desert, its trailer parks rampant with unemployed meth heads. Drugged-out drifters, who filtered through the disintegrating settlements on the Salton Sea, an inland body of water sixty miles from the Mexico border, were our only neighbors. Whenever I passed them on the street while out on a ten-mile ruck, they'd stare like I was an alien that had materialized into the real world from one of their speed-addled vision quests. Then again, I was dressed in three layers of clothes and a Gore-Tex jacket in peak hundred-degree heat. I did look like some evil messenger from the way-out beyond! By then my injuries had become manageable and I ran ten miles at a time, then hiked the hills around Niland for hours, weighed down with a fifty-pound ruck.

The Team guys I was training considered me an alien being too, and a few of them were more frightened of me than the meth heads. They thought something had happened to me on the battlefield out in that other desert where war wasn't a game. What they didn't know was the battlefield for me was my own mind.

I drove back out to Death Valley to train and did a ten-mile run in a sauna suit. That motherfucker was hot as balls, but I had the hardest race in the world ahead of me, and I'd run a hundred miles twice. I knew how that felt, and the prospect of having to take on an additional thirty-five miles petrified me. Sure, I talked a good game, projected all kinds of confidence, and raised tens of thousands of dollars, but part of me didn't know if I had what it took to finish the race, so I had to invent barbaric PT to give myself a chance.

It takes a lot of will to push yourself when you are all alone. I hated getting up in the morning knowing what the day held for me. It was very lonely, but I knew that on the Bad water course I'd reach a point where the pain would become unbearable and feel insurmountable. Maybe it would be at mile fifty or sixty, maybe later, but there would be a time when I'd want to quit, and I had to be able to slay the one-second decisions in order to stay in the game and access my untapped 60 percent.

During all the lonely hours of heat training, I'd started to dissect the quitting mind and realized that if I was going to perform close to my absolute potential and make the Warrior Foundation proud, I'd have to do more than answer the simple questions as they came up. I'd have to stifle the quitting mind before it gained any traction at all. Before I ever asked myself, "Why?" I'd need my Cookie Jar on recall to convince me that despite what my body was saying, I was immune to suffering.

Because nobody quits an ultra race or Hell Week in a split second. People make the decision to quit hours before they ring that bell, so I needed to be present enough to recognize when my body and mind were starting to fail in order to short circuit the impulse to look for a way out long before I tumbled into that fatal funnel. Ignoring pain or blocking out the truth like I did at the San Diego One Day would not work this time, and if you are on the hunt for your 100 percent you should catalog your weaknesses and vulnerabilities. Don't ignore them. Be prepared for them, because in any endurance event, in any high-stress environment, your weaknesses will surface like bad karma, build in volume, and overwhelm you. Unless you get ahead of them first.

This is an exercise in recognition and visualization. You must recognize what you are about to do, highlight what you do not like about it, and spend time visualizing each and every obstacle you can. I was afraid of the heat, so in the run-up to Bad water, I imagined new and more medieval self-torture rituals disguised as training sessions (or maybe it was the other way around). I told myself I was immune to suffering, but that didn't mean I was immune to pain. I hurt like everybody else, but I was committed to working my way around and through it so it would not derail me. By the time I toed up to the line at Bad water at 6 a.m. on July 22, 2006, I'd moved my governor to 80 percent. I'd doubled my ceiling in six months, and you know what that guaranteed me?

Jack fucking shit.

Badwater has a staggered start. Rookies started at 6 a.m., veteran runners had an 8 a.m. start, and the true contenders wouldn't take off until to a.m., which put them in Death Valley for peak heat. Chris Kostman was one hilarious son of a bitch. But he didn't know he'd given one hard motherfucker a serious tactical advantage. Not me. I'm talking about Akos Konya.

Akos and I met up the night before at the Furnace Creek Inn, where all the athletes stayed. He was a first-timer too, and he looked a hell of a lot better since the last time we saw one another. Despite his issues at the Hurt 100 (he finished by the way, in 35 hours and 17 minutes), I knew Akos was a stud, and since we were both in the first group I let him pace me through the desert. Bad call!

For the first seventeen miles we were side by side, and we looked like an odd couple. Akos is a 5'7", 122-pound Hungarian. I was the biggest man in the field at 6'1", 195 pounds, and *the* only black guy too. Akos was sponsored and dressed in a colorful, branded getup. I wore a torn grey tank top, black running shorts, and streamlined Oakley sunglasses. My feet and ankles were wrapped in compression tape and stuffed into broken-in but still springy running shoes. I didn't wear Navy SEAL gear or Warrior Foundation garb. I preferred to go incognito. I was the shadow figure filtering into a new world of pain.

During my first Badwater

Although Akos set a fast pace, the heat didn't bother me, partly because it was early and because I'd heat trained so well. We were the two best runners in the 6 a.m. group by far, and when we passed the Furnace Creek Inn at 8:40 a.m., some of the runners from the 10 a.m. group were outside, including Scott Jurek, the defending champion, Bad water record-holder, and an ultra legend. He must have known we were making great time, but I'm not sure he realized that he'd just glimpsed his stiffest competition.

Not long ·after, Akos put some space between us, and at mile twenty-six, I started to realize that, once again, I went out way too fast. I was dizzy and lightheaded, and I was dealing with GI issues. Translation: I had to shit on the side of the road. All of which stemmed from the fact that I was severely dehydrated. My mind spun with dire prognosis after dire prognosis. Excuses to quit piled up one after another. I didn't listen. I responded by taking care of my dehydration issue and pounding more water than I wanted.

I went through the Stovepipe Wells checkpoint at mile forty-two at 1:31 p.m., a full hour after Akos. I'd been on the race course for over seven and a half hours and was almost exclusively walking by then. I was proud just to have made it through Death Valley on my feet. I took a break, went to a proper bathroom, and changed my clothes. My feet had swollen more than I'd expected, and my right big toe had been chafing the side of the shoe for hours, so stopping felt like sweet relief. I felt the bloom of a blood blister on the side of my left foot, but I knew better than to take off my shoes. Most athletes size up their shoes to run Bad water, and even then, they cut out the big toe side panel to create space for swelling and to minimize chafing. I did not, and I had ninety more miles ahead of me.

I hiked the entire eighteen-mile climb to Towne Pass at 4,850 feet. As predicted, the sun dropped as I crested the pass, the air cooled, and I pulled on another layer. In the military we always say we don't rise to the level of our expectations, we fall to the level of our training, and as I hiked up the winding highway with my blister barking, I fell into the same rhythm I'd find on my long rucks in the desert around Niland. I wasn't running, but I kept a strong pace and covered a lot of ground.

I stuck to my script, ran the entire nine-mile descent, and my quads paid the price. So did my left foot. My blister was growing by the minute. I could feel it verging on hot-air-balloon status. If only it would burst through my shoe like an old cartoon, and continue to expand until it carried me into the clouds and dropped me onto the peak of Mount Whitney itself.

No such luck. I kept walking, and aside from my crew, which included, among others, my wife (Kate was crew chief) and mother, I didn't see anybody else. I was on an eternal ruck, marching beneath a black dome sky glittering with starlight. I'd been walking for so long I expected a swarm of runners to materialize at any moment, then leave me in their wake. But nobody showed. The only evidence of life on planet pain was the rhythm of my own hot breath, the bum of my cartoon blister, and the high beams and red taillights of road trippers blazing trails through the California night. That is, until the sun was ready to rise and a swarm finally did arrive at mile 110.

I was exhausted and dehydrated by then, glazed in sweat, dirt, and salt, when horseflies began to dive bomb me one at a time. Two became four which became ten and fifteen. They beat their wings against my skin, bit my thighs, and crawled into my ears. This shit was biblical, and it was my very last test. My crew took turns swatting flies off my skin with a towel. I was in personal best territory already. I'd covered more than 110 miles on foot, and with "only" twenty-five miles to go there was no fucking way these devil flies would stop me. Would they? I kept marching, and my crew kept swatting flies, for the next eight miles!

Since watching Akos run away from me after mile seventeen, I hadn't seen another Bad water runner until mile 122 when Kate pulled up alongside me.

"Scott Jurek is two miles behind you," she said.

We were more than twenty-six hours into the race, and Akos had already finished, but the fact that Jurek was just now catching . me meant my time must have been pretty damn good. I hadn't run much, but all those Niland rucks made my hiking stride swift and strong. I was able to power hike fifteen-minute miles, and got my nutrition on the move to save time. After it was all over, when I examined the splits and finishing times of all the competitors, I realized my biggest fear, the heat, had actually helped me. It was the great equalizer. It made fast runners slow.

With Jurek on the hunt, I was inspired to give it everything I had as I turned onto Whitney Portal Road and started the final thirteen-mile climb. I flashed onto my pre-race strategy to walk the slopes and run the fiats as the road switched back like a snake slithering into the clouds. Jurek wasn't pursuing me, but he was on the chase. Akos had finished in twenty-five hours and fifty-eight minutes and Jurek hadn't been at his best that day. The clock was winding down on his effort to repeat as Bad water champion, but he had the tactical advantage of knowing Akos' time in advance. He also knew his splits. Akos hadn't had that luxury, and somewhere on the highway he'd stopped for a thirty-minute nap.

Jurek wasn't alone. He had a pacer, a formidable runner in his own right named Dusty Olson who nipped at his heels. Word was Olson ran at least seventy miles of the race himself. I heard them approach from behind, and whenever the road switched back I could see them below me. Finally, at mile 128, on the steepest part of the steepest road in this entire fucked-up race, they were right behind me. I stopped running, got out of the way, and cheered them on.

Jurek was the fastest ultra runner in history at that point, but his pace wasn't electric that late in the game. It was consistent. He chopped down the mighty mountain with each deliberate step.

He wore black running shorts, a blue sleeveless shirt, and a white baseball cap. Behind him, Olson had his long, shoulder length hair corralled with a bandana, otherwise their uniform was identical. Jurek was the mule and Olson was riding him.

"Come on, Jurker! Come on, Jurker! This is your race," Olson said as they passed me up. "No one is better than you! No one!" Olson kept talking as they ran ahead, reminding Jurek that he had more to give. Jurek .obliged and kept charging up the mountain. He left it all out on that unforgiving asphalt. It was amazing to watch.

Jurek wound up winning the 2006 edition of Bad water when he finished in twenty-five hours and forty-one minutes, seventeen minutes faster than Akos, who must have regretted his power nap, but that wasn't my concern. I had a race of my own to finish.

Whitney Portal Road winds up a parched, exposed rock escarpment for ten miles, before finding shade in gathering stands of cedar and pine. Energized by Jurek and his crew, I ran most of the last seven miles. I used my hips to push my legs forward and every single step was agony, but after thirty hours, eighteen minutes, and fifty-four seconds of running, hiking, sweating, and suffering, I snapped the tape to the cheers of a small crowd. I'd wanted to quit thirty times. I had to mentally inch my way through 135 miles, but ninety runners competed that day, and I came in fifth place.

Akos and I after my second Badwater in 2007—I placed third and Akos came in second again

I plodded over to a grassy slope in the woods and lay back on a bed of pine needles as Kate unlaced my shoes. That blister had fully colonized my left foot. It was so big it looked like a sixth toe, the color and texture of cherry bubble gum. I marveled at it while she removed the compression tape from my feet. Then I staggered to the stage to accept my medal from Kostman. I'd just finished one of the hardest races on planet earth. I'd visualized that moment ten times at least and thought I'd be elated, but I wasn't.

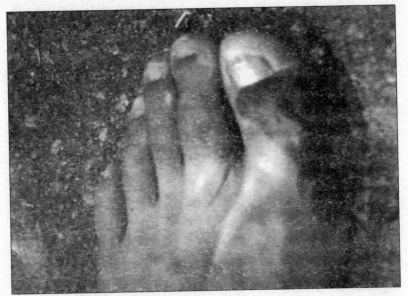

Blistered toe after Badwater

Chris, I'm sure you get plenty of requests for rookie waivers to enter the race, but I'd really appreciate it if you and your folks would give this serious consideration. This request is not for myself but is on the behalf of a guy that works for me...This is where I introduce a man who is going to put in an entry application – Dave Goggins. I put him through BUD/S in 2001 and quickly identified him as incredibly talented. His strength and endurance are extraordinary. He graduated SEAL training and volunteered to go to Army Ranger School where he graduated as the honor man, no small feat...Because he is an instructor on my staff...it is nearly impossible for him to complete the pre-requisites for entry. He is simply the best endurance athlete with the greatest mental toughness I have ever seen. I would put my reputation as a Naval Officer and SEAL on the line to say he would successfully complete the race and finish in the top 10%...If accepted he would like to run under the U. S. Navy SEAL Team logo as well as raise money for the Special Operations Warrior Foundation (SOWF). Thanks for your consideration.

Very Respectfully,
SBG

SBG's email to Kostman. He was right: I did finish in the top 10 percent!

He handed me my medal, shook my hand, and interviewed me for the crowd, but I was only half there. While he spoke, I flashed to the final climb and a pass above 8,000 feet, where the view was unreal. I could see all the way to Death Valley. Near the end of another horrible journey, I got to see where I came from. It was the perfect metaphor for my twisted life. Once again I was broken, destroyed twenty different ways, but I'd passed another evolution, another crucible, and my reward was a lot more than a medal and a few minutes with Kostman's microphone.

It was a whole new bar.

I closed my eyes and saw Jurek and Olson, Akos and Karl Meltzer. All of them had something I didn't. They understood how to drain every last drop and put themselves in a position to win the world's most difficult races, and it was time to seek out that feeling for myself. I'd prepared like a madman. I knew myself and the terrain. I stayed ahead of the quitting mind, answered the simple questions, and stayed in the race, but there was more to be done. There was still somewhere higher for me to rise. A cool breeze rustled the trees, dried the sweat from my skin, and soothed my aching bones. It whispered in my ear and shared a secret which echoed in my brain like a drumbeat that wouldn't stop.

There is no finish line) Goggins. There is no finish line.

CHALLENGE #7

The main objective here is to slowly start to remove the governor from your brain.

First, a quick reminder of how this process works. In 1999, when I weighed 297 pounds, my first run was a quarter mile. Fast forward to 2007, I ran 205 miles in thirty-nine hours, nonstop. I didn't get there overnight, and I don't expect you to either. Your job is to push past your normal stopping point.

Whether you are running on a treadmill or doing a set of push-ups, get to the point where you are so tired and in pain that your mind is begging you to stop. Then push just 5 to 10 percent further. If the most push-ups you have ever done is one hundred in a workout, do 105 or 110. If you normally run thirty miles each week, run 10 percent more next week.

This gradual ramp-up will help prevent injury and allow your body and mind to slowly adapt to your new workload. It also resets your baseline, which is important because you're about to increase your workload another 5 to 10 percent the following week, and the week after that.

There is so much pain and suffering involved in physical challenges that it's the best training to take command of your inner dialogue, and the newfound mental strength and confidence you gain by contining to push yourself physically will carry over to other aspects in your life. You will realize that if you were underperforming in your physical challenges, there is a good chance you are underperforming, at school and work too.

The bottom line is that life is one big mind game. The only person you are playing against is yourself. Stick with this process and soon what you thought was impossible will be something you do every fucking day of your life. I want to hear your stories. Post on social. Hashtags: #canthurtme #The4oPercentRule #dontgetcomfortable.

CHAPTER EIGHT

TALENT NOT REQUIRED

THE NIGHT BEFORE THE FIRST LONG - DISTANCE TRIATH-
lon in my life, I stood with my mother on the deck of a sprawling,
seve n-million-dollar beach house in Kona watching the moon-
light play on the water. Most people know Kona, a gorgeous town
on the west coast of the island of Hawaii, and triathlons in general,
thanks to the Ironman World Championships. Although there
are far more Olympic distance and shorter sprint triathlons held
around the world than there are Ironman events, it was the original Ironman in Kona that placed the sport on the international
radar. It starts with a 2.4-mile swim followed by a 112-mile bike
ride, and closes with a marathon run. Add to that stiff and shifting
winds and blistering heat corridors reflected by harsh lava fields,
and the race reduces most competitors to open blisters of raw
anguish, but I wasn't here for that. I came to Kona to compete in
a less celebrated form of even more intense masochism. I was
there to compete for the title of Ultraman.

Over the next three days I would swim 6.2 miles, ride 261
miles, and run a double marathon, covering the entire perimeter of the. Big Island of Hawaii. Once again, I was raising money

for the Special Operations Warrior Foundation, and because I'd been written up and interviewed on camera after Badwater, I was invited by a multi-millionaire I'd never met to stay in his absurd palace on the sand in the run-up to the Ultraman World Championships in November 2006.

It was a generous gesture, but I was so focused on becoming the very best version of myself his glitz didn't impress me. In my mind, I still hadn't achieved shit. If anything, staying in his house only inflated the chip on my shoulder. He would never have invited my wanna-be-thug ass to come chill with him in Kona luxury back in the day. He only reached out because I'd become somebody a rich guy like him wanted to know. Still, I appreciated being able to show my mom a better life, and whenever I was offered a taste, I invited her to experience it with me. She'd swallowed more pain than anyone I'd ever known, and I wanted to remind her that we'd climbed out of that gutter, while I kept my own gaze locked at sewer level. We didn't live in that $7 a month place in Brazil anymore, but I was still paying rent on that motherfucker, and will be for the rest of my life.

The race launched from the beach beside the pier in downtown Kona—the same start line as the Ironman World Championships, but there wasn't much of a crowd for our race. There were only thirty athletes in the entire field compared to over 1,200 in the Ironman! It was such a small group I could look every one of my competitors in the eye and size them up, which is how I noticed the hardest man on the beach. I never did catch his name, but I'll always remember him because he was in a wheelchair. Talk about heart. That mnn had a presence beyond his stature.

He was fucking immense!

Ever since I'd started up in BUD /S, I'd been in search of people like that. Men and women with an uncommon way of thinking.

One thing that surprised me about military special operations was that some of the guys lived so mainstream. They weren't trying to push themselves every day of their lives, and I wanted to be around people who thought and trained uncommon 24/7, not just when duty called. That man had every excuse in the world to be at home, but he was ready to db one of the hardest stage races in the world, something 99.9 percent of the public wouldn't even consider, and with just his two arms! To me, he was what ultra racing was all about, and its why after Bad water I'd become hooked on this world. Talent wasn't required for this sport. It was all about heart and hard work, and it delivered relentless challenge after relentless challenge, always demanding more.

But that doesn't mean I was well-prepared for this race. I still didn't own a bike. I borrowed one three weeks earlier from another friend. It was a Griffin, an uber-high-end bicycle custom made for my friend who was even bigger than I was. I borrowed his clip-in shoes too, which were just shy of down-sized. I filled the empty space with thick socks and compression tape, and didn't take the time to learn bike mechanics before leaving for Kona. Changing tires, fixing chains and spokes, all the stuff I know how to do now, I hadn't learned yet. I just borrowed the bike and logged over 1,000 miles in the three weeks prior to Ultraman. I'd wake up at 4 a.m. and get one hundred-mile rides in before work. On weekends I'd ride 125 miles, get off the bike and run a marathon, but I only did six training swims, just two in the open water, and in the ultra octagon all your weaknesses are revealed.

The ten-kilometer swim should have taken me about two and a half hours to complete, but it took me over three, and it hurt. I was dressed in a sleeveless wetsuit for buoyancy, but it was too tight under my arms, and within thirty minutes my armpits began to chafe. An hour later the salty edge of my suit had become sandpaper that ripped my skin with every stroke. I switched from freestyle to side stroke and back again, desperate for comfort that never came. Every revolution of my arms cut my skin raw and bloody on both sides.

Coming out of the water at Ultraman

Plus, the sea was choppy as hell. I drank sea water, my stomach flipped and flopped like a fish suffocating in fresh air, and I puked a half dozen times at least. Because of the pain, my poor mechanics, and the strong current, I swam a meandering line that stretched to seven and a half miles. All of that in order to clear what was supposed to be a 6.2-mile swim. My legs were jelly when I staggered to shore, and my vision rocked like a teeter totter during an earthquake. I had to lie down, then crawl behind the bathrooms, where I vomited again. Other swimmers gathered in the transition area, hopped into their saddles, and pedaled off into the lava fields in a blink. We still had a ninety-mile bike ride to knock off before the day was done, and they were getting after it while I was still on my knees. Right on time, those simple questions bubbled to the surface.

Why the fock am I even out here?

I'm not a triathlete!

I'm chafed to hell, sick as fuck, and the first part of the ride is all uphill!

Why do you keep doing this to yourself, Goggins?

I sounded like a whiny bitch, but I knew finding some comfort would help me hem my vagina, so I paid no attention to the other athletes who eased through their transition. I had to focus on getting my legs under me and slowing my spun-out mind. First I got some food down, a little at a time. Then I treated the cuts under my arms. Most triathletes don't change their clothes. I did. I slipped on some comfortable bike shorts and a lycra shirt, and fifteen minutes later I was upright, in the saddle, and climbing into the lava fields. For the first twenty minutes I was still nauseous. I pedaled and puked, replenished my fluids, and puked again. Through it all, I gave myself one job: stay in the fight! Stay in it long enough to find a foothold.

Ten miles later, as the road rose onto the shoulders of a giant volcano and the incline increased , I shook off my sea legs and found momentum. Riders appeared ahead like bogeys on a radar, and I picked them off, one by one. Victory was a cure-all. Each time I passed another motherfucker I got less and less sick. I was in fourteenth place when I saddled up, but by the time I approached the end of that ninety-mile leg there was only one man in front of me. Gary Wang, the favorite in the race.

As I hammered toward the finish line I could see a reporter and photographer from *Triathlete* magazine interviewing him. None of them expected to see my black ass, and they all watched me carefully. During the four months since Bad water, I'd often dreamt of being in position to win an ultra race, and as I coasted past Gary and those reporters, I knew the moment had arrived, and my expectations were intergalactic.

The following morning, we lined up for the second stage, a 171-mile bike ride through the mountains and back toward the west coast. Gary Wang had a buddy in the race, Jeff Landauer, aka the Land Shark, and those two rode together. Gary had done the race before and knew the terrain. I didn't, and by mile one hundred, I was roughly six minutes off the lead.

As usual, my mother and Kate were my two-headed support crew. They handed me replacement water bottles, packets of GU, and protein drinks from the side of the road, which I consumed in motion to keep my glycogen and electrolyte levels up. I'd become much more scientific about my nutrition since that Myoplex and Ritz cracker meltdown in San Diego, and with the biggest climb of the day looming into view I needed to be ready to roar. On a bicycle, mountains produce pain, and pain was my business. As the road peaked in pitch, I put my head down and hammered as hard as I could. My lungs heaved until they were flipped inside out and back again. My heart was a pounding bass line. When I crested the pass, my mom pulled up alongside me and hollered, "David, you are two minutes off the lead ! "

Roger that!

I curled into an aerodynamic crouch and shot downhill at over 40 mph. My borrowed Griffin was equipped with aero bars and I leaned over them, focusing only on the white dotted line and my perfect form. When the road leveled off I went all out and kept my pace ·up around 27 mph. I had a Land Shark and his buddy on an industrial-sized hook, and was reeling them all the way in.

Until my front tire blew.

Before I had time to react, I was off the bike, somersaulting over the handlebars into space. I could see it happening in slow motion, but time sped back up when I crash landed on my right side and my shoulder crumpled with blunt force. The side of my face skidded the asphalt until I stopped moving, and I rolled onto my back in shock. My mother slammed on her brakes, leapt from the car, and rushed over. I was bleeding in five places, but nothing felt broken. Except my helmet, which was cracked in two, my sunglasses, which were shattered, and my bicycle.

I'd run over a bolt tpat pierced the tire, tube, and rim. I didn't pay attention to my road rash, the pain in my shoulder, or the blood dribbling down my elbow and cheek. All I thought about was that bicycle. Once again, I was underprepared! I had no spare parts and didn't have any clue how to change a tube or a tire. I had rented a back-up bicycle which was in my mom's rental car, but it was a heavy, slow piece of shit compared to that Griffin. It didn't even have clip in pedals, so I called for the official race mechanics to assess the Griffin. As we waited, seconds piled up into twenty precious minutes and when mechanics arrived, they didn't have supplies to fix my front wheel either, so I hopped on my clunky back-up and kept rolling.

I tried not to think of bad luck and missed opportunities. I needed to finish strong and get myself within striking distance by the end of the day, because day three would bring a double marathon, and I was convinced that I was the best runner in the field. Sixteen miles from the finish line, the bike mechanic tracked me down. He'd repaired my Griffin! I switched out my hardware for the second time and made up eight minutes on the leaders, finishing the day in third place, twenty-two minutes off the lead.

I crafted a simple strategy for day three. Go out hard and build up a fat cushion over Gary and the Land Shark so that when I hit the inevitable wall, I'd have enough distance to maintain the overall lead all the way to the finish line. In other words, I didn't have any strategy at all.

I began my run at Boston Marathon qualifying pace. I pushed hard because I wanted my competitors to hear my splits and forfeit their souls as I built that big lead I'd anticipated. I knew I would blow up somewhere. That's ultra life. I just hoped it would happen late e nough in the race that Gary and the Land Shark would be content to race one another for second and give up all hope of winning the overall title.

Didn't happen quite like that.

At mile thirty-five I was already in agony and walking more than I was running. By mile forty, I watched both enemy vehicles pull up so their crew chiefs could peep my form. I was showing a ton of weakness, which gave Gary and the Land Shark ammunition. The miles mounted too slowly. I hemorrhaged time. Luckily, by mile forty-five, Gary had blown up too, but the Land Shark was rock solid, still on my ass, and I didn't have anything left to fight him off. Instead, as I suffered and staggered toward downtown Kona, my lead evaporated.

In the end, the Land Shark taught me a vital lesson. From day one, he had run his own race. My early burst on day three didn't faze him. He welcomed it as the ill-conceived strategy that it was, focused on his own pace, waited me out, and took *my* soul. I was the first athlete to cross the finish line of the Ultraman that year, but as far as the clock was concerned I was no champion. While I came in first pl □e on the run, I lost the overall race by ten minutes and took second place. The Land Shark was crowned Ultraman!

I watched him celebrate knowing exactly how I'd wasted an opportunity to win. I'd lost my vantage point. I'd never evaluated the race strategically and didn't have any backstops in place.

Backstops are a versatile tool that I employ in all facets of my life. I was lead navigator when I operated in Iraq with the SEAL Teams, and "backstop" is a navigation term. It's the mark I made on my map. An alert that we'd missed a turn or veered off course.

Let's say you're navigating through the woods and you have to go one click toward a ridgeline, then make a turn. In the military, we would do a map study ahead of time and mark that turn on our maps, and another point about 200 meters past that turn, and a third an additional 150 meters past the second mark. Those last two marks are your backstops. Typically, I used terrain features, like roads, creeks, a giant cliff in the countryside, or landmark buildings in an urban setting, so that when we hit them I knew we'd gone off course. That's what backstops are for, to tell you to turn around, reassess, and take an alternative route to accomplish the same mission. I never left our base in Iraq without having three exit strategies. A primary route and two others, pinned to backstops, we could fall back to if our main route became compromised.

On day three ofUltraman, I tried to win with sheer will. I was all motor, no intellect. I didn't evaluate my condition, respect my opponents' heart, or manage the clock well enough. I had no primary strategy, let alone alternative avenues to victory, and therefore I had no idea where to employ backstops. In retrospect I should have paid more attention to my own clock, and my backstops should have been placed on my split times. When I saw how fast I was running that first marathon, I should have been alarmed and eased off the gas. A slower first marathon may have left me with enough energy to drop the hammer once we were back in the lava fields on the Ironman course, heading toward the finish line. That's when you take someone's soul—at the end of a race, not at the beginning. I'd raced hard, but if I 'd run smarter and handled the bike situation better, I would have given myself a better chance to win.

Still, coming in second place at Ultraman was no disaster. I raised good money for families in need and booked more positive ink for the SEALs in *Triathlete* and Competitor magazines. Navy brass took notice. One morning, I was called into a meeting with Admiral Ed Winters, a two-star Admiral and the top man at Naval Special Warfare Cbmmand. When you're an enlisted guy and hear an Admiral wants a word, your ass sort of puckers up. He wasn't supposed to seek me out. There was a chain of command in place specifically to prevent conversations between Rear Admirals and enlisted men like me. Without any warning that was all out the window, and I had a feeling it was my own fault.

Thanks to the positive media I'd generated, I had received orders to join the recruitment division in 2007, and by the time I was ordered into the Admiral's office I'd done plenty of public speaking on behalf of the Navy SEALs. But I was different than most of the other recruiters. I didn't just parrot the Navy's script. I always included my own life story, off the cuff. As I waited outside the Admiral's office I dosed my eyes and flipped through memory files, searching for when and how I'd overstepped and embarrassed the SEALs. I was the picture of tension, sitting stiff and alert, sweating through my uniform when he opened the door to his office.

"Goggins," he said, "good to see you, come on in." I opened my eyes, followed him inside, and stood straight as an arrow, locked at attention. "Sit down," he said with a smile, gesturing to a chair facing his desk. I sat; but maintained my posture and avoided all eye contact. Admiral Winters sized me up.

He was in his late fifties, and though he appeared relaxed, he maintained perfect posture. To become an Admiral is to rise through the ranks of tens of thousands. He'd been a SEAL since 1981, was an Operations Officer at DEVGRU (Naval Special Warfare Development Group), and a Commander in Afghanistan and Iraq. At each stop he stood taller than the rest, and was among the strongest, smartest, shrewdest, and most charismatic men the Navy had ever seen. He also fit a certain standard. Admiral Winters was the ultimate insider, and I was as outside the box as you could get in the United States Navy.

"Hey, relax," he said, "you aren't in any trouble. You're doing a great job in recruiting." He gestured to a file on his otherwise immaculate desk. It was filled with some of my clips. "You're representing us really well. But there's some men out there we need to do a better job of reaching out to, and I'm hoping you can help."

That's when it finally hit me. A two-star Admiral needed my help.

The trouble we faced as an organization, he said, was that we were terrible at recruiting African Americans into the SEAL Teams. I knew that already. Black people made up only 1 percent of all special forces, even though we are 13 percent of the general population. I was just the thirty-sixth African American ever to graduate BUD/S, and one of the reasons for that was we weren't . hitting the best places to recruit black men into the SEAL teams, and we didn't have the right recruiters either. The military likes to think of itself as a pure meritocracy (it isn't), which is why for decades this issue was ignored. I called Admiral Winters recently, and he had this to say about the problem, which was originally flagged by the Pentagon during the second Bush administration and sent to the Admiral's desk to fix.

"We were missing an opportunity to get great athletes into the teams and make the teams better," he said, "and we had places we needed to send people where, if they looked like me, they would be compromised."

In Iraq, Admiral Winters made his name building elite counter terrorism forces. That's one of the primary missions in special forces: to train allied military units so they can control social cancers like terrorism and drug trafficking and maintain stability within borders. By 2007, Algeda had made inroads into Africa, allied with existing extremist networks including Boko Haram and al Shabaab, and there was talk of building up counter-terrorism forces in Somalia, Chad, Nigeria, Mali, Cameroon, Burkina Faso, and Niger. Our' operations in Niger made international news in 2018 when four American special operations soldiers were killed in an ambush, drawing public scrutiny to the mission. But back in 2007, almost nobody knew we were about to get involved in West Africa, or that we lacked the personnel to get it done. As I sat in his office, what I heard was the time had finally come when we needed black people in special forces and our military leaders were clueless as to how to meet that need and entice more of us into the fold.

It was all new information to me. I didn't know anything about the African threat. The only hostile terrain I knew about was in Afghanistan and Iraq. That is, until Admiral Winters dropped a whole new detail on me, and the military's problem officially became my problem. I'd report to my Captain and the Admiral, he said, and hit the road, visiting ten to twelve cities at a time, with a goal of spiking recruiting numbers in the POC (people of color) category.

We made the first stop on this new mission together. It was at Howard University, in Washington D.C., probably the best known historically black university in America. We'd dropped in to speak to the football tearh, and though I knew almost nothing about historically black colleges and universities, I knew students who attended them aren't usually the type to think of the military as an optimal career choice. Thanks to our country's history and the rampant racism that continues to this day, black political thought trends left of center at these institutions, and if you're recruiting for the_ Navy SEALs, there are definitely better choices than the Howard University practice field to find a willing ear. But this new focus required work in hostile territory, not mass enthusiasm. We were looking for one or two great men at each stop.

The Admiral and I walked onto the field, dressed in uniform, and I noted suspicion and disregard in the eyes of our audience. Admiral Winters had planned to introduce me, but our icy reception told me we had to go another way.

"You were shy at first," Admiral Winters remembered, "but when it was time to speak, you looked at me and said, 'I got this, sir.'"

I launched right into my life story. I told those athletes what I've already told you, and said we were looking for guys with heart. Men who knew it was going to be hard tomorrow and the day after that and welcomed every challenge. Men who wanted to become better athletes, and smarter and more capable in all aspects of their life. We wanted guys who craved honor and purpose and were open minded enough to face their deepest fears.

"By the time you were done you could have heard a pin drop," Admiral Winters recalled.

From then on, I was given command of my own schedule and budget and leeway to operate, as long as I hit certain recruitment thresholds. I had to come up with my own material and knew that most people didn't think they could ever become a Navy SEAL, so I broadened the message. I wanted everyone who heard me out to know that eve·n if they didn't walk in our direction they could still become more than they ever dreamed. I made sure to cover my life in its entirety so if anyone had any excuse, my story would void all that out. My main drive was to deliver hope that with or without the military anybody could change their life, so long as they kept an open mind, abandoned the path of least resistance, and sought out the difficult and most challenging tasks they could find. I was mining for diamonds in the rough like me.

From 2007-2009, I was on the road for 250 days a year and spoke to 500,000 people at high schools and universities. I spoke at inner city high schools in tough neighborhoods, at dozens of historically black colleges and universities, and at schools with all cultures, shapes, and shades well represented. I'd come a long way from fourth grade, when I couldn't stand up in front of a class of twenty kids and say my own name without stuttering.

Teenagers are walking, talking bull shit detectors, but the kids who heard me speak bought into my message because everywhere I stopped, I also ran an ultra race and rolled my training runs and races into my overall recruitment strategy. I'd usually land in their town midweek, make my speeches, then run a race on Saturday and Sunday. In one stretch in 2007, I ran an ultra almost every weekend. There were fifty-mile races, too-kilometer races, too-mile races, and longer ones too. I was all about spreading the Navy SEAL legend that I loved, and wanted to be true and living our ethos.

Essentially, I had two full-time jobs. My schedule was jammed full, and while I know that having the flexibility to manage my own time contributed to my ability to train for and compete on the ultra circuit, I still put in fifty hours a week at work, clocking in every day from about 7:30 a.m. to 5:30 p.m. My training hours came in addition to, not instead of, my work commitments.

I appeared at upwards of forty-five schools every month, and after each appearance I had to file an After Action Report (AAR), detailing how many separate events (an auditorium speech, a workout, etc.) I organized, how many kids I spoke to, and how many of those were actually interested. These AARs went directly to my Captain and the Admiral.

I learned quickly that I was my own best prop. Sometimes I'd dress in a SEAL t-shirt with a Trident on it, run fifty miles to a speaking engagement, and show up soaking wet. Or I would do push-ups for the first five minutes of my speech, or roll a pull-up bar out on stage and do pull-ups while I was talking. That's right, the shit you see me do on social media isn't new. I've been living this life for eleven years!

Wherever I stopped, I invited the kids who were interested to come train with me before or after school, or crew on one of my ultra races. Word got out and soon the media—local television, print, and radio—showed up, especially if I was running between cities to get to the next gig. I had to be articulate, well groomed, and do well in the races I entered.

I remember landing in Colorado the week of the legendary Leadville 100 trail race. The school year had just started, and on my first night in Denver I mapped out the five schools on my roster in relation to the trails I wanted to hike and run. At each stop I'd invite the kids to train with me, but warn them that my day started early. At 3 a.m. I would drive to a trailhead, meet up with all the students who dared to show, and by 4 a.m. we'd begin power hiking up one of Colorado's fifty-eight summits above 14,000-feet. Then we'd sprint down the mountain to strengthen our quads. At 9 a.m. I hit another school, and then another. After the bell rang, I worked out with the football, track, or swim teams at the schools I visited, then ran back into the mountains to train until sunset. All, of that to recruit stud athletes and acclimatize for the highest altitude ultra marathon in the world.

The race started at 4 a.m. on a Saturday, departing from the city of Leadville, a working-class ski town with frontier roots, and traversing a network of beautiful and harsh Rocky Mountain trails that range from 9,200 feet to 12,600 feet in elevation. When I finished at 2 a.m. on Sunday, a teenager from Denver who attended a school I'd visited a few days earlier was waiting for me at the finish line. I didn't have a great race (I came in 14th place, rather than my typical top five), but I always made sure to finish strong, and when I sprinted home he approached me with a wide smile and said, "I drove two hours just to see you finish! "

The lesson: you never know who you're affecting. My poor race results mint less than nothing to that young man because I'd helped open his eyes to a new world of possibility and capability that he sensed within himself. He'd followed me from his high school auditorium to Leadville because he was looking for absolute proof—my finishing the race—that it was possible to transcend the typical and become more, and as I cooled down and toweled off he asked me for tips so he could one day run all day and night through the mountains in his backyard.

I have several stories like that. More than a dozen kids came out to pace and crew for me at the McNaughton Park Trail Race, a 150-miler held outside of Peoria, Illinois. Two dozen students trained with me in Minot, North Dakota. Together we ran the frozen tundra before sunrise in January when it was twenty below zero! Once I spoke at a school in a majority black neighborhood in Atlanta, and as I was leaving, a mother showed up with her two sons who had long dreamed of becoming Navy SEALs but kept it a. secret because enlisting in the military wasn't considered cool in their neighborhood. When summer vacation broke out, I flew them to San Diego to live and train with me. I woke their asses up at 4 a.m. and beat them down on the beach like they were in a junior version of First Phase. They did not enjoy themselves, but they learned the truth about what it takes to live the ethos. Wherever I went, whether the students were interested in a military career or not, they always asked if they had the same hardware I had. Could they run a hundred miles in one day? What would it take to reach their full potential? This is what I'd tell them:

Our culture has become hooked on the quick-fix, the life hack, efficiency. Everyone is on the hunt for that simple action algorithm that nets minimum profit with the least amount of effort. There's no denying this attitude may get you some of the trappings of success, if you're lucky, but it will not lead to a calloused mind or self-mastery. If you want to master the mind and remove your governor, you'll have to become addicted to hard work. Because passion and obsession, even talent, are only useful tools if you have the work ethic to back them up.

My work ethic is the single most important factor in all of my accomplishments. Everything else is secondary, and when it comes to hard work, whether in the gym or on the job, The 40% Rule applies. To me, a forty-hour work week is a 40 percent effort. It may be satisfactory, but that's another word for mediocrity. Don't settle for a forty-hour work week. There are 168 hours in a week! That means you have the hours to put in that extra time at work without skimping on your exercise. It means streamlining your nutrition, spending quality time with your wife and kids. It means scheduling your life like you're on a twenty-four-hour mission every single day.

The number one excuse I hear from people as to why they don't work out as much as they want to is that they don't have time. Look, we all have work obligations, none of us want to lose sleep, and you'll need time with the family or they'll trip the fuck out. I get it, and if that's your situation, you must win the morning.

When I was full-time with the SEALs I maximized the dark

hours before dawn. When my wife was sleeping, I would bang out a six- to ten-mile run. My gear was all laid out the night before, my lunch was packed, and my work clothes were in my locker at work where I 'd shower before my day started at 7:30 a.m. On a typical day, I'd be out the door for my run just after 4 a.m. and back by 5:15 a.m. Since that wasn't enough for me, and because we only owned one car, I rode my bike (I finally got my own shit!) twenty-five miles to work. I'd work from 7:30 a.m. to noon, and eat at my desk before or after my lunch break. During the lunch hour I'd hit the gym or do a four- to six-mile beach run, work the afternoon shift and hop on my bike for the twenty-five-mile ride home. By the time I was home at 7 p.m., I'd have run about fifteen miles, rocked fifty miles on the bike, and put in a full day at the office. I was always home for dinner and in bed by 10 p.m. so I could do it all over again the next day. On Saturdays I'd sleep in until 7 a.m., hit a three-hour workout, and spend the rest of the weekend with Kate. If I didn't have a race, Sundays were my active recovery days. I'd do an easy ride at a low heart rate, keeping my pulse below 110 beats per minute to stimulate healthy blood flow.

Maybe you think I'm a special case or an obsessive maniac. Fine, I won't argue with you. But what about my friend Mike? He's a big-time financial advisor in New York City. His job is high pressure and his work day is a hell of a lot longer than eight hours. He has a wife and two kids, and he's an ultra runner. Here's how he does it. He wakes up at 4 a.m. every weekday, runs sixty to ninety minutes each morning while his family is still snoozing, rides a bike to work and back and does a quick thirty-minute treadmill run after he gets home. He goes out for longer runs on weekends, but he minimizes its impact on his family obligations.

He's high-powered, wealthy as fuck, and could easily maintain his status quo with less effort and enjoy the sweet fruits of his labors, but he finds a way to stay hard because his labors are his sweetest fruits. And he makes time to get it all in by minimizing the amount of bull shit clogging his schedule. His priorities are clear, and he remains dedicated to his priorities. I'm not talking about general priorities here either. Each hour of his week is dedicated to a particular task and when that hour shows up in real time, he focuses 100 percent on that task. That's how I do it too, because that is the only way to minimize wasted hours.

Evaluate your life in its totality! We all waste so much time doing meaningless bullshit. We burn hours on social media and watching television, which by the end of the year would add up to entire days and weeks if you tabulated time like you do your taxes. You should, because if you knew the truth you'd deactivate your Face book account STAT, and cut your cable. When you find 'yourself having frivolous conversations or becoming ensnared in activities that don't better you in any way, move the fuck on!

For years I've lived like a monk. I don't see or spend time with a lot of people. My circle is very tight. I post on social media once or twice a week and I never check anybody else's feeds because I don't follow anyone. That's just me. I'm not saying you need to be that unforgiving, because you and I probably don't share the same goals. But I know you have goals too, and room for improvement, or you wouldn't be reading my book, and I guarantee that if you audited your schedule you'd find time for more work and less bullshit.

It's up to you to find ways to eviscerate your bullshit. How much time do you spend at the dinner table talking about nothing after the meal is done? How many calls and texts do you send for no reason at all?. Look at your whole life, list your obligations and tasks. Put a time stamp on them. How many hours are required to shop; eat, and clean? How much sleep do you need? What's your commute like? Can you make it there under your own power? Block everything into windows of time, and once your day is scheduled out, you'll know how much flexibility you have to exercise on a given day and how to maximize it.

Perhaps you aren't looking to get fit, but have been dreaming of starting a business of your own, or have always wanted to learn a language or an instrument you're obsessed with. Fine, the same rule applies. Analyze your schedule, kill your empty habits, burn out the bullshit, and see what's left. Is it one hour per day? Three? Now maximize that shit. That means listing your prioritized tasks every hour of the day. You can even narrow it down to fifteen-minute windows, and don't forget to include backstops in your day-to-day schedule. Remember how I forgot to include back-stops in my race plan at Ultraman? You need backstops in your day-to-day schedule too. If one task bleeds into overtime, make sure you know it, and begin to transition into your next prioritized task straight away. Use your smartphone for productivity hacks, not click bait. Turn on your calendar alerts. Have those alarms set.

If you audit your life, skip the bull shit, and use backstops, you'll find time to do everything you need and want to do. But remember that you also need rest, so schedule that in. Listen to your body, sneak in those ten- to twenty-minute power naps when necessary, and take one full rest day per week. If it's a rest day, truly allow your mind and body to relax. Turn your phone off. Keep the computer shut down. A rest day means you should be relaxed, hanging with friends or family, and eating and drinking well, so you can recharge and get back at it. It's not a day to lose yourself in technology or stay hunched at your desk in the form of a damn question mark.

The whole point of the twenty-four-hour mission is to keep up a championship pace, not for a season or a year, but for your entire life! That requires quality rest and recovery time. Because there is no finish line. There is always more to learn, and you will always have weaknesses to strengthen if you want to become as hard as woodpecker lips. Hard enough to hammer countless miles, and finish that shit strong!

★ ★ ★

In 2008, I was back in Kona for the Ironman World Championships. I was in peak visibility mode for the Navy SEALs, and Commander Keith Davids, one of the best athletes I ever saw in the SEAL teams, and I were slated to do the race. The NBC Sports broadcast tracked our every move and turned our race within the race into a feature the announcers could cut to between clocking the main contenders.

Our entrance was straight out of a Hollywood pitch meeting. While most athletes were deep into their pre-race rituals and getting psyched up for the longest day of their racing live, we buzzed overhead in a C-130, jumped from 1,500 feet, and parachuted into the water, where we were scooped up by a Zodiac and motored to shore just four minutes before the gun. That was barely enough time for a blast of energy gel, a swig of water, and to change into our Navy SEAL triathlon suits.

You know by now that I'm slow in the wate-r, and Davids destroyed my ass on the 2.4-mile swim. I'm just as strong as he is on a bicycle, but my lower back tightened up that day and at the halfway point I had to stop and stretch out. By the time I coasted into the transition area after a 112-mile bike ride, Davids had thirty minutes on me, and early on in the marathon, I didn't do a great job of getting any of it back. My body was rebelling and I had to walk those early miles, but I stayed in the fight, and at mile ten found a rhythm and started clipping time. Somewhere ahead of me Davids blew up, and I inched closer. For a few miles I could see him plodding in the distance, suffering in those lava fields, heat shimmering off the asphalt in sheets. I knew he wanted to beat me because he was a proud man. He was an Officer, a great operator, and a stud athlete. I wanted to beat him too. That's how Navy SEALs are wired, and I could have blown by him, but as I got closer I told myself to humble up. I caught him with just over two miles to go. He looked at me with a mix of respect and hilarious exasperation.

"Fucking Goggins," he said with a smile. We'd jumped into the water together, started the race together, and we were gonna finish this thing together. We ran side by side for the final two miles, crossed the finish line, and hugged it out. It was terrific fucking television.

At the Kona Ironman finish line with Keith Davids

★ ★ ★

Everything was going well in my life. My career was spit-shined and gleaming I'd made a name for myself in the sports world, and I had plans to get back onto the battlefield like a Navy SEAL should. But sometimes, even when you are doing everything right in life, shit storms appear and multiply. Chaos can and will descend without warning, and when (not if) that happens, there won't be anything you can do to stop it.

If you're fortunate, the issues or injuries are relatively minor, and when those incidents crop up it's on you to adjust and stay after it. If you get injured or other complications arise that prevent you from working on your primary passion, refocus your energy elsewhere. The activities we pursue tend to be our strengths because its fun to do what we're great at. Very few people enjoy working on their weaknesses, so if you're a terrific runner with a knee injury that will prevent you from running for twelve weeks, that is a great time to get into yoga, increasing your flexibility and your overall strength, which will make you a better and less injury-prone athlete. If you're a guitar player with a broken hand, sit down at the keys and use your one good hand to become a more versatile musician. The point is not to allow a setback to shatter our focus, or our detours to dictate our mindset. Always be ready to adjust, recalibrate, and stay after it to become better, somehow.

The sole reason I work out like I do isn't to prepare for and win ultra races. I don't have an athletic motive at all. It's to prepare my mind for life itself. Life will always be the most grueling endurance sport, and when you train hard, get uncomfortable, and callous your mind, you will become a more versatile competitor, trained to find a way forward no matter what. Because there will be times when the shit life throws at you isn't minor at all. Sometimes life hits you dead in the fucking heart.

My two-year stint on recruitment detail was due to end in 2009, and while I enjoyed my time inspiring the next gen, I was looking forward to getting back out and operating in the field. But before I left my post I planned one more big splash. I would ride a bicycle from the beach in San Diego to Annapolis, Maryland, in a legendary endurance road race, the Race Across America. The race was in June, so from January to May I spent all my free time on the bike. I woke up at 4 a.m. and rode 110 miles before work, then rode twenty to thirty miles home at the end of a long work day. On weekends I put in at least one zoo-mile day, and averaged over 700 miles per week. The race would take about two weeks to complete, there would be very little sleep involved, and I wanted to be ready for the greatest athletic challenge of my entire life.

718 mile week

WEEK 192

MON/10- 6H 10min BIKE RIDE 112m
TUE/11- 5H 42min BIKE RIDE 89m
WED/12- 7H 22min BIKE RIDE 112m
THU/13- 5H 28min BIKE RIDE 93m
FRI/14- 4H 34min BIKE RIDE 82m
SAT/15- 7H 29min BIKE RIDE 123m
SUN/16- 6H 11min BIKE RIDE 107m
MON/17- 5H 22min BIKE RIDE 96m   WEEK 193
TUE/18- 6H BIKE RIDE 106m   778
WED/19- 7H 11min BIKE RIDE 126m   MILE
THU/20- 4H 30min BIKE RIDE 92m   WEEK
FRI/21- 6H 4min BIKE RIDE 115m
SAT/22- 7H 50min DIKE RIDE 141m
SUN/23- 5H 45min BIKE RIDE 102m

My RAAM training log

Then in early May everything capsized. Like a malfunctioning appliance, my heart went on the blink, almost overnight. For years my resting pulse rate was in the thirties. Suddenly it was in the seventies and eighties and any activity would spike it until I verged on collapse. It was as if I'd sprung a leak, and all my energy had been sucked from my body. A simple five-minute bike ride would send my heart racing to 150 beats per minute. It pounded uncontrollably during a short walk up a single flight of stairs.

At first I thought it was from overtraining and when I went to the doctor, he agreed, but scheduled an echocardiogram for me at Balboa Hospital just in case. When I went in for the test, the tech gelled up his all-knowing receiver and rolled it over my chest to get the angles he'd need while I lay on my left side, my head away from his monitor. He was a talker and kept bullshitting about a whole lot of nothing while he checked out all my chambers and valves. Everything looked solid, he said, until suddenly, forty-five minutes into the procedure, this chatty motherfucker stopped talking. Instead of his voice, I heard a lot of clicking and zooming. Then he left the room and reappeared with another tech a few minutes later. They clicked, zoomed, and whispered, but didn't let me in on their big secret.

When people in white coats are treating your heart as a puzzle to be solved right in front of you, it's hard not to think that you're probably pretty fucked up. Part of me wanted answers immediately, because I was scared as shit, but I didn't want to be a bitch and show my cards, so I opted to stay calm and let the professionals work. Within a few minutes two other men walked into the room. One of them was a cardiologist. He took over the wand, rolled it on my chest, and peered into the monitor with one short nod. Then he patted me on the shoulder like I was his fucking intern, and said, "Okay, let's talk."

"You have an Atrial Septal Defect," he said as we stood in the hallway, his techs and nurses pacing back and forth, disappearing into and reappearing from rooms on either side of us. I stared straight ahead and said nothing until he realized I had no idea what the fuck he was talking about. "You have a hole in your heart." He scrunched his forehead and stroked his chin. "A pretty good-sized one too."

"Holes don't just open in your heart, do they?"

"No, no," he said with a laugh, "you were born with it."

He went on to explain that the hole was in the wall between my right and left atria, which was a problem because when you have a hole between the chambers in your heart, oxygenated blood mixes with the non-oxygenated blood. Oxygen is an essential element that every single one of our cells needs to survive. According to the doctor, I was only supplying about half of the necessary oxygen my muscles and organs needed for optimal performance.

That leads to swelling in the feet and abdomen, heart palpitations, and occasional bouts of shortness of breath. It certainly explained the fatigue I'd been feeling recently. It also impacts the lungs, he said, because it floods the pulmonary blood vessels with more blood than they can handle, which makes it much more difficult to recover from overexertion and illness. I flashed back to all the issues I had recovering after contracting double pneumonia during my first Hell Week. The fluid I had in my lungs never fully receded. During subsequent Hell Weeks, and after getting into ultras, I found myself hocking up phlegm during and after finishing races. Some nights, there was so much fluid in me I couldn't sleep. I'd just sit up and spit phlegm into empty Gatorade bottles, wondering when that boring ritual would play itself out. Most people, when they become ultra obsessed, may deal with overuse injuries, but their cardiovascular system is finely tuned. Even though I was able to compete and accomplish so much with my broken body, I never felt that great. I'd learned to endure and overcome, and as the doctor continued to download the essentials I realized that for the first time in my entire life, I'd also been pretty fucking lucky. You know, the backhanded brand of luck where you have a hole in your heart, but are thanking God that it hasn't killed you ... yet.

Because when you have an ASD like mine and you dive deep under water, gas bubbles, which are supposed to travel through the pulmonary blood vessels to be filtered through the lungs, might leak from that hole upon ascent, and recirculate as weaponized embolisms that.can clog blood vessels in the brain and lead to a stroke, or block an artery to the heart, and cause cardiac arrest. It's like diving with a dirty bomb floating inside you, never knowing when or where it might go off.

I wasn't alone in this fight. One out of every ten children are born with this same defect, but in most cases the hole closes on its own, and surgery isn't required. In just under 2,000 American children each year, surgery is required, but is usually administered before a patient starts school, because there are better screening processes these days. Most people my age who were born with ASD left the hospital in their mothers' arms and lived ·· with a potential deadly problem without a clue. Until, like me, their heart started giving them trouble in their thirties. If I had ignored my warning signs, I could have dropped dead during a four-mile run.

That's why if you're in the military and are diagnosed with an ASD, you can't jump out of airplanes or scuba dive, and if anyone had known of my condition there is no way the Navy ever would have let me become a SEAL. It's astonishing I even made it through Hell Week, Bad water, or any of those other races.

"I'm truly amazed you could do all you've done with this condition," the doctor· said.

I nodded. He thought I was a medical marvel, some kind of outlier, or simply a gifted athlete blessed with amazing luck. To me, it was just further evidence that I didn't owe my accomplishments to God-given talent or great genetics. I had a fucking hole in my heart! I was running on a tank perpetually half full, and that meant my life was absolute proof of what's possible when someone dedicates themselves to harnessing the full power of the human mind.

Three days later I was in surgery.

And boy did the doctor fuck that one up. First off, the anesthesia didn't take all the way, which meant I was half awake as the surgeon sliced into my inner thigh, inserted a catheter into my femoral artery, and once it reached my heart, deployed a helix patch through that catheter and moved it into place, supposedly patching the hole in my heart. Meanwhile, they had a camera down my throat, which I could feel as I gagged and struggled to endure the two-hour-long procedure. After all of that, my troubles were supposed to have been over. The doctor mentioned that it would take time for my heart tissue to grow around and seal the patch, but after a week he cleared me for light exercise.

Roger that, I thought, as I dropped to the floor to do a set of push-ups as soon as I got home. Almost immediately my heart went into atrial fibrillation, also known as a-fib. My pulse spiked from 120 to 230, back to 120 then up to 250. I felt dizzy and had to sit down as I stared at my heart rate monitor, while my breathing normalized. Once again my resting heart rate was in the eighties. In other words, nothing had changed. I called the cardiologist who tagged it a minor side effect and begged patience. I took him at his word and rested for a few more days then hopped on the bike for an easy ride home from work. At first all went well but after about fifteen miles, my heart went into a-fib once again. My pulse rate bounced from 120 to 230 and back again across the imaginary graph in my mind's eye with no rhythm whatsoever.

Kate drove me straight to Balboa Hospital. After that visit, and second and third opinions, it was clear that the patch had either failed or was insufficient to cover the entire hole, and that I'd need a second heart surgery.

The Navy didn't want any part of that. They feared further complications and suggested I scale back my lifestyle, accept my new normal, and a retirement package. Yeah, right. Instead, I found a better doctor at Balboa who said we'd have to wait several months before we could even contemplate another heart surgery. In the meantime, I couldn't jump or dive, and obviously couldn't operate in the field, so I stayed in recruitment. It was a different life, no doubt, and I was tempted to feel sorry for myself. After all, this thing that hit me out of the clear blue changed the entire landscape of my military career, but I'd been training for life, not ultra races, and I refused to hang my head.

I knew that if I maintained a victim's mentality I wouldn't get anything at all out of a fucked-up situation, and I didn't want to sit home defeated all day long. So I used the time to perfect my recruitment presentation. I wrote up sterling AARs and became much more detail oriented in my administrative work. Does that sound boring to you? Fuck yes, it was boring! But it was honest, necessary work, and I used it to keep my mind sharp for when the moment came that I'd be able to drop back into the fight for real.

Or so I hoped.

A full fourteen months after the first surgery, I was once again rolling through a hospital corridor on my back, staring at the fluorescent lights in the ceiling, headed to pre-op, with no guarantees. While the techs and nurses shaved me down and prepped me up, I thought about all I'd accomplished in the military and wondered, was it enough? If the docs couldn't fix me this time would I be willing to retire, satisfied? That question lingered in my head until the anesthesiologist placed an oxygen mask over my face and counted down softly in my ear. Just before lights out, I heard the answer erupt from the abyss of my jet-black soul.

Fuck no!

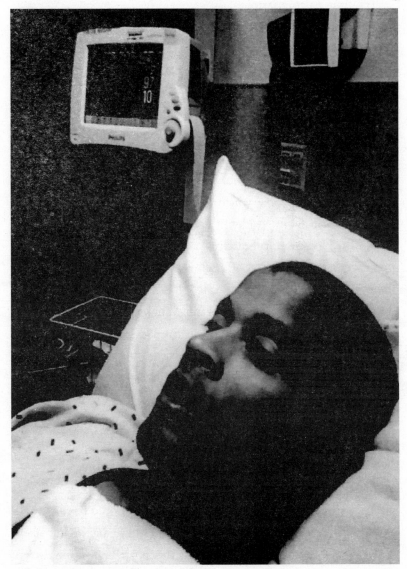

After second heart surgery

CHALLENGE #8

Schedule it in!

It's time to compartmentalize your day. Too many of us have become multitaskers, and that's created a nation of half-asses. This will be a three-week challenge. During week one, go about your normal schedule, but take notes. When do you work? Are you working nonstop or checking your phone (the Moment app will tell you)? How long are your meal breaks? When do you exercise, watch TV, or chat to friends? How long is your commute? Are you driving? I want you to get super detailed and document it all with timestamps. This will be your baseline, and you'll find plenty of fat to trim. Most people waste four to five hours on a given day, and if you can learn to identify and utilize it, you'll be on your way toward increased productivity.

In week two, build an optimal schedule. Lock everything into place in fifteen- to thirty-minute blocks. Some tasks will take multiple blocks or entire days. Fine. When you work, only work on one thing at a time, think about the task in front of you and pursue it relentlessly. When it comes time for the next task on your schedule, place that first one aside, and apply the same focus.

Make sure your meal breaks are adequate but not open-ended, and schedule in exercise and rest too. But when it's time to rest, actually rest. No checking email or bullshitting on social media. If you are going to work hard you must also rest your brain.

Make notes with timestamps in week two. You may still find some residual dead space. By week three, you should have a working schedule that maximizes your effort without sacrificing sleep. Post photos of your schedule, with the hash tags #canthurtme # talentnotrequired.

CHAPTER NINE

UNCOMMON AMONGST UNCOMMON

THE ANESTHESIA TOOK HOLD , AND IF ELTMY SELF WHEEL
ing backward until I landed in a scene from my past. We were
humping through the jungle in the dead of night. Our movement
was stealthy and silent, but swift. Had to be. He who hits first wins
the fight, most of the time.

We crested a pass, took shelter beneath a thick stand of towering mahogany trees in the triple canopy jungle, and tracked our
targets through night vision goggles. Even without sunlight, the
tropical heat was intense and sweat slid down the side of my face
like dew drops on a window pane. I was twenty-seven years old,
and my Platoon and Rambo fever dreams had become real as fuck.
I blinked twice, exhaled, and on the OIC's signal, opened fire.

My entire body reverberated with the rhythm of the M60,
a belt-fed machine gun, firing 500-650 rounds per minute. As
the one-hundred-round belt fed the growling machine and
flared from the barrel, adrenaline flooded my bloodstream and
saturated my brain. My focus narrowed. There was nothing

else but me, my weapon, and the target I was shredding with zero apologies.

It was 2002, -I was fresh out of BUD/S, and as a full-time Navy SEAL, I was now officially one of the world's most fit and deadly warriors and one of the hardest men alive. Or so I thought, but this was years before my descent into the ultra rabbit hole. September 11th was still a fresh, gaping wound in the American collective consciousness, and its ripple effects changed everything for guys like us. Combat was no longer a mythical state of mind we aspired to. It was real and ongoing in the mountains, villages, and cities of Afghanistan. Meanwhile, we were moored in fucking Malaysia, awaiting orders, hoping to join the fight.

And we trained like it.

After BUD/S, I moved on to SEAL Qualification Training, where I officially earned my Trident before landing in my first platoon. Training continued with jungle warfare exercises in Malaysia. We rappelled and fast-roped up and down from hovering helicopters. Some men were trained as snipers, and since I was the biggest man in the unit—my weight was back up to 250 pounds by then—I scored the job of carrying the Pig, the nickname for the M60 because it sounded like the grunt of a barnyard hog.

SQT graduation (note the blood stains from the Trident being punched into my chest)

Most people dreaded Pig detail, but I was obsessed with that gun. The weapon alone was twenty pounds, and each belt of one-hundred rounds weighed in at seven pounds. I carried six to seven of those (one on the gun, four on my waist, and one in a pouch strapped to my rucksack), the weapon, and my fifty-pound ruck everywhere we went and was expected to move just as fast as everyone else. I had no choice. '?Je train as we fight, and live ammo is necessary to mimic true combat so we could perfect the SEAL battle maxim: shoot, move, communicate.

That meant keeping barrel discretion on point. We couldn't let our weapon spray just anywhere. That's how friendly fire incidents happen, and it takes great muscle discipline and attention to detail to know where you're aiming in relation to the location of your teammates at all times, especially when armed with the Pig. Maintaining a high standard of safety and delivering deadly force on-target when duty calls is what makes an average SEAL a good operator.

Most people think once you're a SEAL you're always in the circle, but that's not true. I learned quickly that we were constantly being judged, and the second I was unsafe, whether I was still a new guy or a veteran operator, I'd be out! I was one of three new guys in my first platoon, and one of them had to have his gun taken away because he was so unsafe. For ten days, we moved through the Malaysian jungle, sleeping in hammocks, paddling dugouts, carrying our weapons all day and night, and he was stuck hauling a fucking broomstick like the Wicked Witch of the West. Even then he couldn't hack it and wound up getting booted. Our officers in that first platoon kept everybody honest, and I respected them for it.

"In combat, nobody just turns into Rambo," Dana De Coster told me recently. Dana was second in command on my first platoon with SEAL Team Five. These days he's Director of Operations at BUD/S. "We push ourselves hard so when bullets do start flying we fall back on really good training, and it's important that the point where we fall back is so high, we know we're gonna outperform the enemy. We may not become Rambo, but we'll be damn close."

A lot of people are fascinated by the weaponry and gunfights SEALs utilize and engage in, but that was never my favorite part of the job. I was damn good at it, but I preferred going to war with myself. I'm talking about strong physical training, and my first platoon delivered that too. We would go on long run-swim-runs most mornings before work. We weren't just getting miles in either. We were competing, and our officers led from the front. Our OIC and Dana, his second, were two of the best athletes in the entire platoon and my Platoon Chief, Chris Beck (who now goes by Kristin Beck, and is one of most famous trans women on Twitter; talk about being the o nly!) , was a hard motherfucker too.

"It's funny," Dana said, " [the OIC and I] never really talked about our philosophy on PT. We just competed. I wanted to beat him and he wanted to beat me, and that got people talking about how hard we were getting after it."

There was never a doubt in my mind that Dana was off his damn rocker. I remember before we shipped out for Indonesia, with stops in Guam, Malaysia, Thailand, and Korea, we did a number of training dives off San Clemente Island. Dana was my swim buddy, and one morning he challenged me to do a training dive in fifty-five-degree water without a wetsuit because that's how the predecessors to the SEALs did it when they prepared the beaches in Normandy for the famous D-Day invasion during World War II.

"Let's go old school and dive in shorts with our dive knives," he said.

He had the animalistic mentality I thrived on, and I wasn't about to back down from that challenge. We swam and dove together all over Southeast Asia, where we trained elite military units in Malaysia and sharpened the skills of Thai Navy SEALs— the crew of frogmen who saved the soccer kids in the cave in the summer of 2018. They were engaged with an Islamist insurgency in South Thailand. Wherever we deployed, I loved those PT mornings above all else. Pretty soon, every man in that platoon was competing against everyone else, but no matter how hard I tried I couldn't seem to catch our two officers and usually came in third place. Didn't matter. It wasn't important who won because everybody was capping personal bests almost every day, and that's what stayed with me. The power of a competitive environment to amp up an entire platoon's commitment and achievement!

This was exactly the environment I'd been dreaming of when I classed up for BUD/S. We were all living the SEAL ethos, and I couldn't wait to see where it took us individually and as a unit once we tagged into the fight. But as war raged in Afghanistan, all we could do was sit tight and hope our number was called.

We were in a Korean bowling alley when we watched the invasion of Iraq together. It was depressing as hell. We had been training hard for an opportunity like that. Our foundation had been reinforced with all that PT, and filled out with robust weapons and tactical training. We'd become a deadly unit frothing to be a part of the action, and the fact that we were passed over again pissed us all off. So we took it out on one another every morning.

Navy SEALs were treated like rock stars at the bases we visited around the world, and some of the guys partied like it. In fact, most SEALs enjoyed their share of big nights out, but not me. I'd gotten into the SEALs by living a Spartan lifestyle and felt my job at night was to rest, recharge, and get my body and mind right for battle again the next day. I was forever mission-ready, and my attitude earned respect from some, but our OIC tried to influence me to let go a little and become "one of the boys."

I had great respect for our OIC. He'd graduated from the Naval Academy and the University of Cambridge. He was clearly smart, a stud athlete, and a great leader, on his way to claiming a coveted spot on DEVGRU, so his opinion mattered to me. It mattered to all of us, because he was responsible for evaluating us and those evaluations have a way of following you around and affecting your military career going forward.

On paper, my first evaluation was solid. He was impressed with my skills and all-out effort, but he also dropped some off the record wisdom. "You know, Goggins," he said, "you'd understand the job a little better if you hung out with the guys more. That's when I learn the most about operating in the field, hanging with the boys, hearing their stories. It's important to be part of the group."

His words were a reality check that hurt. Clearly, the OIC, and probably some of the other guys, thought I was a little different. Of course I was! I came from fucking nothing! I didn't get recruited to the Naval Academy. I didn't even know where the fuck Cambridge was. I wasn't raised around pools. I had to teach myself to swim. Fuck, I shouldn't have even been a SEAL, but I made it, and I thought that made me part of the group, but now I realized I was part of the Teams—not the brotherhood.

I had to go out and socialize with the guys after hours to prove my value? That was a big ask for an introvert like me.

Fuck that.

I'd arrived in that platoon because of my intense dedication and I wasn't about to let up. While people were out at night I was reading up on tactics, weaponry, and war. I was a perpetual student! In my mind I was training for opportunities that didn't even exist yet. Back then you couldn't screen to join DEVGRU until after you finished your second platoon, but I was already preparing for that opportunity, and I refused to compromise who I was to conform to their unwritten rules.

DEVGRU (and the Army's Delta Force) are considered the very best within the best of special operations. They get the tip of the spear missions, like the Osama Bin Laden raid, and from that point on, I decided I wouldn't and couldn't be satisfied just being a vanilla Navy SEAL. Yeah, we were all uncommon, hard motherfuckers compared to civilians, but now I saw I was uncommon even among the uncommon, and if that's who I was, then so the fuck be it. I may as well separate myself even more. Not long after that evaluation, I won the morning race for the first time. I passed up Dana and the OIC in the last half mile and never looked back.

Platoon assignments last .for two years, and by the end of our deployment most of the guys were ready for a breather before tackling their next platoon, which judging by the wars we were involved in were almost guaranteed to take them into combat. I didn't want or need a break because the uncommon among uncommon don't take breaks!

After my first evaluation I started studying the other branches in the military (Coast Guard not included) and read up on their special forces. Navy SEALs like to think that we're the best of them all, but I wanted to see for myself. I suspected all the branches employed a few individuals who stood out in the worst environments. I was on a hunt to find and train with those guys because I knew they could make me better. Plus, I'd read that Army Ranger School was known as one of the best, if not the best, leadership schools in the entire military, so during my first platoon, I put seven chits in with my OIC hoping to get approval to go to Army Ranger School between deployments. I wanted to sponge more knowledge, I told him, and become more skilled as a special operator.

Chits are special requests, and my first six were ignored. I was a new guy, after all, and some thought my focus should remain within Naval Special Warfare, rather than stray into the dreaded Army. But I'd earned my own reputation after serving two years in my first platoon, and my seventh request went up the ladder to the CO in charge of Seal Team Five. When he signed off, I was in.

"Goggins," my OIC said after giving me the good news, "you are the type of motherfucker who wishes you were a POW just to see if you have what it takes to last."

He was onto me. He knew the kind of person I was becoming—the type of man willing to challenge myself to the nth degree. We shook hands. The OIC was off to DEVGRU, and there was a chance we'd meet there soon. He told me that with two ongoing wars, for the first time DEVGRU had opened their recruitment process to include guys off their first platoon. By always searching for more and preparing my mind and body for opportunities that didn't yet exist, I was one of a handful of men on the West Coast approved by SEAL Team Five brass to screen for Green Team, the training program for DEVGRU, just before I left for Army Ranger School.

The Green Team screening process unfolds over two days. The first day is the physical fitness portion, which included a three-mile run, a 1,200-meter swim, three minutes of sit-ups and push-ups, and a max set of pull-ups. I smoked everybody, because my first platoon had made me a much stronger swimmer and a better runner. Day two was the interview, which was more like an interrogation. Only three men from my screening class of eighteen guys were approved for Green Team. I was one of them, which theoretically meant that after my second platoon I'd be one step closer to joining DEVGRU. I could hardly wait. It was December 2003, and as imagined, my special forces career was zooming into hyperspace because I kept proving myself to be the most uncommon of motherfuckers, and remained on track to become that One Warrior.

A few weeks later, I arrived in Fort Benning, Georgia, for Army Ranger School. It was early December, and as the only Navy guy in a class of 308 men, I was greeted with skepticism by the instructors because a few classes before mine, a couple of Navy SEALs quit in the middle of training. Back then they used to send Navy SEALs to Ranger School as punishment, so they may not have been the best representatives. I'd been begging to go, but the instructors didn't know that yet. They thought I was just another cocky special ops guy. Within hours they stripped me and everyone else of our uniforms and reputations until we all looked the same. Officers lost rank, and minted special forces warriors like me became nobodies with a hell of a lot to prove.

On day one, we were split into three companies and I was appointed first sergeant in command of Bravo company. I got the job because the original first sergeant had been asked to recite the Ranger Creed after a beat down on the pull-up bar, and he was so tired he fucked it up. To Rangers, their creed is everything. Our Ranger Instructor (RI) was livid as he took stock of Bravo company, all of us locked at attention.

"I don't know where you think you men are, but if you expect to become Range'rs then I expect you to know our creed." His eyes found me. "I know for a fact Old Navy here doesn't know the Ranger Creed."

I 'd been studying it for months and could have recited it while standing on my head. For effect, I cleared my throat and got loud.

"Recognizing that I volunteered as a Ranger, fully knowing the hazards of my chosen profession, I will always endeavor to uphold the prestige, honor, and high spirit de corps of the Rangers!"

"Very surpri. .." He tried to cut me off, but I wasn't done.

"Acknowledging the fact that a Ranger is a more elite Soldier who arrives at the cutting· edge of battle by land, sea, or air, I accept the fact that as a Ranger my country expects me to move further, faster, and fight harder than any other Solider! "

The RI nodded with a wry smile, but this time stayed out of my way.

"Never shall I fail my comrades! I will always keep myself mentally alert, physically strong, and morally straight, and I will shoulder more than my share of the task whatever it may be, 100 percent and then some!

"Gallantly will I show the world that I am a specially selected and well-trained Soldier! My courtesy to superior officers, neatness of dress, and care of equipment shall set the example for others to follow!

"Energetically will I meet the enemies of my country! I shall defeat them on the field of battle for I am better trained and will fight with all my might! Surrender is not a Ranger word! I will never leave a fallen comrade to fall into the hands of the enemy and under no circumstances will I ever embarrass my country!

"Readily will I display the intestinal fortitude required to fight on to the Ranger objective and complete the mission though I be the lone survivor!

" Rangers lead the way! "

I recited all six stanzas, and afterward he shook his head in disbelief, and mulled the ideal way to get the last laugh. "Congratulations, Goggins," he said, "you are now first sergeant."

He left me there, in front of my platoon, speechless. It was now my job to march our platoon around and make sure every man was prepared for whatever lay in front of us. I became part boss, part big brother, and full-time quasi-instructor. In Ranger School it's hard enough to get yourself squared away enough to graduate. Now I had to look after a hundred men and make sure they had their shit together, too.

Plus, I still had to go through the same evolutions as everyone else, but that was the easy part and actually gave me a chance to chill out. For me the physical punishment was more than manageable, but the way I went about accomplishing those physical tasks had shifted. In BUD/S I'd always lead my boat crews, often with tough love, but in general I didn't care how the guys in the other boat crews were doing or if they quit. This time, I wasn't j ust putting out, I was also looking after everybody. If I saw someone having trouble with navigation, patrolling, keeping up on a run, or staying awake all night, I made sure we all rallied together to help. Not everybody wanted to. The training was so difficult that when some guys weren't on the clock being graded, they did the bare minimum and found opportunities to rest and hide. In my sixty-nine days at Ranger School I didn't coast for a single second. I was becoming a true leader.

The whole point of Ranger School is to give every man a taste of what it takes to lead a high-level team. The field exercises were like an operator's scavenger hunt blended with an endurance race. Over the course of six testing phases we were evaluated .on navigation, weapons, rope techniques, reconnaissance, and overall leadership. The field tests were notorious for their Spartan brutality and capped three separate phases of training.

First, we were split into groups of twelve men and together spent five days and four nights in the foothills for Fort Benning phase. We were given very little food to eat—one or two MREs per day—and only a couple of hours sleep per night, as we raced the clock to navigate cross-country terrain between stations where we'd knock off a series of tasks to prove our proficiency in a particular skill. Leadership in the group rotated between men.

Mountain phase was exponentially harder than Fort Benning. Now we were grouped into teams of twenty-five men to navigate the mountains in north Georgia, and buddy, Appalachia gets cold as fuck in wintertime. I'd read stories about black soldiers with Sickle Cell Trait dying during Mountain Phase, and the Army wanted me to wear special· dog tags with a red casing to alert medics if something went wrong, but I was leading men and didn't want my crew to think of me as some sickly child, so the red casing never quite found its way to my dog tags.

In the mountains we learned how to rappel and rock climb, among other mountaineering skills, and became proficient in ambush techniques and mountain patrol. To prove it we went out on two separate, four-night field training exercises, known as FTXs. A storm blew in during our second FTX. Thirty-mile-per-hour winds howled with ice and snow. We didn't haul sleeping bags or warm clothes, and again we had very little food. All we could use to keep warm was a poncho liner and one another, which was an issue because the rancid odor in the air was our own. We'd burned so many calories without proper nutrition, we'd lost all our fat and were incinerating our own muscle mass for fuel. The putrid stink made our eyes water. It triggered the gag reflex. Visibility narrowed to a few feet. Guys wheezed, coughed, and jackhammered, their eyes wide with terror. I thought for sure someone was gonna die from frostbite, hypothermia, or pneumonia that night.

Whenever you stop to sleep during field tests, rest is brief and you're required to maintain security in four directions, but in the face of that storm, Bravo platoon buckled. These were generally very hard men with a ton of pride, but they were focused on survival above all else. I under good the impulse, and the instructors didn't mind because we were in weather emergency mode, but to me that presented an opportunity to stand apart and lead by example. I looked at that winter storm as a platform to become uncommon among uncommon men.

No matter who you are, life will present you similar opportunities where you can prove to be uncommon. There are people in all walks of life who relish those moments, and when I see them I recognize them immediately because they are usually that motherfucker who's all by himself. It's the suit who's still at the office at midnight while everyone else is at the bar, or the badass who hits the gym directly after coming off a forty-eight-hour op. She's the wildland firefighter who instead of hitting her bedroll, sharpens her chainsaw after working a fire for twenty-four hours. That mentality is there for all of us. Man, woman, straight, gay, black, white, or purple fucking polkadot. All of us can be the person who flies all day and night only to arrive home to a filthy house, and instead of blaming family or roommates, cleans it up right then because they refuse to ignore duties undone.

All over the world amazing human beings like that exist. It doesn't take wearing a uniform. It's not about all the hard schools they graduated from, all their patches and medals. It's about wanting it like there's no tomorrow-because there might not be. It's about thinking of everybody else before yourself and developing your own code of ethics that sets you apart from others. One of those ethics is the drive to turn every negative into a positive, and then when shit starts flying, being prepared to lead from the front.

My thinking on that Georgia mountaintop was that, in a real-world scenario, a storm like that would provide the perfect cover for an enemy attack, so I didn't group up and seek warmth. I dialed deeper, welcomed the carnage of ice and snow, and held the western perimeter like it was my duty-because it damn well was! And I loved every second of it. I squinted into the wind, and as hail stung my cheeks, I screamed into the night from the depths of my misunderstood soul.

A few guys heard me, popped out of the tree line to the north, and stood tall. Then another guy emerged to the east, and another on the edge of the south-facing slope. They were all shivering, wrapped in their measly poncho liners. None of them wanted to be there, but they rose up and did their duty. In spite of one of the most brutal storms in Ranger School history, we held a complete perimeter until the instructors radioed us to come in from the, cold. Literally. They put up a circus tent. We filed in and huddled up until the storm passed.

The final weeks in Ranger School are called Florida Phase, a ten-day FTX in which fifty men navigate the panhandle, GPS point by GPS point, as a single unit. It started with a static line jump from an aircraft at 1,500 feet into frigid swamplands near Fort Walton Beach. We waded and swam across rivers, set up rope bridges, and with our hands and feet shimmied back to the other side. We couldn't stay dry, and the water temperature was in the high thirties and low forties. We'd all heard the story that during the winter of 1994 it got so cold, four would-be Rangers died ofhypothem;tia during Florida Phase. Being near the beach, freezing .my nuts off, reminded me of Hell Week. Whenever we stopped, guys were nut to butt and jackhammering, but as usual, I focused h.ard and refused to show any weakness. This time it wasn't about taking the souls of our instructors. It was about giving courage to the men who were struggling. I'd cross the river six times if that's what it took to help one of my guys tie off his rope bridge. I'd walk them step-by-step through the process until they could prove their value to the Ranger brass.

We slept very little, ate even less, and continually knocked off reconnaissance tasks, hitting waypoints, setting up bridges and weapons, and preparing for ambush, while taking turns leading a group of fifty men. Those men were tired, hungry, cold, frustrated, and they did not want to be there anymore. Most were at their ultimate edge, their 100 percent. I was getting there too, but even when it wasn't my turn to lead, I helped out because in those sixty-nine days of Ranger School I learned that if you want to call yourself a leader, that's what it takes.

A true leader stays exhausted, abhors arrogance, and never looks down on the weakest link. He fights for his men and leads by example. That's what it meant to be uncommon among uncommon. It meant being one of the best and helping your men find their best too. It was a lesson I'd wish sunk in a lot deeper, because in just a few more weeks I'd be challenged in the leadership department and come up well short.

Ranger School was so demanding, and the standards were so high that only ninety-six men graduated out of a class of 308 candidates, and the majority of them were from Bravo platoon. I was awarded Enlisted Honor Man and received a 100 percent peer evaluation. To me that meant even more, because my classmates, my fellow knuckle draggers, had valued my leadership in harsh conditions, and one look in the mirror revealed just how harsh those conditions were.

Certificate for being the Enlisted Honor Man at Ranger School

I lost fifty-six pounds in Ranger School. I looked like death. My cheeks were sunken. My eyes bugged out. I had no bicep muscle left. All of us were emaciated. Guys had trouble running down the block. Men who could do forty pull-ups in one go now struggled to do a single one. The Army expected that and scheduled three days between the end of Florida Phase and graduation to fatten us up before our families flew in to celebrate.

As soon as the final FTX was called, we hustled straight to chow hall. I piled my tray with doughnuts, fries, and cheeseburgers, and went looking for the milk machine. After drinking all those damn chocolate shakes when I was down. and out, my body had become lactose intolerant, and I hadn't touched dairy in years. But that day I was like a little child, unable to stifle a primordial yean-ling for a glass of milk.

I found the milk machine, pulled the lever down and watched, confused, as it funneled out, chunky as cottage cheese. I shrugged and sniffed. It smelled all kinds of wrong, but I remember downing that spoiled milk like it was a fresh glass of sweet tea, courtesy of another hellacious special forces school that put us through so much, by the end anybody who survived was grateful for their cold glass of spoiled milk.

★ ★ ★

Most people take a couple weeks off to recover from Ranger School and put some weight back on. Most people do that. The day of graduation, on Valentine's Day, I flew into Coronado to meet up with my second platoon. Once again, I looked at that lack oflag time as an opportunity to be uncommon. Not that anybody else was watching, but when it comes to mindset, it doesn't matter where other people's attention lies. I had my own uncommon standards to live up to.

At every stop I'd made in the SEALs, from BUD/S to that first platoon to Ranger School, I was known as a hard motherfucker, and when the OIC in my second platoon put me in charge of PT, I was encouraged because it told me that once again I'd landed c with a group of men who were driven to put out and get better. Inspired, I bent my brain to think of evil shit we could do to get us battle ready. This time we all knew we'd deploy to Iraq, and I made it my mission to help us become the hardest SEAL platoon in the fight. That was a high bar, set by the original Navy SEAL legend still lodged like an anchor deep in my brain. Our legend suggested we were the type of men to swim five miles on Monday, run twenty miles on Tuesday, and climb a 14,000-foot peak on Wednesday,- and my expectations were sky fucking high.

For the first week, guys rallied at 5 a.m. for a run-swim-run or a twelve-mile ruck, followed by a lap through the 0-Course. We carried logs over the berm and hammered hundreds of push-ups. I had us doing the hard shit, the real shit, the workouts that m ade us SEALs. Each day the workouts were harder than the last and over the course of a week or two, that wore people down. Every alpha male in special ops wants to be the best at everything they do, but with me leading PT they couldn't always be the best. Because I never gave them a break. We were all breaking down and showing weakness. That was the idea, but they didn't want to be challenged like that every day. During the second week, attendance flagged and the OIC and the Chief of our platoon took me aside.

"Look, dude," our OIC said, "this is stupid. What are we doing?"

"We aren't in BUD/S anymore, Goggins," said the Chief.

To me, this wasn't about being in BUD/S, this was about living the SEAL ethos and earning the Trident every day. These guys wanted to do their own PT, which typically meant hitting the gym and getting big. They weren't interested in being punished physically, and definitely weren't interested in being pushed to meet my standard. Their reaction shouldn't have surprised me. but it sure as hell disappointed me and made me lose all respect for their leadership.

I understood that not everyone wanted to work out like an animal for the rest of their career, because I didn't want to do that shit either! But what put distance between me and almost everybody else in that platoon is that I didn't let my desire for comfort rule me. I was determined to go to war with myself to find more because I believed it was our duty to maintain a BUD/S mentality and prove ourselves every day. Navy SEALs are revered the world over and are thought to be the hardest men that God ever created, but that conversation made me realize that wasn't always true.

I had just come from Ranger School, a place where nobody

has any rank at all. Even if a General had classed up, he'd have been in the same clothes we all had to wear, that of an enlisted man on day one of basic fucking training. We were all maggots reborn, with no future and no past, starting at zero. I loved that concept because it sent a message that no matter what we'd accomplished in the outside world, as far as the Rangers were concerned we weren't shit. And I claimed that metaphor for myself, because it's always 'and forever true. No matter what you or I achieve, in sports, business, or life, we can't be satisfied. Life is too dynamic a game. We're either getting better or we're getting worse. Yes, we need to celebrate our victories. There's power in victory that's transformative, but after our celebration we should dial it down, dream up new training regimens, new goals, and start at zero the very next day. I wake up every day as if I am back in BUD/S, day one, week one.

Starting at zero is a mind set that says my refrigerator is never full, and it never will be. We can always become stronger and more agile, mentally and physically. We can always become more capable and more reliable. Since that's the case we should never feel that our work is done. There is always more to do.

Are you an experienced scuba diver? Great, shed your gear, take a deep breath and become a one-hundred-foot free diver. Are you a badass triathlete? Cool, learn how to rock climb. Are you enjoying a wildly successful career? Wonderful, learn a new language or skill. Get a second degree. Always be willing to embrace ignorance and become the dumb fuck in the classroom again, because that is the only way to expand your body of knowledge and body of work. It's the only way to expand your mind.

During week two of my second platoon, my Chief and OIC showed their cards. It was devastating to hear that they didn't feel that we needed to earn our status every day. Sure, all the guys I worked with over the years were relatively hard guys and highly skilled. They enjoyed the challenges of the job, the brotherhood, and being treated like superstars. They all loved being SEALs, but some weren't interested in starting at zero because just by qualifying to breathe rare air they were already satisfied. Now, that is a very common way of thinking. Most people in the world, if they ever push themselves at all, are willing to push themselves only so far. Once they reach a cushy plateau, they chill the fuck out and enjoy their rewards, but there's another phrase for that mentality. It's called getting soft, and that I could not abide.

As far as I was concerned I had my own reputation to uphold, and when the rest of the platoon opted out of my custom made hellscape, the chip on my shoulder grew even bigger. I ramped up my workouts and vowed to put out so hard it would hurt their fucking feelings. As head of PT, that was not in my job description. I was supposed to inspire guys to give more . Instead, I saw what I considered a glaring weakness and let them know I wasn't impressed.

In one short week, my leadership regressed light years from where I was in Ranger School. I lost touch with my situational awareness (SA) and didn't respect the men in my platoon enough. As a leader, I was trying to bull my way through, and they bucked against that. Nobody gave an inch, including the officers. I suppose all of us took a path ofleast resistance. I just didn't notice it because physically I was going harder than ever.

And I had one guy with me. Sledge was a hard .motherfucker who grew up in San Bernardino, the son of a firefighter and a secretary, and, like me, he taught himself to swim in order to pass the swim test and qualify for BUD/S. He was only a year older but was already in his fourth platoon. He was also a heavy drinker, a little overweight, and looking to change his life. The morning after the Chief, the OIC, and I had words, Sledge showed up at 5 a.m. ready to roll. I'd been there since 4:30 a.m. and had a lather of sweat work_ing already.

"I like what you're doing with the workouts," he said, "and I wanna keep doing them."

"Roger that."

From then on, no matter where we were stationed, whether that was Coronado, Niland, or Iraq, we got after it every single morning. We'd meet up at 4 ·a.m. and get to it. Sometimes that meant running up the side of a mountain before hitting the O-Course at high speed and carrying logs up and over the berm and down the beach. In BUD/S, usually six men carried those logs. We did it with just the two of us. On another day we rocked a pull-up pyramid, hitting sets of one, all the way up to twenty, and back down to one again. After every other set we'd climb a rope forty feet high. One thousand pull-ups before breakfast became our new mantra. At first, Sledge struggled to rock one set of ten pull-ups. Within months he 'd lost thirty-five pounds and was hitting one hundred sets of ten!

In Iraq, it was impossible to get long runs in, so we lived in the weight room. We did hundreds of deadlifts and spent hours on the hip sled. We went way beyond overtraining. We didn't care about muscle fatigue or breakdown because after a certain point we were training our minds, not our bodies. My workouts weren't designed to make us fast runners or to be the strongest men on the mission. I was training us to take torture so we'd remain relaxed in extraordinarily uncomfortable environments. And shit did get uncomfortable from time to time.

Despite the clear divide within our platoon (Sledge and me vs. everyone else) we operated well together in Iraq. Off duty, however, there was a huge gulf between who the two of us were becoming and who I thought the men in my platoon were, and my disappointment showed. I wore my shitty attitude around like a shroud, thus earning me the platoon nickname David "Leave Me Alone" Goggins, and never woke up to realize that my disappointment was my own problem. Not my teammates' fault.

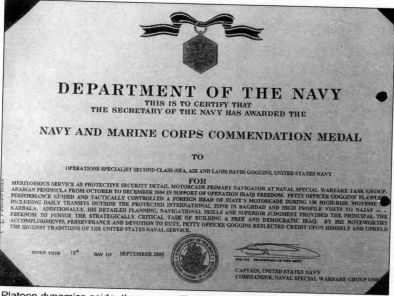

DEPARTMENT OF THE NAVY
THIS IS TO CERTIFY THAT
THE SECRETARY OF THE NAVY HAS AWARDED THE

NAVY AND MARINE CORPS COMMENDATION MEDAL

TO

OPERATIONS SPECIALIST SECOND CLASS (SEA, AIR AND LAND) DAVID GOGGINS, UNITED STATES NAVY

FOR

MERITORIOUS SERVICE AS PROTECTIVE SECURITY DETAIL MOTORCADE PRIMARY NAVIGATOR AT NAVAL SPECIAL WARFARE TASK GROUP-ARABIAN PENINSULA FROM OCTOBER TO DECEMBER 2004 IN SUPPORT OF OPERATION IRAQI FREEDOM. PETTY OFFICER GOGGINS' FLAWLESS PERFORMANCE GUIDED AND TACTICALLY CONTROLLED A FOREIGN HEAD OF STATE'S MOTORCADE DURING 150 HIGH-RISK MOVEMENTS INCLUDING DAILY TRANSITS OUTSIDE THE PROTECTED INTERNATIONAL ZONE IN BAGHDAD AND HIGH PROFILE VISITS TO NAJAF AND KARBALA. ADDITIONALLY, HIS DETAILED PLANNING, NAVIGATIONAL SKILLS AND SUPERIOR JUDGMENT PROVIDED THE PRINCIPAL THE FREEDOM TO PURSUE THE STRATEGICALLY CRITICAL TASK OF BUILDING A FREE AND DEMOCRATIC IRAQ. BY HIS NOTEWORTHY ACCOMPLISHMENTS, PERSEVERANCE AND DEVOTION TO DUTY, PETTY OFFICER GOGGINS REFLECTED CREDIT UPON HIMSELF AND UPHELD THE HIGHEST TRADITIONS OF THE UNITED STATES NAVAL SERVICE.

GIVEN THIS 15ᵗʰ DAY OF SEPTEMBER 2005

FOR THE SECRETARY OF THE NAVY

CAPTAIN, UNITED STATES NAVY
COMMANDER, NAVAL SPECIAL WARFARE GROUP ONE

Platoon dynamics aside, there was still a job to do in Iraq

That's the drawback of becoming uncommon amongst uncommon. You can push yourself to a place that is beyond the current capability or temporal mind set of the people you work with, and that's okay. Just know that your supposed superiority is a figment of your own ego. So don't lord it over them, because it won't help you advance as a team or as an individual in your field. Instead of getting angry that your colleagues can't keep up, help pick your colleagues up and bring then1 with you!

We are all fighting the same battle. All of us are torn between comfort and performance, between settling for mediocrity or being willing .to suffer in order to become our best self, all the damn time. We make those kinds of decisions a dozen or more times each day. My job as head of PT wasn't to demand that my guys live up to the Navy SEAL legend I loved, it was to help them become the best version of themselves. But I never listened, and I didn't lead. Instead, I got angry and showed up my teammates. For two years I played the tough guy and never took a step back with a calm mind to address my original error. I had countless opportunities to bridge the gap I'd helped create, but I never did, and it cost me.

I didn't realize any of that right away, because after my second platoon, I was ordered to freefall school, then made an assaults instructor. Both were posts scheduled to prep me for Green Team. Assaults was critical because most people who get cut from Green Team are dismissed for sloppy house runs. They move too slow when clearing buildings, are too easily exposed, or are amped up and trigger happy and end up shooting friendly targets. Teaching those skills made me clinical, stealthy, and calm in confined environments, and I expected to receive my orders to train with DEVGRU in Dam Neck, Virginia, any day, but they never came. The other two guys who'd rocked the screening with me received their orders. Mine went AWOL.

I called leadership at Dam Neck. They told me to screen again, and that's when I knew something was off. I thought about the process I'd been through. Did I really expect to do better? I smoked that shit. But then I remembered the actual interview, which felt more like an interrogation with two men playing good cop, bad cop. They didn't probe my skillset or Navy knowhow. Eighty-five percent of their questions had nothing to do with my ability to operate whatsoever. The bulk of that interview was about my race.

"We are a bunch of good ol' boys," one of them said, "and we need to know how you're gonna handle hearing black jokes, bro."

Most of their questions were a variation on that one theme and through it all, I smiled and thought, *How are you white boys gonna feel when tm the baddest motherfucker in here?* But that's not what I said, and it wasn't because I was intimidated or uncomfortable. I was more at home in that interview than anywhere I'd been in the military, because for the first time in my life it was out in the fucking open. They weren't trying to pretend that being one of only a handful of black guys in perhaps the most revered military organization in the world didn't have its own unique set of challenges. One guy was challenging me with his aggressive posture and tone, the other guy kept it cool, but they were both being real. There were two or three black men in DEVGRU already and they were telling me that entry into their inner circle required my signing off on certain terms and conditions. And in a sick way, I loved that message and the challenge that came with it.

DEVGRU was a hard ass, renegade crew within the SEALs, and they wanted it to stay that way. They didn't want to civilize anybody. They didn't want to evolve or change, and I knew where I was and what I was getting myself into. This crew was responsible for the most dangerous, tip of the spear missions. It was a white man's underworld, and these guys needed to know how I'd act if someone started to fuck with me. They needed assurances I could control my emotions, and once I saw through their language into the greater purpose, I couldn't be offended by their act.

"Look, I've experienced racism my entire life," I replied, "and there is nothing any of you fuckers can say to me that I haven't heard twenty times before, but be ready. Because I'm coming right the fuck fuck at you!" At the time, they seemed to like the sound of that. Trouble is, when you're a black guy giving it back it usually doesn't go over nearly as well.

I will never know why I didn't receive my orders for Green

Team, and it doesn't matter. We can't control all the variables in our lives. It's about what we do with opportunities revoked or presented to us that determine how a story ends. Instead of thinking, *I crushed the screening process once, I can do it again,* I decided to start at zero and screen for Delta Force—the Army's version of DEVGRU, instead.

Delta Selection is rigorous, and I'd always been intrigued by it due to the elusive nature of the group. Unlike SEALs, you never heard about Delta. The screening for Delta Selection included an IQtest, a complete military resume including my qualifications and war experience, and my evaluations. I pulled all of that together in a few days, knowing that I was competing against the best guys from every military branch and that only the cream would be extended an invitation. My Delta orders came through in a matter of weeks. Not long after that, I landed in the mountains of West Virginia ready to compete for a spot among the Army's very best soldiers.

Strangely, there was no yelling or screaming in the Delta void. There was no muster and no OICs. The men that showed up there were all self-starters and our orders were chalked on a board hanging in the barracks. For three days we weren't allowed to leave the compound. Our focus was rest and acclimatization, but on day four, PT started up with the basic screening test, which included two minutes of push-ups, two minutes of sit-ups, and a timed two-mile run. They expected everyone to meet a minimum standard, and those that didn't were sent home. From there things got immediately and progressively more difficult. In fact, later that same night we had our first road march. Like everything Delta, officially the distance was unknown, but I believe it was about an eighteen-mile course from start to finish.

It was cold and very dark when all 160 of us took off, strapped with around forty-pound rucksacks. Most guys started out in a slow march, content to pace themselves and hike it out. I took off hot, and in the first quarter mile left everyone behind. I saw an opportunity to be uncommon and seized it, and I finished about thirty minutes before anybody else.

Delta Selection is the best orienteering course in the world. For the next ten days we hammered PT in the morning and worked on advanced land navigation skills into the night. They taught us how to get from A to B by reading the terrain instead of roads and trails on a map. We learned to read fingers and cuts, and that if you get high you want to stay high. We were taught to follow water. When you start reading the land this way, your map comes alive, and for the first time in my life I became great at orienteering. We learned to judge distance and how to draw our own topographic maps. At first we were assigned an instructor to tail through the vildlands, and those instructors hauled ass. For the next few weeks we were on our own. Technically, we were still practicing, but we were also being gatled and watched to make sure we were moving cross-country instead of taking roads.

It all culminated with an extended final exam in the field that lasted seven days and nights, if we even made it that far. This wasn't a team effort. Each of us was on our own to use our map and compass to navigate from one waypoint to the next. There was a Humvee at every stop and the cadres (our instructors and evaluators) there noted our time and gave us the next set of coordinates. Each day was its own unique challenge, and we never knew how many points we'd have to navigate before the test was done. Plus, there was an unknown time limit that only the cadres were privy to. At the finish line we weren't told if we passed or failed. Instead we were directed to one of two covered Humvees.

The good truck took you to the next camp, the bad truck motored back to base, where you would have to pack your shit and head home. Most of the time I didn't know if I made it for sure until the truck stopped.

By day five I was one of roughly thirty guys still in consideration for Delta Force. There were only three days left and I was rocking every test, coming in at least ninety-minutes before drop-dead time. The final test sould be a forty-mile ball-kicker of a land navigation, and I was looking forward to that, but first I had work to do. I splashed through washes, huffed up sloped woodlands, and rambled along ridgelines, point-to-point until the unthinkable happened. I got lost. I was on the wrong ridge. I double checked my map and compass and looked across a valley to the correct one, due south.

Roger that!

For the first time, the clock became a factor. I didn't know the drop-dead time, but knew I was cutting it close, so I sprinted down a steep ravine but lost my footing. My left foot jammed between two boulders, I rolled over my ankle and felt it pop. The pain was immediate. I checked my watch, gritted my teeth, and laced my boot tight as quickly as I could, then hobbled up a steep hillside to the correct ridge.

On the final stretch to the finish, my ankle blew up so bad I had to untie my boot to relieve the pain. I moved slow, convinced· I would be sent home. I was wrong. My Humvee unloaded us at the second to last base camp of Delta Selection, where I iced my ankle all night knowing that thanks to my injury, the next day's land navigation test was likely beyond my capability. But I didn't quit. I showed up, fought to stay in the mix, but missed my time on one of the early checkpoints and that was that. I didn't hang my head, because injuries happen. I'd given it everything I had and when you handle business like that, your effort will not go unnoticed.

Delta cadres are like robots. Throughout Selection they didn't show any personality, but as I was getting ready to leave the compound, one of the officers in charge called me into his office.

"Goggins," he said, extending his hand, "you are a stud! We want you to heal up, come back, and try again. We believe you will be a great addition to Delta Force someday."

But when? I came to from my: second heart surgery in a billowing cloud of anesthesia. I looked over my right shoulder to an IV drip and followed the flow to my veins. I was wired to the medical mind. Beeping heart monitors recorded data to tell a story in a language beyond my comprehension. If only I were fluent, maybe I'd know if my heart was finally whole, if there would ever be a "someday." I placed my hand over my heart, closed my eyes and listened for clues.

After leaving Delta, I went back to the SEAL Teams and was assigned to land warfare as an instructor instead of a warrior. At first my morale flagged. Men who lacked my skills, commitment, and athletic ability were in the field in two countries·· and I was moored in no-man's-land, wondering how it had all gone so haywire so quickly. It felt like I'd hit a glass ceiling, but had it always been there or did I slide it into place myself? The truth was somewhere in between.

I realized from living in Brazil, Indiana, that prejudice is everywhere. There is a piece of it in every person and each and every organization, and if you are the only in any given situation, it's on you to dwide how you're going to handle it because you can't make it go away. For years, I used it to fuel me because there's a lot of power in being the only. It forces you to juice your own resources and to believe in yourself in the face of unfair scrutiny. It increases the degree of difficulty, which makes every success that much sweeter. That's why I continually put myself in situations where I knew I would encounter it. I fed off being *the only* one in a room. I brought the war to people and watched my excellence explode small minds. I didn't sit back and cry about being the o nly. I took action, said go fuck yourself, and used all the prejudice I felt as dynamite to blow up those walls.

But that kind of raw material will only get you so far in life. I was so confrontational I created needless enemies along the way, and I believe that's what limited my access to the top SEAL Teams. With my career at a crossroads, I didn't have time to dwell on those mistakes. I had to find higher ground and turn the negative I'd created into another positive. I didn't just accept land warfare duty, I was the best instructor I could possibly be, and on my own time I created new opportunities for myself by launching my ultra quest, which revived my stalled career. I was right back on track until I learned I'd been born with a broken heart.

Yet there was a positive side to that too. Tucked into my post-op hospital bed, I looked to be fading in and out of consciousness, as conversations between doctors, nurses, my wife, and mother bled into one another like white noise. They had no clue that I was wide awake the whole time, listening to my wounded heart beat, and smiling inside. Knowing I finally had definitive, scientific proof that I was as uncommon as any motherfucker who has ever lived.

CHALLENGE #9

This one's for the unusual motherfuckers in this world. A lot of people think that once they reach a certain level of status, respect, or success, that they've made it in life. I'm here to tell you that you always have to find more. Greatness is not something that if you meet it once it stays with you forever. That shit evaporates like a flash of oil in a hot pan.

If you truly want to become uncommon amongst the uncommon, it will require sustaining greatness for a long period of time. It requires staying in constant pursuit and putting out unending effort. This may sound appealing but will require everything you have to give and then some. Believe me, this is not for everyone because it will demand singular focus and may upset the balance in your life .

That's what it takes to become a true overachiever, and if you are already surrounded by people who are at the top of their game, what are you going to do differently to stand out? It's easy to stand out amongst everyday people and be a big fish in a small pond. It is a much more difficult task when you are a wolf surrounded by wolves.

This means not only getting into Wharton Business School, but being ranked #1 in your class. It means not just graduating BUD/S, but becoming Enlisted Honor Man in Army Ranger School then going out and finishing Bad water.

Torch the complacency you feel gathering around you, your coworkers, and teammates in that rare air. Continue to put obstacles in front of yourself, because that's where you'll find the friction that will help you grow even stronger. Before you know it, you will stand alone.

#canthurtme #uncommonamongstuncommon.

CHAPTER TEN

THE EMPOWERMENT
OF FAILURE

ON SEPTEMBER 27, 2012, I STOOD IN A MAKESHIFT GYM ON the second floor of 30 Rockefeller Center prepared to break the world record for pull-ups in a twenty-four-hour period. That was the plan, anyway. Savannah Guthrie was there, along with an official from the Guinness Book of World Records and Matt Lauer (yeah, that fucking guy). Again, I was gunning to raise money—a lot of money this time—for the Special Operations Warrior Foundation, but I also wanted that record. To get it I had to perform under *The Today Show spotlight*.

The number in my head was 4,020 pull-ups. Sounds superhuman, right? Did to me too, until I dissected it and realized if I could knock out six pull-ups on the minute, every minute, for twenty-four hours, I 'd shatter it. That's roughly ten seconds of effort, and fifty seconds of rest, each minute. It wouldn't be easy, but I considered it doable given the work I'd put in. Over the past five to six months, I'd rocked over 40,000 pull-ups and was stoked to be on the precipice of another huge challenge.

After all the ups and downs since my second heart surgery, I needed this.

The good news was the surgery worked. For the first time in my life I had a fully functioning heart muscle, and I wasn't in a rush to run or ride. I was patient with my recovery. The Navy wouldn't clear me to operate anyway, and in order to stay in the SEALs I had to accept a non-deployable, non-combat job. Admiral Winters kept me in recruiting for two more years, and I remained on the road, shared my story with willing ears, and worked to win hearts and minds. But all I really wanted to do was what I was trained to do, and that's fight! I tried to salve that wound with trips to the gun range, but shooting targets only made me feel worse.

In 2011, after recruiting for four-plus years and spending two and a half years on the disabled list due to my heart issues, I was finally medically cleared to operate again .. Admiral Winters offered to send me anywhere I wanted to go. He knew my sacrifices and my dreams, and I told him I had unfinished business with Delta. He signed my papers, and after a five-year wait, my someday had arrived.

THE UNITED STATES OF AMERICA

THIS IS TO CERTIFY THAT
THE PRESIDENT OF THE UNITED STATES OF AMERICA
HAS AWARDED THE

MERITORIOUS SERVICE MEDAL

TO
SPECIAL WARFARE OPERATOR (SEA, AIR, AND LAND) DAVID GOGGINS
UNITED STATES NAVY
FOR

OUTSTANDING MERITORIOUS SERVICE FROM JUNE 2007 TO MAY 2010

GIVEN THIS 28TH DAY OF MAY 2010

E. G. WINTERS
REAR ADMIRAL, UNITED STATES NAVY
COMMANDER, NAVAL SPECIAL WARFARE COMMAND

NAVAL SPECIAL WARFARE COMMAND

The President of the United States takes pleasure in presenting the
MERITORIOUS SERVICE MEDAL to

SPECIAL WARFARE OPERATOR FIRST CLASS (SEAL)
DAVID GOGGINS
UNITED STATES NAVY

for service as set forth in the following

CITATION:

For outstanding meritorious service while serving as Leading Petty Officer at the Naval Special Warfare Recruiting Directorate from June 2007 to May 2010. Petty Officer Goggins personally presented compelling discussions about perseverance, mental toughness and Naval Special Warfare career opportunities to 71,965 students from 159 high schools, 12 junior high schools, and 67 universities throughout the country. Capitalizing on his hard-earned fame from stellar achievements in ultra-running and ultra-biking events, he recruited, mentored, coached, and provided ongoing personal guidance to hundreds of potential candidates, 66 of whom entered the Navy for SEAL training, 21 having successfully graduated to date. Through superlative personal effort and initiative, he dramatically enhanced efforts to increase NSW awareness among minority audiences through numerous high impact presentations. Finally, on his own personal time, he raised $1.1 million for a charity supporting the families of fallen special operations warriors. Petty Officer Goggins' exceptional professionalism, personal initiative, and loyal devotion to duty reflected great credit upon him and were in keeping with the highest traditions of the United States Naval Service.

For the President,

E. G. Winters
Rear Admiral, United States Navy
Commander, Naval Special Warfare Command

Awarded the Metritorious Service Medal for my work in recruiting

Chosen as Sailor of the Quarter, January to March 2010

Once again, I dropped into Appalachia for Delta Selection. In 2006, after I smoked the eighteen-mile road ruck on our first real day of work, I heard some well-intentioned blowback from some of the other guys who were tapped into the rumor mill. In Delta Selection everything is a secret. Yes, there are clear tasks and training but nobody tells you how long the tasks are or will be (even the eighteen-mile ruck was a best estimate based on my own navigation) , and only the cadres know how they evaluate their candidates. According to the rumor mill, they use that first ruck as a baseline to calculate how long each navigation task should take. Meaning if you go hard you'll eat away at your own margin for error. This time, I had that intel going in, and I could have played it safe and taken my time, but I wasn't about to go out among those great men and give a half-assed effort. I went out even harder so I could make sure they saw my very best, and I broke my own course record (according to that reliable rumor mill) by nine minutes.

Rather than hear it from me, I reached out to one of the guys who was in Delta Selection with me, and below is his first-hand account of how that ruck went down:

Before I can talk about the road march, I have to give a little bit of context in the days leading up to it. Showing up to Selection you have no idea what to expect, every one hears stories but you do not have a complete grasp of what you are about to go through... I remember arriving at an airport waiting for a b us and everyone wash anging out bullshiting. For many people it is are union offriends that you haven't seen in years. This is also where you startsizing everyone up. I remembera majority of the people talking or relaxing, there was one person who was sitting on his bag, looking intense. That person I would later find out was David Goggins, you could tell right from the start he would be one of the guys at the end. Being a runner, I recognized him, but didn't really putit all together until after the first few days.

There are several events that you know you have to do just to start the course; one of those is the road march. Without getting into specific distances, I knew it was going to be fairly far but was comfortable with running a majority of it. Coming into Selection, I had been in Special Forces for a majority of my career and it was are when someone finished before me in aroad march. I was comfortable with a ruck on my back. When we started it was a little cold and very dark, and as we took off I was where I was most comfortable, out front. With in the first quartermile a guy blew by me, I thought to myself, " No way he could keep that space" But I could see the light on his head lamp continuet opull away; I figured I would see him in a few miles after the course crushed him.

This particular road march course has a reputation of being brutal ;there was one hill that as I was going up I could almost reach out in front of me and touch the ground, it was that steep. At this point, the re was only one guy infront of me and I saw foot prints that were twice as long as my stride length. I was in awe, my exact thought was, "This is the craziest shit I have seen; that duderan up this hill. "Through out the next couple of h o u r s , I was expecting to come around a corner and find him laid up on the side of the road, but that never happened. Once finished, I was laying out my gear and I saw David hanging out. He had been done for quite a while. Though.

That performance left an impression beyond the guys in my Selection class. I heard recently from Hawk, another SEAL, that some Army guys he worked with on deployment were still talking about that ruck, almost like it is an urban legend. From there I continued to smash through Delta Selection at or near the top of the class. My land navigation skills were better than they'd ever been, but that doesn't mean it was easy. Roads were off limits, there was no flat ground, and for days we bushwhacked up and down steep slopes, in below-freezing temperatures, taking way points, reading maps, and the countless peaks, ridges, and draws that all looked the same. We moved through thick brush and deep snow banks, splashed through icy creeks, and slalomed the winter skeletons of towering trees. It was painful, challenging, and fucking beautiful, and I was smoking it, mashing every test they could conjure.

On the second to last day of Delta Selection, I hit my first four points as fast as usual. Most days there were five waypoints to hit in total, so when I got my fifth I was beyond confident. In my mind, I was the black Daniel Boone. I plotted my point and moseyed down another steep grade. One way to navigate foreign terrain is to track power lines, and I could see that one of those lines in the distance led directly to my fifth, and final point. I hustled down country, tracked the line, turned my conscious mind off, and started dreaming ahead. I knew I was going to rock the final exam—hat forty—mile land navigation I didn't even get to attempt last time because I busted my ankle two days before. I considered my graduation a foregone conclusion, and after that I'd be running and gunning in an elite unit again. As I visualized it, it became all the more real, and my imagination took me far away from the Appalachian Mountains.

The thing about following the power supply is you'd better make damn sure you're on the right line! According to my training, I was supposed to be constantly checking my map, so if I made a misstep I could re ... adjust and head in the right direction without losing too much time, but I was so overconfident I forgot to do that, and I didn't chart backstops either. By the time I woke from fantasy land, I was way off course and almost out of bounds!

I went into panic mode, found my location on the map, humped it to the right power line, sprinted to the top of the mountain and kept running all the way to my fifth point. I still had ninety minutes until drop-dead time but when I got close to the next Humvee I saw another guy heading back toward me!

"Where you headed," I asked as I jogged over.

"I'm off to my sixth point," he said.

"Shit, there's not five points today?! "

"Nah, there's six today, brother."

I checked my watch. I had a little over forty minutes before they called time. I reached the Humvee, took down the coordinates for checkpoint six and studied the map. Thanks to my fuck up, I had two clear options. I could play by the rules and miss drop-dead time or I could break the rules, use the roads at my disposal, and give myself a chance. The one thing on my side was that in special operations they prize a thinking shooter, a soldier willing to do what it takes to meet an objective. All I could do was hope they'd have mercy on me. I plotted the best possible route and took the fuck off. I skirted the woods, used the roads, and whenever I heard a truck rumbling in the near distance, I took cover. A half hour later, at the crest of yet another mountain, I could see the sixth point, our finish line. According to my watch, I had five minutes left.

I flew downhill, sprinting all out, and made drop-dead by one minute. As I caught my breath, our crew was divided and loaded into the covered beds of two separate Humvees. At first glance, my group of guys looked pretty squared away, but given when and where I received my sixth point, every cadre in the place had to know I'd skirted protocol. I didn't know what to think. Was I still in or assed out?

At Delta Selection, one way to be sure you're out is if you feel speed bumps after a day's work. Speed bumps mean you're back at the base, and you're heading home early. That day, when we felt the first one j ar us out of our hopes and dreams, some guys started cursing, others had tears in their eyes. I just shook my head.

"Goggins, what the fuck are you doing here ? " One guy asked. He was shocked to see me sitting alongside him, but I was resigned to my reality because I'd been daydreaming about graduating Delta training and being a part of the force when I hadn't even finished Selection!

"I didn't do what they told me to do," I said. "I fucking deserve to go home."

" Bullshit! You are one of the best guys out here. They're making a huge mistake."

I appreciated his outrage. I expected to make it too, but I couldn't be upset by their decision. Delta brass weren't looking for men who could pass a class with a C, B+, or even an A- effort. They only accepted A+ students, and if you fucked up and delivered a performance that was below your capability they sent you packing. Shit, if you daydream for a split second on the battlefield, that could mean your life and the life of one of your brothers. I understood that.

"No. It was my mistake," I said. " I got this far by staying focused and delivering my best, and I'm going home because I lost focus."

★ ★ ★

It was time to go back to being a SEAL. For the next two years I based in Honolulu as part of a clandestine transport unit called SDV, for SEAL Delivery Vehicles. Operation Red Wings is the best known SDV mission, and you only heard about it because it was such big news. Most SDV work happens in the shadows, and well out of sight. I fit in well over there, and it was great to be back operating again. I lived on Ford Island, with a view of Pearl Harbor right out my living room window. Kate and I had split up, so now I was really living that Spartan life, and still waking up at 5 a.m. to run into work. I had two routes, an eight-miler and a ten-miler, but no matter which I took my body didn't react too well. After only a few miles, I'd feel intense neck pain and dizzy spells. There were several times during my runs that I would have to sit down due to vertigo.

For years I'd harbored a suspicion that we all had a limit on the miles we could run before a full-body breakdown, and I wondered if I was closing in on mine. My body had never felt so tight. I had a knot on the base of my skull that I first noticed after graduating BUD/S. A decade later it had doubled in size. I had knots above my hip flexors too. I went to the doctor to get everything checked out, but they weren't even tumors, much less malignant. When the doctors cleared me of mortal danger, I realized I'd have to live with them and try to forget about long-distance running for a while.

When an activity or exercise that you've always relied on gets taken away from you, like running was for me, it's easy to get stuck in a ·mental rut and stop doing any exercise at all, but I didn't have a quitter's mentality. I gravitated toward the pull-up bar and replicated the workouts I used to do with Sledge. It was an exercise that allowed me to push myself and didn't make me dizzy because I could take a break between sets. After a while I Googled around to see if there was a pull-up record within reach. That's when I read about Stephen Hyland's many pull-up records, including the twenty-four-hour record of 4,020.

At the time I was known as an ultra runner, and I didn't want to be known for just one thing. Who does? Nobody thought of me as an all-around athlete, and this record could change that dynamic. How many people are capable of running 100, 150, even 200 miles and also knocking out over 4,000 pull-ups in a day? I called the Special Operations Warrior Foundation and asked if I could help raise a bit more money. They were thrilled, and next thing I knew, a contact of mine used her networking skills to book me on the damn *Today Show*.

To prepare for the attempt I did 400 pull-ups a day during the week, which took me about seventy minutes. On Saturday I did 1,500 pull-ups, in sets of five to ten reps over three hours, and on Sunday I dialed it back to 750. All that work strengthened my lats, triceps, biceps, and back, prepared my shoulder and elbow joints to take extreme punishment, helped me develop a power-ful gorilla-type grip, and built up my lactic acid tolerance so my muscles could still function long after they were overworked. As game day approached, I shortened recovery and started doing five pull-ups every thirty seconds for two hours. Afterward my arms fell to my side, limp as overstretched rubber bands.

On the eve of my record attempt, my mom and uncle flew

into New York City to help crew me, and we were all systems go until the SEALs nearly killed my *Today Show* appearance at the last minute. No Easy Day, a first-hand account of the Osama Bin Laden raid, had just come out. It was written by one of the operators in the DEVGRU unit that got it done, and Naval Special Warfare brass were not happy. Special Operators are not supposed to share details of the work we do in the field with the general public, and lots of people in the Teams resented that book. I was given a direct order to pull out of the appearance, which didn't make any sense. I wasn't going on camera to talk about operations, and I wasn't on a mission to self-promote. I wanted to raise one million dollars for families of the fallen, and *The Today Show* was the biggest morning show on television.

I'd served in the military for nearly twenty years by that point, without a single infraction on my record, and for the previous four years the Navy had used me as their poster boy. They put me on billboards, I was interviewed on CNN, and I'd jumped out of an airplane on NBC. They placed me in dozens of magazine and newspaper stories, which helped their recruitment mission. Now they were trying to stifle me for no good reason. Hell, if anybody knew the regulations of what I could and could not say it was me. In the nick of time, the Navy's legal department cleared me to proceed.

Billboard during my recruiting days

My interview was brief. I told a Cliffs Notes version of my life story and mentioned I'd be on a liquid diet, drinking a carbohydrate-loaded sports drink as my only nutrition until the record was broken.

"What should we cook for you tomorrow once it's all over?" Savannah Guthrie replied. I laughed and played along, agreeable as hell, but don't get it twisted, I was way out of my comfort zone. I was about to go to war with myself, but I didn't look like it or act like it. As the clock wound down I took my shirt off and was wearing only a pair of lightweight, black running shorts and running shoes.

"Wow, it's like looking at myself in a mirror," .Lauer joked, gesturing toward me.

"This segment just got even more interesting," said Savannah. "All right David, 'best of luck to you. We will be watching."

Someone hit play on *Going the Distance, the Rocky* theme song, and I steppbd to the pull-up bar. It was painted matte black, wrapped with white tape, and stenciled with the phrase, SHOW NO -WEAKNESS in white lettering. I got the last word in as I strapped on my gray gloves.

"Please donate to specialops.org," I said. "We're trying to raise a million dollars."

"Alright, are you ready?" Lauer asked. " Three... two... one... David, go! "

With that, the clock started and I rocked a set o fe ight pull-ups. The rules laid down by the Guinness Book ofWorld Records were clear. I had to start each pull-up from a dead hang with arms fully extended, and my chin had to exceed the bar.

"So it begins," Savannah said.

I smiled for the camera and looked relaxed, but even those first pull-ups didn't feel right. Part of it was situational. I was a lone fish in a glass box aquarium that attracted sunshine and reflected a bank of hot show lights. The other half was technical. From the very first pull-up I noticed that the bar had a lot more give than I was used to. I didn't have my usual power and anticipated a long fucking day. At first, I blocked that shit out. Had to. A looser bar just meant a stronger effort and gave me another opportunity to be uncommon.

Throughout the day people passed by on the street below, waved, and cheered. I waved back, kept to my plan, and rocked six pull-ups on the minute, every damn minute, but it wasn't easy because of that rickety bar. My force was getting dissipated, and after hundreds of pull-ups, dissipation took its toll. Each subsequent pull-up required a monumental effort, a stronger grip, and at the 1,500 mark my forearms hurt like hell. My massage therapist rubbed them down between sets, but they bulged with lactic acid which seeped into every muscle in my upper body.

After more than six long hours, and with 2,000 pull-ups in the bank, I took my first ten-minute break. I was well ahead of my twenty-four-hour pace, and the sun angled lower on the horizon, which reduced the mercury in the room to manageable. It was late enough that the whole studio was shut down. It was just me, a few friends, a massage therapist, and my mother. *Today Show* cameras were set up and rolling to clock me and make sure I kept to regulations. I had more than 2,000 pull-ups still to go, and for the first time that day, doubt carved out a home in my brain.

I didn't vocalize my negativity, and I tried to reset my mind for the second half push, but the truth was my whole plan had gone to hell. My carbohydrate drink wasn't giving me the power I needed, and I didn't have a Plan B, so I ordered and downed a cheeseburger. It felt good to have some real food. Meanwhile, my team tried to stabilize the bar by tying it to the pipes in the rafters, but instead of recharging my system like I'd hoped, the long break had an adverse effect.

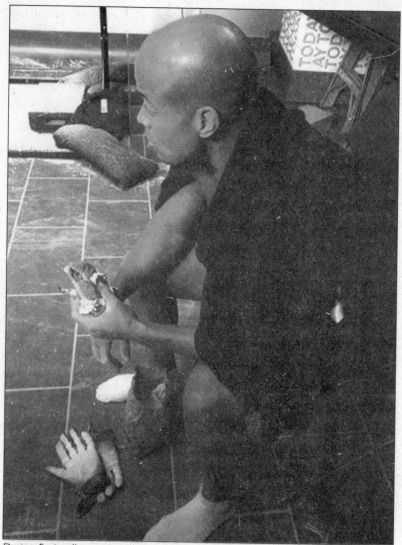

During first pull-up record attempt

My body was shutting down, while my mind swirled with panic because I'd made a pledge and staked my name on a quest to raise money and break a record, and I already knew that there was no way on this earth I was gonna be able to get it done. It took me five hours to do another 500 pull-ups—that's an average of under two pull-ups per minute. I was verging on total muscle failure after doing only 1,000 more pull-ups than I would rock in three hours at the gym on a typical Saturday with no ill effects. How was that possible?

I tried to bull my way through, but tension and lactic acid had overwhelmed my system and my upper body was a lump of dough. I had never hit muscle failure before in my life. I'd run on broken legs in BUD/S, run nearly a hundred miles on broken feet, and accomplished dozens of physical feats with a hole in my heart. But late at night, on the second floor of the NBC tower, I pulled the plug. After my 2,500th pull-up, I could barely lift my hands high enough to grip the bar, let alone clear it with my chin, and just like that, it was over. There would be no celebratory breakfast with Savannah and Matt. There would be no celebration at all. I failed, and I'd failed in front of millions of people.

So did I hang my head in shame and misery? Fuck no! To me a failure is just a stepping stone to future success. The next morning, my phone was blowing up so I left it in my hotel room and went for a run in Central Park. I needed zero distractions and time enough to go back through what I'd done well and where I'd fallen short. In the military, after every real-world mission or field exercise, we fill out After Action Reports (AARs), which serve as live autopsies. We do them no matter the outcome, and if you're analyzing a failure like I was, the AAR is absolutely crucial. Because when you're headed into uncharted territory there are no books to study, no YouTube instructional videos to watch. All I had to read were my mistakes, and I considered all variables.

First of all, I should never have gone on that show. My motivation was solid. It was a good idea to try to increase awareness and raise money for the foundation, and while I required exposure to raise the amount I'd hoped, by thinking of money first (always a bad idea) I wasn't focused on the task at hand. To break this record, I needed an optimal environment, and that realization blasted me like a surprise attack. I didn't respect the record enough going in. I thought I could have broken it on a rusty bar bolted to the back of a pick-up truck with loose shocks, so even though I tested the bar twice before game day, it never bothered me enough to make a change, and my lack of focus and attention to detail cost me a shot at immortality. There were also way too many bubbly looky-loos buzzing in and out of the room, asking for pictures between sets. This was the beginning of the selfie era, and that sickness most definitely invaded my motherfucking safe space

Obviously, my break was too long. I figured massage would counteract the swelling and lactic acid build -up, but I was wrong about that too, and I should have taken more salt tablets to prevent cramping. Before my attempt, haters found me online and predicted my failure, but I ignored them and didn't fully absorb the hard truths couched in their negativity. I thought, as long as I trained hard, the record would be mine, and as a result, I wasn't as well-prepared as I should have been.

You can't prepare for unknown factors, but if you have a better pre-game focus, you will likely only have to deal with one or two rather than ten. In New York, too many bubbled up, and unknown factors usually blaze a wake of doubt . Afterward, I was eye to eye with my haters and acknowledged that my margin for error was small. I weighed 210 pounds, much heavier than anyone else who had ever tried to break that record, and my probability of failure was high.

I didn't touch a pull-up bar for two weeks, but once back in Honolulu I hammered sets at my home gym and noticed the difference in the bar right way. Still, I had to resist the temptation to blame everything on that loose bar because odds were that a firmer one wouldn't translate into an extra 1,521 pull-ups. I researched gymnast chalk, gloves, and taping systems. I sampled and experimented. This time I wanted a fan set below the bar to cool me down between sets, and I switched up my nutrition. Instead of running off pure carbs I added in some protein and bananas to prevent cramping. When it came time to choose a location to attempt the record, I knew I needed to get back to who I am at my core. That meant losing the glitz and setting up shop in a dungeon. And on a trip to Nashville, I found just the place, a Crossfit gym a mile from my mother's house, owned by a former marine named Nand or Tamaska.

After emailing a couple of times, I ran over to Crossfit Brentwood Hills to meet him. It was set in a strip mall, a few doors down from a Target, and there was nothing fancy about the place. It had black mat floors, buckets of chalk, racks of iron, and lots of hard motherfuckers doing work. When I walked in, the first thing I did was grab the pull-up bar and shake it. It was bolted into the ground just like I'd hoped. Even a little sway in the bar would require me to adjust my grip mid -set, and when your goal is 4,021 pull-ups, all minuscule movements accumulate into a reservoir of wasted energy, which takes a toll.

"This is exactly what I need," I said, gripping the bar.

"Yeah," Nandor said. "They have to be sturdy to double as our squat racks."

In addition to its strength and stability, it was the right height. I didn't want a short bar, because bending your legs can cause cramping in the hamstrings. I needed it high enough that I could grab it when standing on my toes.

I could tell right away that Nandor was a perfect co-conspirator for this mission. He had been an enlisted man, got into Crossfit, and moved to Nashville from Atlanta with his wife and family to open his first gym. Not many people are willing to open their doors and let a stranger take over their gym, but Nandor was down with the Warrior Foundation cause.

My second attempt was scheduled for November, and for five straight weeks I did 500-1,300 pull-ups a day at my home gym in Hawaii. During my last island session, I did 2,000 pull-ups in five hours, then caught a flight to Nashville, arriving six days before my attempt.

Nandor rallied members of his gym to act as witnesses and my support crew. He took care of the playlist, sourced the chalk, and set up a break room in back in case I needed it. He also put out a press release. I trained at his gym in the run-up to game day, and a local news channel came by to file a report. The local newspaper did a story too. It was small scale, but Nashville was growing curious, especially the Crossfit junkies. Several showed up to absorb the scene. I spoke with Nandor recently, and I liked how he put it.

" People have been running for decades, and running long distances, but 4,000 pull-ups, the human body isn't designed to do that. So to get a chance to witness something like that was pretty neat."

I rested the full day before the attempt and when I showed up to the gym I felt strong and prepared for the minefield ahead. Nandor and my mom collaborated to have everything dialed in. There was a sleek digital timer on the wall which also tracked my count, plus they.had two battery-powered wall clocks running as back ups. There was a Guinness Book of World Records banner hanging over the bar, and a video crew because every rep had to be recorded for potential review. My tape was right. My gloves perfect. The bar was bolted solid, and when I started out, my performance was explosive.

The numbers remained the same. I was gunning for six pull-ups every minute, on the minute, and during the first ten sets I rose up chest high. Then I remembered my game plan to minimize needless movement and wasted energy. On my initial attempt I felt pressure to get my chin well over the bar, but while all that extra space made for a good show, it did not and would not help me get the damn record. This time I told myself to barely clear the bar with my chin, and not to use my arms and hands for anything other than pull-ups. Instead of reaching down for my water bottle like I had in New York, I set it on a stack of wooden boxes (the kind used for box jumps), so all I had to do was turn and suck my nutrition through a straw. The first sip triggered me to dial back my pull-up motion and from then on, I remained disciplined as I piled up numbers. I was on my game and confident as hell. I wasn't thinking of just 4,020 pull-ups. I wanted to go the full twenty-four hours. If I did that, 5,000 was possible, or even 6,000!

I remained hyper vigilant, scanning for any physical issues that could crop up and derail the attempt. All was smooth until, after almost four hours and 1,300 pull-ups, my hands started to blister. In between sets my mom hit me with Second Skin so I could stay on top of the cuts. This was a new problem for me, and I remembered all the doubting comments I'd read on social media prior to my attempt. My arms were too long, they said. I weighed too much. My form wasn't ideal, I put too much pressure on my hands. I'd disregarded that last comment because during my first attempt I didn't have palm issues, but in the midst of my second I realized it was because the first bar had so much give. This time I had more stability and power, but over time that hard-ass bar did damage.

Still, I labored on and after 1,700 pull-ups my forearms

started aching, and when I bent my arms, my biceps pinched too. I remembered those sensations from my first go 'round. It was the beginning of cramps, so between sets I downed salt tablets and ate two bananas, and that took care of my muscular discomfort. My palms just kept getting worse.

A hundred and fifty pull-ups later I could feel them splitting down the middle beneath my gloves. I knew I should stop and try to fix the problem, but I also knew that might trigger my body to stiffen up and shut down. I was fighting two fires at once and didn't know where to strike first. I opted to stay on the minute by minute pace, and in between experimented with different solutions. I wore two pairs of gloves, then three. I resorted to my old friend, duct tape. Didn't help. I couldn't wrap the bar in pads because that was against Guinness rules. All I could do was try anything and everything to stay in the fight.

Ten hours into the attempt, I hit a wall. I was down to three pull-ups a minute on the minute. The pain was excruciating and I needed some relief. I took my right glove off. Layers of skin came off with it. My palm looked like raw hamburger. My mom called a doctor friend, Regina, who lived nearby and the two of us went into the back room to wait for her and try to salvage my record attempt. When Regina showed up she evaluated the situation, pulled out a syringe, loaded it with local anesthetic and dipped the needle toward the open wound on my right hand.

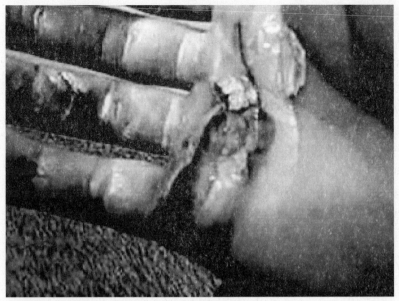
My hand during the second pull-up record attempt

She looked over. My heart pounded, sweat saturated every inch of my skin. I could feel my muscles cooling down and stiffening up, but I nodded, turned away, and she sunk that needle in deep. It hurt so fucking bad, but I held my primal scream inside. *Show no weakness* remained my motto, but that didn't mean I felt strong. My mom pulled off my left glove, anticipating the second shot, but Regina was busy examining the swelling in my biceps and the bulging spasms in my forearms.

"You look like you're in rhabdomyolysis, David," she said. "You shouldn't continue. It's dangerous." I had no idea what the fuck she was talking about, so she broke it down. _

There's a phenomenon that happens when one muscle group is worked way too hard for way too long. The muscles become starved of glucose and break down, leaking myoglobin, a fibrous protein that stores oxygen in the muscle, into the bloodstream. When that happens, it's up to the kidneys to filter all those proteins out and if they become overwhelmed, they shut down. "People can die from rhabdo," she said.

My hands throbbed with agony. My muscles were locking up, and the stakes couldn't be higher. Any rational person would have thrown in the towel, but I could hear *Going the Distance* booming from the speakers, and knew that this was my 14th round, *Cut me, Mick,* moment.

Fuck rationality. I held up my left palm and had Regina sink her needle in. Waves of pain washed through me as a bumper crop of doubt flowered in my mind. She wrapped both palms in layers of gauze and medical tape and fitted me with a fresh pair of gloves. Then I stalked back out onto the gym floor and got back to work. I was at 2,900, and as long as I remained in the fight, I still believed anything was possible.

I did sets of twos and threes on the minute for two hours, but it felt like I was gripping a red hot, melting rod, which meant I was down to using my fingertips to grip the bar. First I used four fingers, then three. I was able to gut out one hundred more pull-ups, then one hundred more. Hours ticked by. I crept closer but with my body in rhabdo, breakdown was imminent. I did several sets of pull-ups with my wrists dangling over the bar. It sounds impossible, but I managed until the numbing agents stopped working. Then even bending my fingers felt like I was stabbing myself in the hand with a sharp knife.

After eclipsing 3,200 pull-ups, I worked out the math and realized if I could do 800 sets of one, it would take thirteen hours and change to break the record and I would just beat the clock. I lasted forty-five minutes. The pain was too much and the vibe in the room went from optimistic to somber. I was still trying to show as little weakness as I could, but the volunteers could see me messing with my gloves and grip, and knew something was drastically wrong. When I went into the back to regroup a second time I heard a collective sigh that sounded like doom.

Regina and my mother unwrapped the tape on my hands, and I could feel my flesh peeling like a banana. Both palms were filleted open down to the dermis, which is where our nerves lie. Achilles had his heel, and when it came to pull-ups, my gift, and my undoing, were my hands. The doubters were right. I wasn't one of those lightweight, graceful pull-up guys. I was powerful, and the power came from my grip. But now my hand better resembled a physiology mannequin than something human.

Emotionally, I was wasted. Not just because of my sheer physical exhaustion or because I couldn't get the record for myself, but because so many people had come out to help. I'd taken over Nandar's gym and felt like I'd disappointed everyone. Without a word, my mother and I slipped out the back door like we were escaping a crime scene, and as she drove to the hospital, I couldn't stop thinking, *I'm better than this!*

While Nand or and his team broke down the clocks, untied the banners, swept up chalk, and peeled bloody tape off their pull-up bar, my mom and I slumped into chairs in the ER waiting room. I was holding what was left of my glove. It looked like it was lifted from the OJ Simpson crime scene, like it had been marinated in blood. She eyeballed me and shook her head.

"Well," she said, "I know one thing... "

After a long pause I turned to face her.

"What's that?"

"You're gonna do this again."

She read my damn mind. I was already doing my live autopsy and would run through a complete AAR on paper as soon as my bloody hands would allow. I knew there was treasure in this wreckage and leverage to be gained somewhere. I just had to piece it together like a puzzle. And the fact that she realized that without my saying so fired me up.

A lot of us surround ourselves with people who speak to our desire for comfort. Who would rather treat the pain of our wounds and prevent further injury than help us callous over them and try again. We need to surround ourselves with people who will tell us what we need to hear, not what we want to hear, but at the same time not make us feel we're up against the impossible. My mother was my biggest fan. Whenever I failed in life she was always asking me when and where I would go after it again. She never said, *Well, maybe it isn't meant to be.*

Most wars are won or lost in our own heads, and when we're in a foxhole we usually aren't alone, and we need to be confident in the quality of the heart, mind, and dialogue of the person hunkered down with us. Because at some point we will need some empowering words to keep us focused and deadly. In that hospital, in my own personal foxhole, I was swimming in doubt. I fell 800 pull-ups short and I knew what 800 pull-ups felt like. That's a long fucking day! But there was nobody else I'd rather have been in that foxhole with.

"Don't worry," she said. " I'll start calling those witnesses up as soon as we get home."

"Roger that," I said. "Tell them I'll be back on that bar in two months."

★ ★ ★

In life, there is no gift as overlooked or inevitable as failure. I've had quite a few and have learned to relish them, because if you do the forensics you'll find clues about where to make adjustments and how to eventually accomplish your task. I'm not talking about a mental list either. After the second attempt, I wrote everything out long-hand, but didn't start with the obvious issue, my grip. Initially, I brainstormed everything that went well, because in every failure a lot of good things will have happened, and we must acknowledge them.

The best takeaway from the Nashville attempt was Nandor's place. His dungeon of a gym was the perfect environment for me. Yeah, I'm on social media, and in the spotlight from time to time, but I am not a Hollywood person. I get my strength from a very dark place, and Nandor's gym wasn't a phony-ass, happy factory. It was dark, sweaty, painful, and real. I called him the very next day and asked if I could come back to train and make another run at the record. I'd taken a lot of his time and energy and left behind a mess, so I had no idea how he'd respond.

"Yeah, motherfucker," he said. " Let's go! " It meant a lot to have his support again.

Another positive was how I handled my second meltdown. I was off the mat and on the comeback trail before I even saw the ER doc. That's where you want to be. You can't let a simple failure derail your mission, or let it worm so far up your ass it takes over your brain and sabotages your relationships with people who are close to you. Everyone fails sometimes and life isn't supposed to be fair, much less bend to your every whim.

Luck is a capricious bitch. It won't always go your way, so you can't get trapped in this idea that just because you've imagined a possibility for yourself that you somehow deserve it. Your entitled mind is dead weight. Cut it loose. Don't focus on what you think you deserve. Take aim on what you are willing to earn! I never blamed anyone for my failures, and I didn't hang my head in Nashville. I stayed humble and sidestepped my entitled mind because I knew damn well I hadn't earned my record. The scoreboard does not lie, and I didn't delude myself otherwise. Believe it or not, most people prefer delusion. They blame others or bad luck or chaotic circumstance. I didn't, which was positive.

I listed most of the equipment we used on the positive side of the AAR, as well. The tape and chalk worked, and even though the bar tore me the fuck up, it also got me 700 additional pull-ups, so I was headed in the right direction. Another positive was the support of Nandor's Crossfit community. It felt great to be surrounded by such intense, respectful people, but this time I'd need to cut the number of volunteers in half. I wanted as little buzz in that room as possible.

After listing out all the plusses, it was time to kick the tires on my mindset, and if you're doing your post-faceplant due diligence, you should do that too. That means checking yourself on how and what you were thinking during the preparation and execution phases of your failure. My commitment to preparation and determination in the fight are always there. They didn't waver, but my belief was shakier than I cared to admit, and as I prepared for my third go 'round it was imperative to move beyond doubt.

That wasn't easy because after my second failure in as many attempts, the doubters were everywhere online. The record holder, Stephen Hyland, was light and spidery strong with thick, muscular palms. He was the perfect build for the pull-up record, and everyone was telling me I was just too big, my form was too brutal, and that I should stop trying to go for it before I hurt myself even worse. They pointed to the scoreboard that doesn't lie. I was still over Boo pull-ups away from the record. That's more than I gained between my first and second attempts. From the beginning some o them had predicted my hands would give out, and when that truth revealed itself in Nashville it presented a big mental hurdle. Part of me wondered if those motherfuckers were right. If I was trying to achieve the impossible.

Then I thought of an English middle-distance runner from back in the day named Roger Bannister. When Bannister was trying to break the four-minute mile in the 1950s, experts told him it couldn't be done, but that didn't stop him. He failed again and again, but he persevered, and when he ran his historic mile in 3=59.4 on May 6, 1954, he didn't just break a record, he broke open the floodgates simply by proving it possible. Six weeks later, his record was eclipsed, and by now over 1,000 runners have done what was once thought to be beyond human capability.

We are all guilty of allowing so-called experts, or just people who have more experience in a given field than we do, to cap our potential. One of the reasons we love sports is because we also love watching those glass ceilings get shattered. If I was going to be the next athlete to smash popular perception, I'd need to stop listening to doubt, whether it streamed in from the outside or bubbled up from within, and the best way to do that was to decide that the pull-up record was already mine. I didn't know when it would officially become mine. It might be in two months or twenty years, but once I decided it belonged to me and decoupled it from the calendar, I was filled with confidence and relieved of any and all pressure because my task morphed from trying to achieve the impossible into working toward an inevitability. But to get there, I'd have to find the tactical advantage I'd been missing

A tactical review is the final and most vital piece of any live autopsy or AAR. And while I had improved tactically from the first attempt—working on a more stable bar and minimizing wasted energy—I still fell 800 reps short, so we needed to delve deeper into the numbers. Six pull-ups per minute on the minute had failed me twice. Yes, it placed me on a fast track to 4,020, but I never got there. This time, I decided to start slower to go further.

I also knew from experience that I would hit some sort of wall after ten hours and that my response couldn't be a longer break. The ten-hour mark smacked me in my face twice and both times I stopped for five minutes or longer, which led to ultimate failure pretty quickly. I needed to stay true to my strategy and limit any long breaks to four minutes max.

Now, about that pull-up bar. Yeah, it would probably tear me up again, so I needed to find a workaround. According to the rules, I wouldn't be allowed to switch up the distance between my hands mid-attempt. The width would have to remain the same from the first pull-up. The only thing I could change would be how I was going to protect my hands. In the run-up to my third attempt, I experimented with all different types of gloves. I also got clearance to use custom foam pads to protect my palms. I remembered seeing a couple SEAL buddies use slices of foam mattresses to protect their hands when they were lifting heavy weights, and called on a mattress company to custom design form-fitting pads for my hands. Guinness approved the equipment, and at 10 a.m .., on January 19, 2013, two months after failing for the second time, I was back on the bar at Crossfit Brentwood Hills.

I started slow and easy with five pull-ups on the minute. I didn't strap my foam pads with tape. I just held them in place around the bar, and they seemed to work well. Within an hour the foam had formed around my hands, insulating them from molten-iron hell. Or so I fucking hoped. At around the two-hour, 600 rep mark, I asked Nandor to play *Going the Distance* on a loop. I felt something click inside and went full cyborg.

I found a rhythm on the bar and between sets I sat on a weight bench and stared at the chalk-dusted floor. My point of view narrowed into tunnel vision as I prepared my mind for the hell that was to come. When the first blister opened on my palm I knew shit was about to get real. But this time, thanks to my failures and forensics, I was ready.

That doesn't mean I was having any fun. I wasn't. I was over it. I didn't want to do pull-ups anymore, but achieving goals or overcoming obstacles doesn't have to be fun. Seeds burst from the inside out in a self-destructive ritual of new life. Does that sound like fucking fun? Like it feels good? I wasn't in that gym to get happy or do what I wanted to be doing. I was there to turn myself inside out if that's what it took to blast through any and all mental, emotional, and physical barriers.

After twelve hours, I finally hit 3,000 pull-ups, a major checkpoint for me, and felt like I'd run headfirst into a wall. I was exasperated, in agony, and my hands were starting to come apart again. I was still a long way from the record, and I felt all the eyeballs in the room upon me. With them came the crushing weight of failure and humiliation. Suddenly, I was back in the cage during my third Hell Week, taping my shins and ankles before mustering up with a new BUD/S class who'd heard it was my last chance.

It takes great strength to be vulnerable enough to put your ass on the line, in public, and work toward a dream that feels like it's slipping away. We all have eyeballs on us. Our family and friends are watching, and even if you're surrounded by positive people, they will have ideas about who you are, what you're good at, and how you should focus your energy. That shit is just human nature, and if you try to break out of their box you'll get some unsolicited advice that has a way of smothering your aspirations if you let it. Often our people don't mean any harm. Nobody who cares about us actually wants us to get hurt. They want us to be safe, comfortable, and happy, and not to have to stare at the floor in a dungeon sifting through shards of our broken dreams. Too bad.

There's a lot of potential in those moments of pain. And if you figure out how to piece that picture back together, you'll find a hell of a lot of power there too!

I kept my break to just four minutes, as planned. Long enough to stuff my hands, and those foam pads, into a pair of padded gloves. But when I got back on the b ar I felt slow and weak. Nandor, his wife, and the other volunteers saw my struggle, but they left me the fuck alone to put in my ear buds, channel Rocky Balboa, and keep grinding one rep at a time. I went from four pull-ups on the minute to three, and found my cyborg trance again. I went ugly, I got dark. I imagined my pain was the creation of a mad scientist named Stephen Hyland, the evil genius who was in temporary possession of my record and my soul. It was him! That motherfucker was torturing me from across the globe, and it was up to me and only me to keep piling up numbers and steamroll toward him, if I wanted to take his motherfucking soul !

To be clear, I wasn't angry with Hyland—I don't even know him! I went there to find the edge I needed to keep going. I got personal with him in my head, not out of overconfidence or envy, but to drown out my own doubt. Life is a head game. This was just the latest angle I used to win a game within that game. I had to find an edge somewhere, and if you find it in the person standing in your way, that's potent.

As the hours ticked past midnight I started closing the distance between us, but the pull-ups weren't coming fast and they weren't coming easy. I was tired mentally and physically, deep into rhabdo, and I was down to three pull-ups a minute. When I hit 3,800 pull-ups I felt like I could see the mountain top. I also knew it was possible to go from being able to do three pull-ups to no pull-ups in a flash. There are stories of people at Bad water who reached mile 129 and couldn't finish a 135-mile race ! You never know when you'll reach your 100 percent and hit the point of total muscle fatigue. I kept waiting for that moment to come, when I couldn't pick my arms up anymore. Doubt stalked me like a shadow. I tried my best to control it or silence it, yet it kept reappearing, following me, pushing me.

After seventeen hours of pain, around 3 a.m. on January 20, 2013, I did my 4,020th and 4,021st pull-up, and the record was mine. Everyone in the gym cheered, but I stayed composed. After two more sets and 4,030 total pull-ups, I took my headphones out, stared into the camera· and said, "I tracked you down, Stephen Hyland!"

In one day, I'd lifted the equivalent of 846,030 pounds, nearly three times the weight of the Space Shuttle! Cheers spread to laughter as I pulled off my gloves and disappeared into the back room, but much to everyone's surprise, I was not in the mood to celebrate.

Does that shock you too? You know that my refrigerator is never full, and it never will be because I live a mission-driven life, always on the hunt for the next challenge. That mindset is the reason I broke that record, finished Bad water, became a SEAL, rocked Ranger School, and on down the list. In my mind I'm that racehorse always chasing a carrot I'll never catch, forever trying to prove myself to myself. And when you live that way and attain a goal, success feels anti-climactic.

Unlike my initial shot at the record, my success barely made a ripple in the news cycle. Which was just fine. I wasn't doing it for adulation. I raised some money, and I learned all I could from that pull-up bar. After logging more than 67,000 pull-ups in nine months, it was time to put them in my Cookie Jar and move on. Because- life 'is one long motherfucking imaginary game that has no scoreboard, no referee, and isn't over until we're dead and buried.

And all I'd ever wanted from it was to become successful in my own eyes. That didn't mean wealth or celebrity, a garage full of hot cars, or a harem of beautiful women trailing after me. It meant becot:ning the hardest motherfucker who ever lived. Sure, I stacked up some failures along the way, but in my mind the record proved that I was close. Only the game wasn't over, and being hard came with the requirement to drain every drop of ability from my mind, body, and soul before the whistle blew.

I would remain in constant pursuit. I wouldn't leave anything on the table. I wanted to earn my final resting place. That's how I thought back then, anyway. Because I had no clue how close to the end I already was.

CHALLENGE #10

Think about your most recent and your most heart-wrenching failures. Break out that journal one last time. Log off the digital version and write them out long-hand. I want you to feel this process because you are about to file your own, belated After Action Reports.

First off, write out all the good things, everything that went well, from your failures. Be detailed and generous with yourself. A lot of good things will have happened. It's rarely all bad. Then note how you handled your failure. Did it affect your life and your relationships? How so?

How did you think throughout the preparation for and during the execution stage of your failure? You have to know how you were thinking at each step because it's all about mindset, and that's where most people fall short.

Now go back through and make a list of things you can fix. This isn't time to be soft or generous. Be brutally honest, write them all out. Study them. Then look at your calendar and schedule another attempt as soon as possible. If the failure happened in childhood, and you can't recreate the Little League all-star game you choked in, I still want you to write that report because you'll likely be able to use that information to achieve any goal going forward.

As you prepare, keep that AAR handy, consult your Accountability Mirror, and make all necessary adjustments. When it comes time to execute, keep everything we've learned about the power of a calloused mind, the Cookie Jar, and The 40% Rule in the forefront of your mind. Control your mindset. Dominate your thought process. This life is all a fucking mind game. Realize that. Own it!

And if you fail again, so the fuck be it. Take the pain. Repeat these steps and keep fighting. That's what it's all about. Share your stories from preparation, training, and execution on social media with the hash tags #canthurtme #empowermentoffailure.

CHAPTER ELEVEN

WHAT IF?

BEFORE THE RACE EVEN KICKED OFF I KNEW I WAS FUCKED . In 2014, the National Park Service wouldn't approve the traditional Bad water course, so Chris Kostman redrew the map. Instead of starting in Death Valley National Park and running forty-two miles through the hottest desert on the planet, it would launch further upcountry at the base of a twenty-two-mile climb. That wasn't my problem. It was the fact that I toed the line eleven pounds over my usual race weight, and had gained ten of those pounds in the previous seven days. I wasn't a fat ass. To the average eye I looked fit, but Bad water wasn't an average race. To run and finish strong, my condition needed to be tip top, and I was far from it. Whatever was happening to me came as a shock, because after two years of substandard running, I thought I'd gotten my powers back.

The previous January I'd won a one-hundred-kilometer glacial trail race called Frozen Otter. It wasn't as hard as the Hurt 100 but it was close. Set in Wisconsin, just outside Milwaukee, the course laid out like a lopsided figure eight, with the start-finish at the center. We passed it between the two loops, which enabled us to stock up on food and other necessary supplies from our cars, and stuff them into our packs with our emergency supplies. The weather can turn evil out there, and race organizers compiled a list of necessities we were required to have on us at all times so we wouldn't die of dehydration, hypothermia, or exposure.

The first lap was the larger loop of the two and when we set off the temperature was sitting at zero degrees Fahrenheit. Those trails were never plowed. In some places, snow piled into drifts. In others the trails seemed purposefully glazed with slick ice. Which presented a problem because I wasn't wearing boots or trail shoes like most of my competitors. I laced up my standard running shoes, and tucked them into some cheap ass crampons, which theoretically were supposed to grip the ice and keep me upright. Well, the ice won that war and my crampons snapped off in the first hour. Nevertheless, I was leading the race and breaking trail in an average of six to twelve inches of snow. In some places the drifts were piled much higher. My feet were cold and wet from the starting gun, and within two hours they felt frozen through, especially my toes. My top half wasn't faring much better. When you sweat in below-freezing temperature, salt on your body chafes the skin. My underarms and chest were cracking raspberry red. I was covered in rashes, my toes hurt with every step, but none of that registered too high on my pain scale, because I was running free.

For the first time since my second heart surgery, my body was beginning to put itself back together. I was getting 100 percent of my oxygen supply like everyone else, my endurance and strength were next-level, and though the trail was a slippery mess, my technique was dialed-in too. I was way out front and stopped at my car for a sandwich before the last twenty-two-mile loop. My toes throbbed with evil pain. I suspected they were frostbitten, which meant I was in danger of losing some of them, hut I didn't want to take off my shoes and look. Once again, doubt and fear were popping in my brain, reminding me that only a handful of people had ever finished the Frozen Otter, and that no lead was safe in that kind of cold. Weather, more than any other variable, can break a motherfucker down quick. But I didn't listen to any of that. I created a new dialogue and told myself to finish the race strong and worry about amputated toes at the hospital after I was crowned champion.

I ran back onto the course. A blast of sun had melted some of the snow earlier in the day, but the cold wind iced up the trail nicely. As I ran, I flashed to my first year at Hurt 100 and the great Karl Meltzer. Back then, I was a plodder. I hit the turf with my heel first, and peeling the muddy trail with the entire surface area of my foot increased my odds of slipping and falling. Karl didn't run like that. He moved like a goat, bouncing on his toes and running along the edges of the trail. As soon as his toes hit the ground he fired his legs into the air. That's why he looked like he was floating. By design, he barely touched the ground, while his head and core remained stable and engaged. From that moment onward, his movements were permanently etched in my brain like a cave painting. I visualized them all the time and put his techniques into practice during training runs.

They say it takes sixty-six days to build a habit. For me it takes a hell of a lot longer than that, but I eventually get there, and during all those years of ultra training and competition I was working on my craft. A true runner analyzes their form. We didn't learn how to do that in the SEALs, but being around so many ultra runners for years, I was able to absorb and practice skills that seemed unnatural at first. At Frozen Otter, my main focus was to hit ⬜e ground soft; to touch it just enough to explode. During my third BUD/S class and then my first platoon, when I was considered one of the better runners, my head bounced all over the place. My weight wasn't balanced and when my foot hit the ground all my weight would be supported by that one leg, which led to some awkward falls on slippery terrain. Through trial and error, and thousands of hours of training, I learned to maintain balance.

At Frozen Otter it all came together. With speed and grace, I navigated steep, slippery trails. I kept my head flat and still, my motion quiet as possible, and my steps silent by running on the front of my feet. When I picked up speed, it was as if I'd disappeared into a white wind, elevated into a meditative state. I became Karl Meltzer. Now it was me who looked to be levitating over an impossible trail, and I finished the race in sixteen hours, smashing the course record and winning the Frozen Otter title without losing any toes.

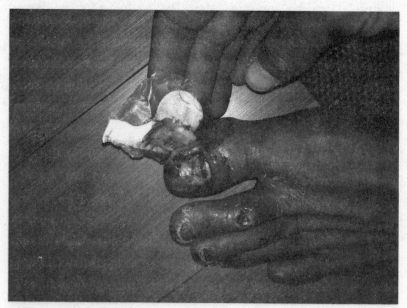

Toes after Frozen Otter

Two years earlier I was stricken with dizzy spells during easy six-mile runs. In 2013, I was forced to walk over one-hundred miles of Badwater, and finished in seventeenth place. I'd been on a downslide and thought my days of contention for titles were long past over. After Frozen Otter, I was tempted to believe I'd made it all the way back and then some, and that my best ultra years were actually ahead of me. I took that energy into my preparations for Badwater 2014 .

I was living in Chicago at the time, working as an instructor in BUD/S prep, a school that prepared candidates to deal with the harsh reality they would face in BUD/S. After more than twenty years, I was in my final year of military service, and by being placed in a position to drop wisdom on the would-bes and wannabes, it felt like I'd come full circle. As usual I would run ten miles to work and back, and squeeze in another eight miles during lunch when I could. On the weekends I'd do at least one thirty-five- to forty-mile run. It all added up to a succession of 130-mile weeks and I was feeling strong. As spring bloomed I added a heat training component by slipping on four or five layers of sweats, a beanie, and a Gore-Tex jacket before hitting the streets. When I'd show up at work, my fellow SEAL instructors would watch, amazed, as I peeled off my wet clothes and stuffed them into black trash bags that together weighed nearly fifteen pounds.

I started my taper four weeks out, and went from 130-mile weeks to an eighty-mile week, then down to sixty, forty, and twenty. Tapering is supposed to generate an abundance of energy as you eat and rest, enabling the body to repair all the damage done and get you primed for competition. Instead, I'd never felt worse. I wasn't ·hungry and couldn't sleep at all. Some people said my body was starved of calories. Others suggested I might be low on sodium. My doctor measured my thyroid and it was a little off, but the readings weren't so bad to explain how shitty I felt. Perhaps the explanation was simple. That I was over-trained.

Two weeks before the race I considered pulling out. I worried it was my heart again because on easy runs I felt a surge of adrenaline that I couldn't vent. Even a mellow pace sent my pulse racing into arrhythmia. Ten days before the race, I landed in Vegas. I'd scheduled five runs but couldn't get past the three-mile mark on any of them. I wasn't eating that much but the weight kept piling on. It was all water. I. sought out another doctor who confirmed there was nothing physically wrong with me and when I heard that, I was not about to be a pussy.

During the opening miles and initial climb of Bad water 2014, my heart rate ran high, but part of that was the altitude, and twenty-two miles later I made it to the top in sixth or seventh place. Surprised and proud, I thought, let's see if I can go downhill. I've never enjoyed the brutality of running down a steep incline because it shreds the quads, but I also thought it would allow me to reset and calm my breath. My body refused. I couldn't catch my breath at all. I hit the fiat section at the bottom, slowed my pace, and began to walk. My competitors passed me by as my thighs twitched uncontrollably. My muscle spasms were so bad, my quads looked like there was an alien rattling around inside them.

And I still didn't stop! I walked for four full miles before seeking shelter in a Lone Pine motel room where the Badwater medical team had set up shop. They checked me out and saw that my blood pressure was a bit low but easily corrected. They couldn't find a single metric that could explain how fucked I felt.

I ate some solid food, rested and decided to try one more time. There was a flat section leaving Lone Pine and I thought if I could knock that out perhaps I'd catch a second wind, but six or seven miles later my sails were still empty, and I'd given all

I had. My muscles trembled and twitched, my heart jumped up and down the chart. I looked over at my pacer and said, "That's it, man. I'm done."

My support vehicle pulled up behind us and I climbed inside. A few minutes later I was laying on that same motel bed, with my tail between my legs. I'd lasted just fifty miles, but any humiliation that came with quitting-II:ot something I was used to—was drowned out by an instinct that something was way the fuck off. It wasn't my fear talking or my desire for comfort. This time, I was certain that if I didn't stop trying to break through this barrier, I wouldn't make it out of the Sierras alive.

We left Lone Pine for Las Vegas the next night, and for two days I did my best to rest and recover, hoping my body would settle somewhere close to equilibrium. We were staying at the Wynn, and on that third morning I went for a jog to see if I had anything in the tank. One mile later, my heart was in my throat, and I shut it down. I walked back to the hotel, knowing that despite what the doctors said, I was sick and suspected that whatever I had was serious.

Later that night, after seeing a movie in the Vegas suburbs, I felt weak as we strolled to a nearby restaurant, the Elephant Bar. My mom was a few paces ahead and I saw her in triplicate. I clenched my eyes shut, released them, and there were still three of her. She held the door open for me and when I stepped into the cool confines, I felt a bit better. We slid into a booth opposite one another. I was too unsteady to read the menu and asked her to order for me. From there, it got worse, and when the runner showed up with our food, my vision blurred again. I strained to open my eyes wide and felt woozy as my mother looked to be floating above the table.

"You're going to have to call an ambulance," I said, "because I'm going down."

Desperate for some stability, I laid my head on the table, but my mom didn't dial 911. She crossed to my side and I leaned on her as we made our way to the hostess stand and then back to the car. On the way I shared as much of my medical history as I could recall, in short bursts, in case I lost consciousness and she did have to call for help. Luckily, my vision and energy improved enough for her to drive me to the emergency room herself.

My thyroid had been flagged in the past, so that's the first thing the doctors explored. Many Navy SEALs have thyroid issues when they reach their thirties, because when you put mother-fuckers in extreme environments like Hell Week and war, their hormone levels go haywire. When the thyroid gland is subopti-mal, fatigue, muscle aches, and weakness are among more than a dozen major side effects, but my thyroid levels were close to normal. My heart checked out too. The ER docs in Vegas told me all I needed was rest.

I went back to Chicago and saw my own doctor who ordered a battery of blood tests. His office tested my endocrine system and screened me for Lyme, hepatitis, Rheumatoid arthritis, and a handful of other autoimmune diseases. Everything came back clean except for my thyroid which was slightly suboptimal, but that didn't explain how I'd morphed so fast from an elite athlete capable of running hundreds of miles into a pretender who could barely muster the energy to tie his shoes, let alone run a mile without verging on collapse. I was in medical no-man's-land. I left his office with more questions than answers and a prescription for thyroid medication.

Each day that went by I felt worse. Everything was crashing on me. I had trouble getting out of bed, I was constipated and achy. They took more blood and decided I had Addison's dis-ease, an autoimmune illness that occurs when your adrenals are drained and your body doesn't produce enough cortisol, which was common 1n SEALs because we're primed to run on adrenaline. My doctor prescribed the steroid Hydrocortisone, DHEA, and Arimidex among other meds, but taking his pills only accelerated my decline, and after that, he and the other doctors I saw were tapped out. The look in their eyes said it all. In their minds, I was either a crazy hypochondriac, or I was dying and they didn't know what was killing me or how to heal me.

I fought through it the best I could. My coworkers didn't know anything about my decline because I continued to show no weakness. My whole life I'd been hiding all my insecurities and trauma. 1 kept all my vulnerabilities locked down beneath an iron veneer, but eventually the pain became so bad I couldn't even get out of bed. I called in sick and lay there, staring at the ceiling, and wondered, could this be the end?

Peering into the abyss sent my mind reeling back through the days, weeks, years, like fingers flipping through old files. I found all the best parts and tacked them together into a highlight loop streamed on repeat. I grew up beat down and abused, filtered uneducated through a system that rejected me at every turn, until I took ownership and started to change. Since then I'd been obese. I was married and divorced. I had two heart surgeries, taught myself to swim, and learned to run on broken legs. I was terrified of heights, then took up high altitude sky diving. Water scared the living shit out of me, yet I became a technical diver and underwater navigator, which is several degrees of difficulty beyond scuba diving. I competed in more than sixty ultra distance races, winning several, and set a pull-up record. I stuttered through my early years in pribary school and grew up to become the Navy SEALs' most trusted public speaker. I'd served my country on the battlefield. Along the way I became driven to make sure that

I could not be defined by the abuse I was hom into or the bullying that I grew up with. I wouldn't be defined by talent either, I didn't have much, or my own fears and weaknesses.

I was the sum total of the obstacles I'd overcome. And even though I'd told my story to students all over the country, I never stopped long enough to appreciate the tale I told or the life I'd built. In my mind, I didn't have the time to waste. I never hit snooze on my life clock because there was always something else to do. If I worked a twenty-hour day, I'd work out for an hour and sleep for three, but I made sure to get that motherfucker in. My brain wasn't wired to appreciate, it was programmed to do work, scan the horizon, ask what's next, and get it done. That's why I piled up so many rare feats. I was always on the hunt for the next big thing, but as I lay there in bed, my body taut with tension and throbbing with pain, I had a clear idea what was next for me. The cemetery. After years of abuse, I'd finally shredded my physical body beyond repair.

I was dying.

For weeks and months, I searched for a cure to my medical mystery, but in that moment of catharsis I didn't feel sad and I didn't feel cheated. I was only thirty-eight years old, but I'd lived ten lives and experienced a hell of a lot more than most eighty-year- aids. I wasn't feeling sorry for myself. It made sense that at some point the toll would come due. I spent hours reflecting back on my journey. This time, I wasn't sifting through the Cookie Jar while in the heat of battle hoping to find a ticket to victory. I wasn't leveraging my life assets toward some new end. No, I was done fighting, and all I felt was gratitude.

I wasn't meant to be this person! I had to fight myself at every turn, and my destroyed body was my biggest trophy. In that moment I knew it didn't matter if I ever ran again, if I couldn't operate anymore, or if I lived or died, and with that acceptance came deep appreciation.

My eyes welled with tears. Not because I was afraid, but because at my lowest point I found clarity. The kid I always judged so harshly didn't lie and cheat to hurt anyone's feelings. He did it for acceptance. He broke the rules because he didn't have the tools to compete and was ashamed for being dumb. He did it because he needed friends. I was afraid to tell the teachers I couldn't read. I was terrified of the stigma associated with special education, and instead of coming down on that kid for one more second, instead of chastising my younger self, I understood him for the first time.

It was a lonely journey from there to here. I missed out on so much. I didn't have a lot of fun. Happiness wasn't my cocktail of choice. My brain had me on constant blast. I lived in fear and doubt, terrified of being a nobody and contributing nothing. I'd judged myself constantly and I'd judged everyone else around me, too.

Rage is a powerful thing. For years I'd raged at the world, channeled all my pain from my past and used it as fuel to propel me into the motherfucking stratosphere, but I couldn't always control the blast radius. Sometimes my rage scorched people who weren't as strong as I'd become, or didn't work as hard, and I didn't swallow my tongue or hide my judgment. I let them know, and that hurt some of the people around me, and it allowed people who didn't like me to affect my military career. But lying in bed on that Chicago morning in the fall of 2014, I let all that judgment go.

I released myself and everyone I ever knew from any and all guilt and bitterness. The long list of haters, doubters, racists, and abusers that populated my past, I just couldn't hate them anymore. I appreciated them because they helped create me. And as that feeling stretched out, my mind quieted down. I'd been fighting a war for thirty-eight years, and now, at what looked and felt like the very end, I found peace.

In this life there are countless trails to self-realization, though most demand intense discipline, so very few take them. In southern Africa, the San people dance for thirty hours straight as a way to commune with the divine. In Tibet, pilgrims rise, kneel, then stretch out face down on the ground before rising again, in a ritual of prostration for weeks and months, as they cover thousands of miles before arriving at a sacred temple and folding into deep meditation. In Japan there's a sect of Zen monks that run 1,000 marathons in 1,000 days in a quest to find enlightenment through pain and suffering. I don't know if you could call what I felt on that bed "enlightenment," but I do know that pain unlocks a secret doorway in the mind. One that leads to both peak performance and beautiful silence.

At first, when you push beyond your perceived capability your mind won't shut the fuck up about it. It wants you to stop so it sends you into a spin cycle of panic and doubt, which only amplifies your self-torture. But when you persist past that to the point that pain fully saturates the mind, you become single-pointed. The external world zeroes out. Boundaries dissolve and you feel connected to yourself, and to all things, in the depth of your soul. That's what I was after. Those moments of total connection and power, which came through me again in an even deeper way as I reflected on where I'd come from and all I'd put myself through.

For hours, I floated in that tranquil space, surrounded by light, feeling as much gratitude as pain, as much appreciation as there was discomfort. At some point the reverie broke like a fever. I smiled, placed my palms over my watery eyes and rubbed the top and then the back of my head. At the base of my neck, I felt a familiar knot. It bulged bigger than ever. I threw off the covers and examined the knots above my hip flexors next. Those had grown too.

Could it be that basic? Could my suffering be linked to those knots? I flashed back to a session with an expert in stretching and advanced physical and mental training methods the SEALs brought to our base in Coronado in 2010 named Joe Hippensteel. Joe was an undersized decathlete in college, driven to make the Olympic team. But when you're a 5 '8 " guy going up against worldclass decathletes who average 6 '3" that isn't easy. He decided to build up his lower body so he could override his genetics to jump higher and run faster than his bigger, stronger opponents. At one point he was squatting twice his own body weight for ten sets of ten reps in one session, but with that increase in muscle mass came a lot of tension, and tension invited injury. The harder he trained, the more injuries he developed and the more physical therapists he visited. When he was told he tore his hamstring before the trials, his Olympic dream died, and he realized he needed to change the way he trained his body. He began balancing his strength work with extensive stretching and noticed whenever he reached a certain range of motion in a given muscle group or joint, whatever pain lingered, vanished.

He became his own guinea pig and developed optimal ranges of motion for every muscle and joint in the human body. He never went to the doctor or physical therapists again because he found his own methodologies much more effective. If an injury cropped up, he treated himself with a stretching regimen. Over the years he built up a clientele and reputation among elite athletes in the area, and in 2010, was introduced to some Navy SEALs. Word spread at Naval Special Warfare Command and he was eventually invited to introduce his range of motion routine to about two dozen SEALs. I was one of them.

As he lectured, he examined and stretched us out. The problem with most of the guys, he said, was our overuse of muscles without the appropriate balance of flexibility, and those issues traced back to Hell Week, when we were asked to do thousands of flutter kicks, then lie back in cold water with waves washing over us. He estimated it would take twenty hours of intensive stretching using his protocol to get most of us back to a normal range of motion in the hips, which can then be maintained, he said, with just twenty minutes of stretching every day. Optimal range of motion required a larger commitment. When he got to me he took a good look and shook his head. As you know, I'd tasted three Hell Weeks. He started to stretch me out, and said I was so locked up it was like trying to stretch steel cables.

"You're gonna need hundreds of hours," he said.

At the time, I didn't pay him any mind because I had no plans to take up stretching. I was obsessed with strength and power, and everything I'd read suggested that an increase in flexibility meant an equal and opposite decrease in speed and force. The view from my death bed altered my perspective.

I pulled myself up, staggered to the bathroom mirror, turned, and examined the knot on my head. I stood as tall as I could. It looked like I'd lost not one, but nearly two inches in height. My range of motion had never been worse. What if Joe was right?

What if?

One of my mottos these days is *peaceful but never satisfied.* It was one thing to enjoy the peace of self-acceptance, and my acceptance of the fucked-up world as it is, but that didn't mean I was going to lie down and wait to die without at least trying to save myself. It didn't mean then, and it doesn't mean now, that I will accept the imperfect or just plain wrong without fighting to change things for the better. I 'd tried accessing the mainstream mind to find healing, but the doctors and their drugs didn't do shit except make me feel a whole lot worse. I had no other cards to play. All I could do is try to stretch myself back to health.

The first posture was simple. I sat on the ground and tried to cross my legs, Indian style, but my hips were so tight, my knees were up around my ears. I lost my balance and rolled onto my back. It took all my strength to right myself and try again. I stayed in position for ten seconds, maybe fifteen, before straightening my legs because it was too damn painful.

Cramps squeezed and pinched every muscle in my lower body. Sweat oozed from my pores, but after a short rest, I folded up my legs and took more pain. I cycled through that same stretch on and off for an hour and slowly, my body started to open. I did a simple quad stretch next. The one we all learn to do in middle school. Standing on my left leg, I bent my right and grabbed my foot with my right hand. Joe was right. My quads were so bulky and tight it was like stretching steel cables. Again, I stayed in the posture until the pain was a seven out of ten. Then I took a short break and hit the other side.

That standing posture helped to release my quad and stretch out my psoas. The psoas is the only muscle connecting our spine to our lower legs. It wraps around the back of the pelvis, governs the hips, and is known as the fight or flight muscle. As you know, my whole life was fight or flight. As a young kid drowning in toxic stress, I worked that muscle overtime. Ditto during my three Hell Weeks, Ranger School, and Delta Selection. Not to mention war. Yet I never did anything to loosen it up, and as an athlete I continued to tap my sympathetic nervous system and had been grinding so hard my psoas continued to stiffen. E specially on long runs, where sleep deprivation and cold weather came into play. Now, it was trying to choke me from the inside out. I'd learn later that it had tilted my pelvis, compressed my spine, and wrapped my connective tissue tight. It shaved two inches off my height. I spoke to Joe about it recently

"What was happening to you is an extreme case of what happens to 90 percent of the population," he said. "Your muscles were so locked up that your blood wasn't circulating very well. They were like a frozen steak. You can't inject blood into a frozen steak, and that's why you were shutting down."

And it wouldn't let go without a fight. Each stretch plunged me into the fire. I had so much inflammation and internal stiffness, the slightest movement hurt, say nothing oflong hold poses meant to isolate my quad and psoas. When I sat down and did the butterfly stretch next, the torture intensified.

I stretched for two hours that day, woke up sore as hell, and got back after it. On day two I stretched for six full hours. I did the same three poses over and over, then tried to sit on my heels, in a double quad stretch that was pure agony. I worked a calf stretch in too. Each session started off rough, but after an hour or two my body released enough for the pain to ease up.

Before long I was folded into stretches for upwards of twelve hours a day. I woke up at 6 a.m., stretched until 9 a.m., and then stretched on and off while at the desk at work, especially when I was on the phone. I'd stretch out during my lunch hour and then after I got home at 5 p.m., I'd stretch until I hit the sack.

I came up with a routine, starting at my neck and shoulders before moving into the hips, psoas, glutes, quads, hamstrings, and calves. Stretching became my new obsession. I bought a massage ball to tenderize my psoas. I propped a board up against a closed door at a seventy-degree angle and used it to stretch out my calf.

I'd been suffering for the better part of two years, and after several months of continual stretching, I noticed the bump at the base of my skull had started to shrink, along with the knots around my hip flexors, and my overall health and energy level improved. I wasn't anywhere close to flexible yet, and I wasn't completely back to myself, but I was off all but my thyroid medication, and the more I stretched the more. my condition improved. I kept at it for at least six hours a day for weeks. Then months and years. I'm still doing it.

★ ★ ★

I retired from the military as a Chief in the Navy, in November 2015, the only military man ever to be part of Air Force TAC-P, three Navy SEAL Hell Weeks in one year (completing two of them) , and graduate BUD/S and Army Ranger School. It was a bittersweet moment because the military was a big part of my identity. It helped shape me and make me a better man, and I gave it everything I had.

By then Bill Brown had moved on too. He grew up marginalized like me, wasn't supposed to amount to much, and even got bounced from his first BUD/S class by instructors who questioned his intelligence. Today, he is a lawyer at a major firm in Philadelphia. Freak Brown proved and continues to prove himself.

Sledge is still in the SEAL Teams. When I met him he was a big time boozer, but after our workouts his mentality .changed. He went from never running at all to running marathons. From not owning a bicycle to becoming one of the fastest cyclists in San Diego. He's finished multiple Ironman triathlons. They say iron sharpens iron, and we proved that

Shawn Dobbs never became a SEAL, but he did become an Officer. He's a Lieutenant Commander these days, and he's still a hell of an athlete. He's an Ironman, an accomplished cyclist, was honor man in the Navy's Advanced Dive School, and later earned a graduate degree. One reason for all of his success is because he's come to own his failure in Hell Week, which means it no longer owns him.

SBG is still in the Navy too, but he's not messing with BUD/S candidates anymore. He analyzes data to make sure Naval Special Warfare continues to become smarter, stronger, and more effective than ever. He's an egghead now. An egghead with an edge. But I was with him when he was at his physical peak, and he was a fucking stud.

Since our dark days in Buffalo and Brazil, my mother has also completely transformed her life. She earned a master's degree in education and serves as a volunteer on a domestic violence task force, when she's not working as a senior associate vice president at a Nashville medical school.

As for me, stretching helped me get my powers back. As my time in the military wound down, while I was still in the rehab zone, I studied to recertify as an EMT. Once again, I utilized my long-hand memorization skills I'd been honing since high school to finish at the top of my class. I also attended TEEX Fire Training Academy, where I graduated Top Honor Man in my class. Eventually, I started running again, this time with zero side effects, and when I got back into decent enough shape, I entered a few ultras and returned to the top spot in several including the Strolling Jim 40-Miler in Tennessee, and Infinitus 88k in Vermont, both in 2016. But that wasn't enough, so I became a wildland firefighter in Montana.

After wrapping up my first season on the fire lines in the summer of 2015, I stopped by my mother's place in Nashville for a visit. At midnight her phone rang. My mother is like me in the sense that she doesn't have a wide circle of friends and doesn't get many phone calls during decent hours, so this was either a wrong number or an emergency.

I could hear Trunnis Jr. on the other end of the line. I hadn't seen or spoken to him in over fifteen years. Our relationship broke down the moment he chose to stay with our father rather than tough it out with us. For most of my life I found his decision impossible to forgive or accept, but like I said, I'd changed. Through the years, my mother kept me updated on the basics. He'd eventually stepped away from our father and his shady businesses, earned a PhD, and became a college administrator. He is also a great father to his kids.

I could tell by my mom's voice that something was wrong. All I remember hearing was my mom asking, "Are you sure it's Kayla?" When she hung up, she explained that Kayla, his eighteen-year-old daughter, had been hanging with friends in Indianapolis. At some point looser acquaintances rolled up, bad blood boiled, a gun was pulled, shots rang out, and a stray bullet found one of the teenagers.

When his ex-wife called him, in panic mode, he drove to the crime scene, but when he arrived he was held outside the yellow tape and kept in the dark. He could see Kayla's car and a body under a tarp, but nobody would tell him if his daughter was alive or dead.

My mother and I hit the road immediately. I drove eighty mph through slanted rain for five hours straight to Indianapolis. We pulled into his driveway shortly after he returned from the crime scene where, while standing outside the yellow tape, he was asked to identify his daughter from a picture of her body taken on a detective's cell phone. He wasn't offered the dignity of privacy or time to pay respects. He had to do all that later. He opened the door, took a few steps toward us, and broke down crying. My mother got there first. Then I pulled my brother in for a hug and all of our bullshit issues no longer mattered.

★ ★ ★

The Buddha famously said that life is suffering. I'm not a Buddhist, but I know what he meant and so do you. To exist in this world, we must contend with humiliation, broken dreams, sadness, and loss. That's just nature. Each specific life comes with its own personalized portion of pain. It's coming for you. You can't stop it. And you know it.

In response, most of us are programmed to seek comfort as a way to numb it all out and cushion the blows. We carve out safe spaces. We consume media that confirms our beliefs, we take up hobbies aligned with our talents, we try to spend as little time as possible doing the tasks we fucking loathe, and that makes us soft. We live a life defined by the limits we imagine and desire for ourselves because it's comfortable as hell in that box. Not just for us, but for our closest family and friends. The limits we create and accept become the lens through which they see us. Through which they love and appreciate us.

But for some, those limits start to feel like bondage, and when we least expect it, our imagination jumps those walls and hunts down dreams that in the immediate aftermath feel attainable. Because most dreams are. We are inspired to make changes little by little, and it hurts. Breaking the shackles and stretching beyond our own perceived limits takes hard fucking work—oftentimes physical work—and when you put yourself on the line, self doubt and pain will greet you with a stinging combination that will buckle your knees.

Most people who are merely inspired or motivated will quit at that point, and upon their return, their cells will feel that much smaller, their shackles even tighter. The few who remain outside their walls will encounter even more pain and much more doubt, courtesy of those who we thought were our biggest fans. When it was time for me to lose 106 pounds in less than three months, everyone I talked to told me there was no way I could do it. "Don't expect too much," they all said. Their weak-ass dialogue only fed my own self doubt.

But it's not the external voice that will break you down. It's what you tell yourself that matters. The most important conversations you'll ever have are the ones you'll have with yourself. You wake up with them, you walk around with them, you go to bed with them, and eventually you act on them. Whether they be good or bad.

We are all our own worst haters and doubters because self doubt is a natural reaction to any bold attempt to change your life for the better. You can't stop it from blooming in your brain, but you can neutralize it, and all the other external chatter by asking, What if?

What if is an exquisite fuck-you to anyone who has ever doubted your greatness or stood in your way. It silences negativity. It's a reminder that you don't really know what you're capable of until you put everything you've got on the line. It makes the impossible feel at least a little more possible. *What if* is the power and permission to face down your darkest demons, your very worst memories, and accept them as part of your history. If and when you do that, you will be able to use them as fuel to envision the most audacious, outrageous achievement and go get it.

We live in a world with a lot of insecure, jealous people. Some of them are our best friends. They are blood relatives. Failure terrifies them. So does our success. Because when we transcend what we once thought possible, push our limits, and become more, our light reflects off all the walls they've built up around them. Your light enables them to see the contours of their own prison, their own self-limitations. But if they are truly the great people you always believed them to be, their jealousy will evolve, and soon their imagination might hop its fence, and it will be their turn to change for the better.

I hope that's what this book has done for you. I hope that right now you are nose-to-concrete with your own bullshit limits you didn't even know were there. I hope you're willing to do the work to break them down. I hope you're willing to change. You'll feel pain, but if you accept it, endure it, and callous your mind, you'll reach a point where not even pain can hurt you. There is a catch, however. When you live this way, there is no end to it.

Thanks to all that stretching, I'm in better shape at forty-three than I was in my twenties. Back then I was always sick, wound tight, and stressed out. I never analyzed why I kept getting stress fractures. I just taped that shit up. No matter what ailed my body or my mind I had the same solution. Tape it up and move the fuck on. Now I'm smarter than I've ever been. And I'm still getting after it.

In 2018 I went back to the mountains to become a wildland firefighter again. I hadn't been in the field for three years, and since then I'd gotten used to training in nice gyms and living in comfort. Some might call it luxury. I was in a plush hotel room in Vegas whenthe 416 fire sparked and I got the call. What started as a 2,000-acre grass fire in the San Juan Range of Colorado's Rocky Mountains was growing into a record breaking, 55,000-acre monster. I hung up and caught a prop plane to Grand Junction, loaded up in a U.S. Forest Service truck, and drove three hours to the outskirts of Durango, Colorado, where I suited up in my green

Nomex pants and yellow, long-sleeved button down, my hard hat, field glasses, and gloves, and grabbed my super Pulaski—a wildland fire fighter's most trusted weapon. I can dig for hours with that thing, and that's what we do. We don't spray water. We specialize in containment, and that means digging lines and clearing brush so there's no fuel in the path of an inferno. We dig and run, run and dig, until every muscle is spent. Then we do it all over again.

On our first day and night we dug fire lines around vulnerable homes as walls of flames marched forward from less than a mile away. We glimpsed the burn through the trees and felt the heat in the drought-stricken forest. From there we were deployed to 10,000feet and worked on a forty-five-degree slope, digging as deep as possible, trying to get to the mineral soil that won't burn. At one point a tree fell and missed hitting one of my teammates by eight inches. It would have killed him. We could smell smoke in the air. Our sawyers—the chainsaw expert—kept cutting dead and dying trees. We hauled that brush out beyond a creek bed. Piles were scattered every fifty feet for over three miles. Each one measured roughly seven to eight feet tall.

We worked like that for a week of eighteen-hour shifts at $12 an hour, before taxes. It was eighty degrees during the day and thirty-six degrees at night. When the shift was over we laid out our mats and slept in the open wherever we were. Then woke up and got back after it. I didn't change my clothes for six days. Most of the people on my crew were at least fifteen years younger than me. All of them were hard as nails and among the very hardest working people I've ever met. Including and especially the women. None of them ever complained. When we were done we'd cleared a line 3.2 miles long, wide enough to stop a monster from burning down a mountain.

At forty-three, my wildland firefighting career is just getting started. I love being part of a team of hard motherfuckers like them, and my ultra career is about to be born again too. I'm just young enough to bring hell on and still contend for titles. I'm running faster now than I ever have, and I don't need any tape or props for my feet. When I was thirty-three I ran at an 8:35 per mile pace. Now I'm running 7:15 per mile very comfortably. I'm still getting used to this new, flexible, fully functioning body, and getting accustomed to my new self

My passion still bums, but to be honest, it takes a bit longer to channel my rage. It's not camped out on my home screen anymore, a single unconscious twitch from overwhelming my heart and head. Now I have to access it consciously. But when I do, I can still feel all the challenges and obstacles, the heartbreak and hard work, like it happened yesterday. That's why you can feel my passion on podcasts and videos. That shit is still there, seared into my brain like scar tissue. Tailing me like a shadow that's trying to chase me down and swallow me whole, but always drives me forward.

Whatever failures and accomplishments pile up in the years to come, and there will be plenty of both I'm sure, I know I'll continue to give it my all and set goals that seem impossible to most. And when those motherfuckers say so, I'll look them dead in the eye and respond with one simple question.

What if?

ACKNOWLEDGMENTS

THIS BOOK WAS SEVEN YEARS IN THE MAKING WITH SIX failed attempts along the way before being introduced to the first, and only, writer who truly understood my passion and captured my voice. I want to thank Adam Skolnick for the countless hours spent learning everything about me and my fucked-up life to help pull together all the pieces and bring my story to life in print. Words can't express how proud I am of the truthfulness, vulnerability, and raw candor of this book.

Jennifer Kish, I do not have the words. A lot of people say that, but it is the truth. Only you truly know how hard this process was for me to pull off, and without you by my side there would be no book at all. It is because of you I was able to take time off of writing to go fight fires while you took care of all the business behind the book. Knowing I had "Kish" in my corner enabled me to make the very ballsy decision to self-publish! It's because of your work ethic that I had the confidence to turn down a substantial book advance-knowing that you alone can shoulder what an entire publishing house can do! All I can say is thank you and I love you.

My mom, Jackie Gardner, we have had a hard, fucked-up life.

One that we can both be proud of6ecause there are many times we have been knocked flat on our asses with no one around to pick us up. Somehow we found a way to always get the fuck up. I know there were many times when you were concerned for me and wanted me to stop, thank you for never acting upon your feelings as it allowed me to find more of me. For most people, this is not how you would talk to your mother as a thank you, but only you know how powerful this message truly is. Stay hard; love you, Mom.

My brother, Trunnis. Our lives and the way we grew up at times made us enemies, but when the shit hit the fan, we were there for one another. At the end of the day, that is true brotherhood to me.

Much appreciation and thanks to the following people who allowed Adam and I to interview them for this book. Your recollection of the events helped me create an accurate and true depiction of my life and how these particular events unfolded.

My cousin, Damien, while you were always the favorite growing up, I had some of my better times in life hanging out with you just doing stupid shit.

Johnny Nichols, our friendship while growing up in Brazil was the only positive thing I had at times. Not many people know the darkness that I experienced as a kid like you do. Thanks for being there _when I truly needed you most.

Kirk Freeman, I want to thank you for your honesty. You were one of the few people who were willing to tell the painful truth about some of my challenges in Brazil, and for that I will forever be grateful.

ScottGearen, to this day, you will never know how much your story and you just being you helped me at a time in my life where darkness was all I could see. You have no idea the impact you had on a fourteen-year-old kid. It's a true saying, you never know who is watching you. I happened to be watching you that day at PJOC school. Grateful for your friendship after all these years.

Victor Pefia, I have many stories to tell, but the one thing I ' will say is that you were always there through thick and thin and always gave everything you had. For that, mad respect, brother.

Steven Schaljo, if it weren't for you, there might not even be a book. You were the best recruiter in the Navy. Thanks again for believing in me.

Kenny Bigbee, thanks for being the other "Black guy" at BUD/S. Your sense of humor was always right on time. Stay hard, brother.

To the white David Goggins, Bill Brown, your willingness to go the distance in the hardest of times made me better in the hardest of times. Last time I saw you, we were on a mission in Iraq, I was manning a .so cal and you were manning an M6o. Hope to see you stateside in the near future!

Drew Sheets, thank you for having the courage to be in the front of the boat with me in my third Hell Week. Very few know how heavy that shit is! Who would ever think that a redneck and a black guy would become so tight? It's true what they say, opposites attract!

Shawn Dobbs, it takes a lot of courage to do what you did in this book. I put myself out there to the reader, but you didn't have to! All I can say is thank you for allowing me to share part of your story. It will change lives!

Brent Gleeson, one of the few guys I know ·where "the first time, e.very time" truly applies. Very few will even know what this means. Stay hard, Brent!

SBG, you were one of the first SEALs I ever met and you set the bar high. Thank you for pushing me in all three of my

BUD/S classes and for the quick heart rate monitoring training class!

Dana De Coster, to the best swim buddy a guy could ever have. Your leadership during my first platoon was second to none!

Sledge, all I can say is that iron definitely sharpens iron! Thanks for being one of the few guys who got after it with me every fucking day and was willing to go against the grain and be misunderstood in your quest to get better.

Morgan Luttrell, 2-5! We will always be connected from our moment in Yuma.

Chris Kostman, you unknowingly forced me to find a whole other level of myself

John Metz, thank you for allowing an inexperienced man into your race. It changed my life forever.

Chris Roman, your professionalism and attention to detail have always amazed me. You are a big reason why I was able to get third in one of the hardest foot races on the planet.

Edie Rosenthal, thank you for all of your support and the amazing work you do for the Special Operations Warrior Foundation.

Admiral Ed Winters, humbled to have worked with you for so many years. Working for an Admiral definitely put pressure on me to bring my very best at all times. Thank you for your continued support.

Steve ("Wiz ")Wisotzki, justice was done and I thank you for that.

Hawk, when you sent me that email about "the 13 percent," I knewwe were kindred spirits. You are one of the few people in this world who understand me and my mentality without explanation.

DocSchreckengaust, thank you for putting me in for that echo. That shit just might have saved my life!

T., thanks for pushing me on that ruck, brother! Continue charging.

Ronald Cabarles, continue leading by example and staying hard. Class 03-04 RLTW.

Joe Hippensteel, thanks for showing me the proper ways to stretch. It's truly changed my life!

Ryan Dexter, thanks for walking with me for seventy-five miles and helping me get to.205 miles!

Keith Kirby, thanks for your continued support throughout the years.

Nand or Tamaska, thank you for opening your gym to me and my team for the pull-up record. Your hospitality, kindness, and support will never be forgotten.

Dan Cottrell, to give without expecting anything in return is a rare find. Thank you for allowing one of my dreams to be a jumper in my forties come true!

Fred Thompson, thank you for allowing me to work with your amazing team this year. I learned so much from you and your crew. Mad respect!

Marc Adelman, thank you for being part of the team from day one and for your counsel at every step along the way. Way to push past your perceived limitations this year. I am proud of all of your accomplishments!

BrandFire, thank you for your creative genius and the creation of davidgoggins.com.

Finally, my sincere gratitude and appreciation for the amazing team at Scribe Media. From the first contact with Tucker Max to the last and every touch point in between, you and every member of your team over-delivered just as you said you would! Special thinks to the consummate professional Ellie Cole, my Publishing Manager; Zach Obront for helping create an amazing marketing plan; Hal Clifford, my editor; and Erin Tyler, the most talented cover designer I could ever imagine, who helped create the sickest book cover of all time!

ABOUT THE AUTHOR

DAVID GOGGINS is a retired Navy SEAL and the only member of the U. S. Armed Forces ever to complete SEAL training, U.S. Army Ranger School, and Air Force Tactical Air Controller training. Goggins has competed in more than sixty ultra-marathons, triathlons, and ultra-triathlons, setting new course· records and regularly placing in the top five. A former Guinness World Record holder for completing 4,030 pull-ups in seventeen hours, he's a much-sought·after public speaker who's shared his story with the staffs of Fortune 500 companies, professional sports teams, and hundreds of thousands of students across the country.